On Faith

Readings in the *Summa theologiae*

TRANSLATED BY MARK D. JORDAN

Volume I

On Faith

Summa theologiae, Part 2–2, Questions 1–16
of St. Thomas Aquinas

TRANSLATED, WITH AN INTRODUCTION AND NOTES,
BY MARK D. JORDAN

UNIVERSITY OF NOTRE DAME PRESS
NOTRE DAME LONDON

Library of Congress Cataloging-in-Publication Data

Thomas, Aquinas, Saint, 1225?–1274.
[Summa theologica. English. Selections]
Readings in the Summa theologiae / translated by Mark D. Jordan.
p. cm.
Includes bibliographical references.
Contents: Vol. 1. On faith, Summa theologiae 2–2, qq. 1–16 of St. Thomas Aquinas
ISBN 0–268–01503–1 (v. 1)
1. Theology, Doctrinal—Early works to 1800. 2. Catholic Church—Doctrines—Early works to 1800. I. Jordan, Mark D. II. Title.
BX1749.T5 1990
230'.2—dc20
89–40753

Manufactured in the United States of America

CONTENTS

INTRODUCTION

The Origin of the *Summa*

Thomas Aquinas's *Summa of Theology* has been a work familiar to so many centuries of Christian thought that it is easy to take its existence for granted and to imagine that its origin was somehow inevitable. It was not. What can be discovered about the origin of the *Summa* suggests that it was a masterly and perhaps unexcelled improvisation in the face of very particular circumstances for the teaching of Christian theology.

Near the end of 1259, at the age of 34 or 35, Thomas Aquinas left Paris to return to his ecclesiastical home, the "Roman" or Italian province of the Dominican order.[1] He had behind him a brilliant if occasionally controversial career as a student and master of theology at the University of Paris. But his work in Italy would be within the houses of his order and not at a university. So far as can be determined, Thomas spent a year and a half in the house at Naples, where he had first joined the Dominicans; he then moved north to the priory in Orvieto for a stay of four years. During those years, he served as an unofficial theological adviser to the papal court and com-

[1] The standard biography for Thomas is James A. Weisheipl, *Friar Thomas d'Aquino: His Life, Thought, and Works*, with corrections and additions (Washington: Catholic University of America Press, 1983). Besides the biographical account, this volume also provides a "Brief Catalogue" of Thomas's works (pp. 355–405, with corrections pp. 478–487). The catalogue is the best guide to the works of Thomas that were available in English as of 1983.

pleted a number of works, including the *Summa against the Gentiles*. This shorter *Summa* (if that is indeed its title) was a first essay in reorganizing philosophical and theological materials to form a strong textual whole. In September of 1265, Thomas was assigned to open a house of studies for Dominicans in Rome. There was no Roman university and no previous academic establishment there for the order.[2] Thomas's new *studium* was also to see the inauguration of a curricular project very much dependent on his personal activity as *lector* (teacher for the house). Thomas was given full authority by the provincial governing body to send back those who proved negligent in their studies.

What did Thomas teach? The prevailing curriculum in Dominican houses relied on Scripture and books of scriptural history, of course, but also on collections of texts for sacramental theology, manuals of the moral life, and some reference works of canon law and the Church Fathers. But Thomas seems to have had other plans at Rome from the start. During his first year, he tried revising his earlier, Parisian commentary on the *Sentences* of Peter Lombard, the standard medieval anthology of theological texts and problems. He began not with the fourth book, often used by Dominicans for teaching on the sacraments, but with the first book, with its doctrine on God as unity and trinity. After revising and supplementing parts of the first book, Thomas seems to have set the project aside.[3] He

[2] The best description of the evidence for Thomas's teaching at Rome, and for its importance to the understanding of the *Summa*, is Leonard Boyle, *The Setting of the Summa theologiae of Saint Thomas*, Etienne Gilson Series 5 (Toronto: PIMS, 1982).

[3] The evidence of Thomas's revision of the *Sentences*-commentary is contained in a manuscript at Lincoln College, Oxford. The manuscript gives the Parisian version of Thomas's commentary as the main text, then enters alternate or supplementary texts in the margin. The marginal annotations are concerned at greatest length with trinitarian ques-

began instead to compose the *Summa*, which begins much as the *Sentences* do, but goes on to a more rigorously ordered consideration of the whole of theology. In short, the evidence we have of Thomas's teaching and writing at Rome suggests that his main effort was directed at expanding the pastoral and practical curriculum of Dominican houses by placing it within the frame of the whole of theology.

Thomas tells us as much in the prologue to the first part of the *Summa*. He begins from a verse out of 1 Corinthians, "as little ones in Christ, I gave you milk to drink, not meat" (1.3). The prologue's first section interprets the verse as it applies to "the teacher of catholic truth," who ought to instruct not only advanced students, but also "beginners" (*incipientes*). The intention of the *Summa*, Thomas says, is to hand on what pertains to "the Christian religion" (*religio*) in a manner suited to the instruction of beginners.

Who exactly are these "beginners" and what is the "religion" they are to learn? The obvious reading supposes that they are beginners in the study of university theology. But the *Summa*, in fact, is not fully appropriate as an aid to university theology, since it follows the order of none of the standard medieval academic texts, nor is it nearly as complex as comparable academic disputations. A second look at the prologue shows that the key words can be understood quite differently. "Beginners" (*incipientes*) will later refer in the *Summa* itself to those who stand lowest in the hierarchy of spiritual learning, and "religion" (*religio*) will refer, not to "religion" in the modern sense, but to life in a religious community

---

tions, but there are also new treatments of the nature of theology, divine simplicity, and the names of God, among other topics. There is as yet no edition of the text, but for a discussion of its authenticity see Leonard Boyle, " 'Alia lectura fratris Thome,' " *Mediaeval Studies* 45 (1983): 419–429.

under the vows of poverty, chastity, and obedience.[4] In other words, the prologue of the *Summa* can also be taken as addressing beginners in spiritual learning who hope to progress through the discipline of the vowed life. It addresses just such "beginners" as were Thomas's students in Rome.

The reading is strengthened in the second section of the prologue, which is a triple complaint against the prevailing forms of academic writing and teaching. Those new to the study of "this doctrine," Thomas continues, are impeded by a multiplication of useless material, by an order tied to textual exposition or formal dispute, and by tiresome repetition. The *Summa* promises, by contrast, to give only what is essential, to give it in the pedagogical order required by an introduction, and not to repeat itself.

Of course, this way of reading the prologue to the *Summa* does not mean that the work is only a temporary solution to a particular problem in teaching. The situation that Thomas faced in Rome is a perennial problem for the Christian teacher. It is the problem of bringing together happily the creed's truths and the daily life of faith. Or, again, it is the double problem of seeing the implications of doctrine for life, and of seeing the need to ground particular habits of life in the whole of Christian revelation. Augustine addressed the problem in the structure of the *Confessions* by retelling the story of his conversion within the frame of a cosmic narrative of Scripture. Many other writers took as frame the order of the ancient Christian creeds. Thomas addressed the perennial problem in yet another way. His aim was not limited to a particular pedagogical problem; it reached out towards a structure of learning that could ground theology on a much larger scale and in many different contexts. But there is still something to be remembered from the particular origin of the

---

[4] *Summa* 2–2 qq.186–189. For abbreviations used in citations to the *Summa*, see the introductory remarks at the beginning of the index.

Summa. The text is not simply another academic work. That is why it differs in so many respects from the synthetic works of Thomas's predecessors and successors. There are many *Summas* in the thirteenth century, but none quite like the *Summa of Theology* in simplicity, scope, and rigor of organization. Thomas offers in the *Summa* a way into the whole of Christianity, dogmatic and pastoral, by means of a structure of inquiry. Indeed, the achievement of the *Summa* lies not so much in its particular arguments or doctrines as in its arrangement of arguments and doctrines. Its mastery shows most in its structure.

The Plan of the *Summa*

The *Summa* was never completed. Thomas stopped writing it—and anything else—in December of 1273, after he had experienced a vision. He died within four months. We do not know exactly how he would have arranged the end of the work in detail, or what improvements he would have introduced in discussing the topics he never reached. It is particularly unfortunate that Thomas was not able to write the section on the sacrament of marriage, since this had long been one of the most poorly ordered parts of theology. But we can know the overall structure of the *Summa* as Thomas conceived it, because he foretells it at several points in the text.

The successive descriptions have to be gone through one after another. Thomas is careful not to say everything at once; he tells the beginners what they need of the whole as they go along.[5] So, for example, the *Summa* is divided

[5] Readers interested in following the unfolding of the plan of the *Summa* should begin by reading the prologues to the following parts and questions in order: 1 q.2, q.26, q.27, q.44, q.75, q.90, q.103; 1–2 q.1, q.6, q.22, q.49, q.55, q.71, q.90, q.98, q.106; 2–2 q.1, q.17, q.23, q.47, q.57, q.123, q.141, q.171; 3 q.1, q.16, q.27, q.60, q.66.

into three parts. We learn this in the very first description of its plan: "we will first treat of faith; second, of the motion of the rational creature towards God; third, of Christ, who, so far as he is man, is the way for us to tend towards God."[6] But things are not quite as they might appear in this short text. The first part, for example, devotes more questions to creation and creatures than to God himself. The second part, in turn, is itself divided into two parts. And the third part, so far as we can project its final form, would have been more concerned with sacraments and the end of earthly life than with Christ himself. In the outline that follows, I have combined several of the successive descriptions into an overview of how Thomas articulates the actual disposition of material in the *Summa*.[7]

An Outline

PART 1: "God"; God "as exemplar" and "the things that proceed from God."

Theology as a body of knowledge (q.1)
["God's essence"]
God's existence (q.2)
How God is named and known by us (qq.3–13)
God's knowledge and will (qq.14–24)
God's power and blessedness (qq.25–26)
["Distinction of persons in God"]
Origin of the Trinitarian persons (qq.27–28)
The persons in themselves (qq.29–38)
The persons in various comparisons (qq.39–43)

---

[6] *Summa* 1 q.2 prol.

[7] The texts used are the prologues to *Summa* 1, 1–2, 2–2, and 3, together with the bridge paragraphs at the beginning of *Summa* 1 q.2, 1–2 q.6 and q.49, 2–2 q.171, and 3 q.66.

["Procession of creatures from God"]
Creation and distinction of creatures (qq.44–49)
Substance, intellect, will, and creation of angels (qq.50–64)
Creation, distinction, and embellishment of bodily creatures (qq.65–74)
Man's nature and powers (qq.75–89)
The first man (qq.90–102)
Governance and interaction of things (qq.103–116)
Man's action and reproduction (qq.117–118)

PART 2 (as a whole): "Motion of the rational creature towards God."

Section 1 of part 2: "Man so far as he is the principle of his own acts"; "consideration in general of virtues and vices and of the other things belonging to moral matter."
Man's final end (qq.1–5)
["Universal consideration of acts proper to man"]
Acts of the will (qq.6–17)
Good and evil acts (qq.18–21)
["Universal consideration of acts shared with animals"]
Passions (qq.22–48)
["Intrinsic principles of human acts"]
Habits in general (qq.49–54)
Virtues in general (qq.55–70)
Vices and sins in general (qq.71–89)
["Extrinsic principles of human acts"]
Law in general (qq.90–97)
Old Testament (qq.98–105)
New Testament (qq.106–108)
Grace and merit (qq.108–114)

Section 2 of part 2: "Special consideration of single moral things"
["Theological virtues"]

Faith, its gifts, opposed vices, and attached precepts (qq.1–16)
Hope (qq.17–22)
Charity (qq.23–46)
["Cardinal virtues"]
Prudence (qq.47–56)
Justice (qq.57–122)
Fortitude (qq.123–140)
Temperance (qq.141–170)
[Moral "differences among men"]
Differences of freely given graces (qq.171–177)
Differences of ways of life (qq.178–182)
Differences of offices and rank (qq.183–189)

PART 3: "Christ as the way" of the rational creature "towards God."

["The Savior himself"]
Appropriateness of the incarnation (q.1)
Manner of the incarnation (qq.2–15)
Consequences of the incarnation (qq.16–26)
Christ's deeds and sufferings (qq.27–59)
["Sacraments of the Church"]
Sacraments in common (qq.60–65)
Baptism (qq.66–71)
Confirmation (q.72)
Eucharist (qq.73–83)
Penance (qq.84–?; the text breaks off with q.90 a.4)
[The following sections projected but not completed]
[Orders]
[Matrimony]
["The end, immortal life"]

Many explanations have been given of the structure of the *Summa*. Some see it as enacting the union of God and man in Christ. Others see it as illustrating the outpouring (*exitus*) and return (*reditus*) of all creatures to God.[8] More plainly, it is clearly a reforming variation on the order of Peter Lombard's *Sentences*, which is itself a distant echo of the pattern of the creeds. None of these readings needs exclude the others. I would want to add to their sum only that the structure can also be seen as a way of enframing the study of Christian moral life between a theology that issues in cosmology and a Christology that issues in an ecclesiology. In other words, the structure of the *Summa* puts the teaching about Christian living right in the middle of a complete pattern of Christian instruction.

The Structure of the *Summa* on Faith

The structural achievement of the *Summa* is most apparent in the two sections of the second part. The structure of the second part is the most innovative and the most rigorous in comparison with its predecessors. Thomas was faced with an extraordinary mass of material about the Christian life, all of it loosely arranged in competing and not entirely consistent patterns. Many of them were patterns drawn from the lists of "capital" or chief sins, though some proposed such alternate divisions as sin against God, against neighbor, and against self. For the positive treatment, Thomas's predecessors used lists of the three theological and four cardinal virtues or of the gifts of the Holy Spirit. Many of the previous treatments were rich in

[8] Marie-Dominique Chenu, *Toward Understanding Saint Thomas*, tr. A.-M. Landry and D. Hughes (Chicago: Henry Regnery, 1964), 310–317. Chenu's entire discussion of the *Summa* is extremely rich in suggestions for a good reading of it. A somewhat less imaginative discussion can be had in Martin Grabmann, *Introduction to the Theological Summa of St. Thomas*, tr. J. S. Zybura (St. Louis and London: B. Herder, 1930).

moral tales and explicit exhortations; they were useful, as might be expected, in preparing sermons. Other treatments were given a legal cast and depended mainly on one one or another codification of Church laws.

Thomas confronts these tangled traditions in the construction of the second part. Indeed, he gives his judgment on them in the prologue to the second section of the second part.[9] The consideration of what pertains to moral doctrine is first divided into the "common" or "general" and the "special" or "particular." The general consideration comes in the first section of the second part. This contains, as we have seen, discussions of the final end, the powers behind human acts, their intrinsic principles in habit, and their extrinsic principles in law and grace. The second section of the second part will provide the detailed consideration. But here the danger of disorganization is acute, simply because there are so many details. Indeed, as Thomas says, there is a great temptation to let the consideration expand beyond any limits, by treating sequentially of all kinds of virtues, gifts, vices, and precepts. In order to avoid this danger, to resist this temptation, Thomas proposes two great organizing principles. First, he unites in a single cluster a virtue, the corresponding gifts, the opposed vices, and the attached affirmative or negative precepts. Second, he traces all of the more particular virtues back to the three theological and four cardinal virtues. These two principles give him a clear and consistent organization for the *secunda secundae* of the *Summa*.

The beauties of the organization can be seen in the discussion of faith, the first of the theological virtues. We are given, just as we were told, first the virtue itself (*Summa* 2–2 qq.1–7), then the corresponding gifts of understanding and knowledge (qq.8–9), then the opposed vices (qq.10–15), and finally the pertinent precepts (q.16). Even

---

[9] The text is given in full below, at the beginning of the translation.

the larger subsections follow consistent patterns. So, within the consideration of the virtue, we move backwards from the specifying object to the consequences or effects: the object of faith (q.1), its act (qq.2–3), the virtue as such (q.4), its subject (q.5), cause (q.6), and effects (q.7). In the consideration of the opposed vices, we move from the root vice (unfaithfulness, q.10), through its progressively more radical and expressed kinds (heresy, q.11; apostasy, q.12; blasphemy, qq.13–14), to its consequences (q.15).

The organization may seem complex to those who approach it for the first time, but it is a remarkable feat of clarity in comparison with its predecessors. In the influential *Summa of Virtues* by the Dominican William Peraldus, for example, the "treatise on faith" is introduced as having the following parts: the necessity of faith, the "descriptions" or definitions of faith, the truth of faith, the commendation of faith, the articles of faith, errors about faith and their causes, and the differences of faith.[10] This arrangement, already obscure, is made much more complicated by the unequal weight given to its various parts and by insertions not accounted for in the stated plan. The discussion of the errors against faith, for example, fills more than twice as many folios as the rest of the treatise combined. William considers the commendation of faith twice, once near the beginning and once at the very end (chapters 4 and 30). And so on. Thomas reduces all of these topics to a concise and clear plan. He does more. He incorporates material from very different theological traditions not even reflected in William, such as the traditions of canon law and the traditions of academic theology. The discussion of faith in the *Summa* is a reflective simplification and radicalization of these diverse traditions of theological discourse.

---

[10] William Peraldus, *Summa aurea de virtutibus et vitiis* (Venice, 1497), f. 7vb.

The Authorities for the *Summa* on Faith

Thomas's procedure in the discussion of faith is itself a simplification of the argumentative procedure from the medieval schools. In each article, Thomas offers a shortened and simplified version of the disputed question. A disputed question is a means for addressing an issue by the dialectical interpretation of apparently contradictory authoritative texts. Sometimes the issue arises out of a famous clash of authorities; sometimes it is brought from present disagreements to the tradition, which is then discovered to offer competing answers for it. However the issue arises, it is to be addressed by constructing a scheme of distinctions and arguments that will cover as many of the adduced authorities as possible. The best contemporary analogy would be to the practice of arguing from precedents in court. The analogy is particularly apt since the growth of medieval disputation was also closely tied to evolving techniques for legal interpretation and argument.

An argument by dialectical interpretation of authoritative texts is a difficult kind of argument to follow. It is dialectical. It advances not in a straight line, but by a series of points and counterpoints. Thomas sets forth his teaching in an oscillating series of particular arguments against positions he rejects. A principle set forth in one article will be qualified in the next. A conclusion drawn in a string of articles will be balanced against other conclusions drawn elsewhere. The reader needs to view the text not as a string of discrete claims, but as a dialectical motion through a series of considerations. The motion would be complete only in the whole *Summa*, but it can be followed microscopically in any given article or series of articles or series of questions.

Arguments by disputative interpretation are also difficult to follow until one knows the authoritative texts that are being brought into play. This presents great difficulty to modern readers for two reasons. First, we are often unfamiliar with the authorities used by Thomas and his contemporaries. Second, when we know something about the authorities, we use them in a different way than he did when disputing. Medieval disputants tended to compare texts not whole to whole, but passage to passage, and even sentence to sentence. This does not mean that they ignored context or other differences among different authors. On the contrary, the disputative interpretations frequently turned just on appeals to context or on distinctions among the terminologies of different texts. But it does mean that the medieval procedure handled authoritative citations as separate pieces, or counters, to be used as such in various arguments. It is not surprising, then, that some of the most important books in every field of medieval theology were collections of texts grouped around particular topics. Such works are the *Sentences* of Peter Lombard, which excerpts broadly theological texts on a whole range of theological topics; the *Book of Decrees* of Gratian, which does the same for texts of canon law; the various Glosses on the Bible, which combine patristic excerpts into an almost continuous commentary. Thomas himself supervised the construction of one of these theological reference works—the *Catena aurea*, a continuous gloss on the Gospels composed of patristic citations from both the Latin and Greek traditions. The second part of the *Summa* itself might also be regarded as a very refined collection and systematization of received material on moral matters.

Unfortunately, the medieval manner of handling authoritative works is still mostly inaccessible to us. We know little enough about the transmission of these text collections. Where we do know something about them, we often lack helpful editions. Modern readers of Thomas almost always resort to tracing his citations of authorities back to their origins in Scripture or the Church Fathers or Greek philosophy. But these bare citations can give very misleading impressions unless one remembers that they were mediated to Thomas through a whole tradition of interpretation, and that Thomas had certain general views about the main authors being cited.[11]

A Key to the Chief Authorities

This introduction cannot be of much help with the first problem in reading Thomas's disputes, but it may do something to ease the second. A small group of texts forms the core of authorities for Thomas's discussion on faith. In what follows, I list these texts and say a little about them and about Thomas's characteristic use of them.

SCRIPTURE. Thomas's text are saturated with the language, the images, and the doctrines of Scripture, which he quotes with intimate knowledge. So there are scriptural citations and quotations on almost every page of Thomas's consideration of faith. But two scriptural passages serve as the foundation: Hebrews 11 and 1 Corinthians 13.12. The first gives Thomas the essential definition of faith, as well as the doctrine of its necessity for salvation. The second tells him that faith is not knowledge. Both texts, but especially the whole chapter from Hebrews, should be read before beginning with Thomas on faith.

AUGUSTINE, various treatises, written c.385–430. No Latin theologian is more important for Thomas than

---

[11] In order to avoid misleading the reader in just this way, citations to the Church Fathers or classical authors will not be expanded to include references to contemporary English translations of them. Contemporary translations frequently construe particular passages differently than Thomas did. Moreover, and more importantly for the *Summa*, Thomas often takes up passages in disputed questions as discrete pieces of argumentative evidence, not as sections of whole works to be construed in light of the whole. Readers who, despite these cautions, want to look at translations of patristic originals can locate them through Johannes Quasten, *Patrology*, 3 vols. (Westminster, Md.: Christian Classics, 1983); Johannes Quaesten and Angelo di Bernardino, eds., *Patrology*, vol. 4: *The Golden Age of Latin Patristic Literature* (Westminster, Md.: Christian Classics, 1986).

Augustine, however much Thomas is routinely said by commentators to be opposed to him. Augustine did so much to fix the problems, the arguments, and the terminology of Latin theology that it is hard to speak of him as a source. He is much more like an embracing context. But it is important to remember that many of the particular pieces of Augustine come to Thomas already excerpted and construed by a long tradition. Most of the Augustinian passages on faith, for example, are taken by Thomas from earlier works of theological reference. This should be kept in mind when looking at the particular readings Thomas gives them.

PSEUDO-DIONYSIUS (that is, the author falsely called Dionysius), *On the Divine Names* (known in Latin as *De divinis nominibus*), written between c.480 and c.525. "Dionysius the Areopagite" is the pseudonym of a Greek-speaking theologian who was one of the main exponents within Christianity of a transformed neo-Platonism from the school of Proclus. His first appearances in Byzantine theological disputes were marked by controversy over his identity and doctrine, but he was later received by the Latin West as that very Dionysius the Areopagite who is mentioned as a disciple of Paul in the Acts of the Apostles. He is one of the most important authorities for Thomas throughout the *Summa*. Thomas knew him through many intermediaries, and directly in several Latin translations (chiefly the late twelfth-century version of John the Saracen). In the discussion of faith, Thomas uses Ps-Dionysius for definitions of faith, for characterizations of theological method, and for principles of hierarchical causality.

GREGORY THE GREAT, *Moral Remarks on Job* (*Moralia in Job*), written c.580-c.590. Gregory's moral exposition of Job served for the Latin West as much more than an exposition of one Old Testament book. It was a storehouse of doctrine on the moral life. As such, it figures prominently in the second part of the *Summa*, especially on technical points of definition and classification for the virtues and vices.

JOHN CHRYSOSTOM, *Commentary on Matthew* (known in Latin as the *In Matthaeum*), written in the 380s. Chrysostom was Thomas's favorite Greek expositor of Scripture. Indeed, one story tells that Thomas was willing to trade the city of Paris for Chrysostom on Matthew. But Thomas's knowledge of the Greek Fathers was imperfect, as he himself confessed, and there are difficulties of translation and textual authenticity, including a longstanding confusion about another (spurious) commentary on Matthew, the *Opus imperfectum*. Chrysostom appears in the discussion of faith as an aid in understanding difficult scriptural passages.

JOHN DAMASCENE, *On the Orthodox Faith* (known in Latin as *De fide orthodoxa*), written in the first half of the seventh century (before 741). John Damascene became available to the West in the twelfth century, along with many other authors previously untranslated from Greek into Latin. His work provided a systematic survey of Greek patristic teaching and of ancient philosophy. Thomas depends on him extensively in the second part of the *Summa* for the classification of powers of the soul, the definition of virtues, and so on.

Ordinary and *Interlinear GLOSS* (*Glossa ordinaria, interlinearis*), definitively edited around the beginning of the twelfth century. Medieval copies of the Bible were early provided with marginal and interlinear notes and comments, many of which were excerpted from the Latin Fathers. With time, these supplementary materials grew, until they came to form an almost continuous commentary on Scripture. They were put into systematic form during the first third of the twelfth century. Thomas knew them in this form and used them as a constant guide for scriptural interpretation. A second and fuller version of parts of the Gloss was produced by PETER LOMBARD.

He left a *Magna Glossatura* on the Psalms and Pauline Epistles unfinished at his death in 1160, but it was finished and published by an editor. It is cited below as the *Glossa Lombardi*.

GRATIAN, *Book of Decrees* (*Decretum*), more properly called *The Concord of Discordant Canons* (*Concordia discordantium canonum*), finished c.1141. Yet another aspect of the systematization of traditional texts in the twelfth century was Gratian's monument of Church law, the *Decretum*. Thomas uses this work extensively in his discussions of vices and sins, since it provides not only a summary of the law, but a handy compendium of patristic texts as well. Within the consideration of faith, Gratian is particularly important to Thomas's analyses of unfaithfulness, heresy, and apostasy.

It may seem odd that I do not list Aristotle among the chief authorities for Thomas. Even though Aristotle could not have much to say about the theological virtue of faith, he is certainly cited frequently enough by Thomas in these texts. While this is true, most of the Aristotelian citations concern general principles or maxims rather than truths specific to the treatment of faith. Here, as elsewhere in the *Summa*, Aristotle provides common premises for arguments that draw their specific content from more pertinent authorities. The only exception to this in the consideration of faith comes with Aristotle's descriptions of knowledge and understanding, which Thomas uses when he needs to give precision to notions that otherwise remain too fluid to be useful.

This brief survey of principal authorities cannot supply anything like what a medieval reader would have brought to the appreciation of Thomas's dialectical interpretations. The most it can do, I think, is to suggest that the problem of authorities, of their transmission as much as of their interpretation, is one that any modern reader will have to confront anew every time he or she begins to read.

The Language of the *Summa* on Faith

Every translation is made for a particular audience. It preserves certain features of the original with a view to that audience, since it cannot preserve all. No English translation can, for example, simultaneously preserve Thomas's rhythm, his brevity, his simplicity, his precision, and his fidelity to traditional vocabularies. This translation is made for American readers who lack Latin and who are not already fluent in that Latinate English that has been the language of Anglophone Thomism. I try to preserve, in a spare but accessible English, Thomas's arguments and a little something of his style. I do not attempt to preserve the (bad) habits of earlier and falsely technical translations that undertook to render Latin terms by etymologically related terms in English. Thus, I do not translate *scientia* as "science," because "science" in modern English does not refer to anything like what *scientia* referred to in Thomas's Latin. I also do not think that there can be such a thing as a permanent or correct translation. Every translation of a serious text is a series of compromises and failures. Indeed, the most important office of the translator may be to insist on the impossibilities of translation.

There are a number of particular difficulties in translating Thomas Aquinas. First, he writes in a relentlessly economical Latin that is at once simple and studded with technical terms. It is hard to think of a similar writer in English, unless it would be one of the Anglo-American analytic philosophers. Second, while most of Thomas's arguments hinge on precise distinctions of meaning in terms or arguments, the distinctions change from passage to passage. How to make an English translation that captures the distinctions idiomatically even while it allows them a certain leeway? Third, the problem of translating Thomas is intimately connected with problems in translating a number of other authors—Aristotle, Augustine, Ps-Dionysius—

since, as should be clear, his language depends on theirs. We speakers of English inherit conflicting and often misleading habits of translating each of these authors.

There are other problems. But I will stop the list of difficulties to say how I have attempted to meet some of them. It seemed to me important in rendering Thomas to do three things: reflect his technical vocabulary with a minimum of anachronism or doctrinal imposition; be consistent without false rigidity; and try for something like an imitation of his style in English.

A Glossary

I have set up certain conventions for translating the technical vocabulary.

Terms having to do with the mind and its acts seem to me the most liable to distortion by modern translators. I have therefore tried to choose common terms and to use them consistently. Thus

agnitio: acquaintance
cognoscere, cognitio: apprehend, apprehension
intelligere, intellectus: understanding
notitia: awareness
ratio: reason
scire, scientia: to know, knowledge or body of knowledge

The word *ratio* is particularly difficult, because *ratio* in Thomas's Latin, somewhat as *logos* in Aristotle's Greek, means at least four things: a power of the human mind, a cause or principle, an argument, and a formula or quasi-definition or notion that expresses what is essential about something. We combine the first two meanings in the English "reason," but that word cannot possibly embrace all four of the Latin meanings. So I have had to use three different translations:

ratio: reason, reasoning, account

Equally difficult is what might be called the language of action. The central term *opus*, for example, can take meanings as different as deed, action, or product, and yet it is essential to many of Thomas's arguments that one single word takes all of these meanings. I have decided to retain a single word in translating, but can do so only while asking the reader to hear the English word with some of its older and specifically theological meanings.

opus, operare, operatio: work, to work, working

By contrast,

actus: act
agere: to do or to act

We are somewhat better off in English when it comes to words for the central subject matter of these questions. I have used the following translations:

credere, credita, credibilia: believe, things believed, believable things
fides, fidelis, fidelitas: faith, faithful, faithfulness
infidelis, infidelitas: unfaithful, unfaithfulness

Thomas does introduce a threefold distinction of faith that is very difficult to render idiomatically into English. He explains it carefully, and following his explanation I have been bold enough to use the following translations, however odd they might seem at first glance:

credere Deo: to believe God
credere Deum: to believe about God
credere in Deum: to believe for the sake of God

The careful reader will keep in mind that much of Thomas's terminology is inherited and that he himself struggles to harmonize different usages. It is a good exercise to go back to the authoritative sources for any given article and to look at the differences or contradictions in terminology with which Thomas must begin. He is successful, much more often than not, in holding together a plurality of different terminologies without incoherence.

A terminological difficulty that is ours more than Thomas's arises over so-called exclusive language, that is, with the use of otherwise masculine common nouns or pronouns to name groups that contain both women and men. The most obvious case in Thomas is the use of *homo* to name all or some members of the human species without regard to their biological gender. I have chosen to render *homo* as "man" in order both to preserve Thomas's distinctions and to avoid cumbersome constructions in English. Thomas requires his readers to distinguish concrete names for a species or its members from more abstract accounts of the essence of the species. Thus *homo*, "man," must be kept distinct from *humanitas*, "humanity," since the latter has different logical properties than the former. For example, we can say that Socrates is a man, but not that Socrates is humanity. Hence, *homo* cannot be translated into English as "humanity" or "human." Nor can *homo* be rendered as "person," since "person" for Thomas has primarily theological overtones and is best understood by reference to the Trinity. Similar difficulties of content or idiom afflict the other alternatives. In the end, modern readers simply must accustom themselves to Thomas's use of *homo* as a general term for women and men if they want to read his texts. To do so is part of the larger effort of sympathy that any attentive reading requires.

The Text of the *Summa*

For all the labor that has gone into the editing and interpreting of Thomas's writings, we are still without a critical edition of the *Summa* done according to contemporary standards. None of the available editions comes close to collating all of the manuscripts. Consequently, none of them can really characterize with certainty the transmission of the text. There are also other difficulties. For example, none of the available editions has an apparatus that gives Thomas's sources, either in terms of the Latin texts he used or in terms of the probable intermediaries. The absence of such an edition is not the consequence of laziness. To prepare it would be an extraordinary undertaking, even with all that has been learned in the forty-five years since the last edition of the *Summa*.

In order to compensate for the absence of a fully critical edition, I have used the two best of the available editions. The first is the Leonine edition of the *Summa*, that is, volumes 4–12 of the *Opera omnia* edited at the instance of Pope Leo XIII (Rome, 1891–1906). The Leonine edition was made directly from a selection of manuscripts. In editing the questions on faith, for example, the Leonine Commission used eleven manuscripts that are conserved at the Vatican Library. These represent only about 4 percent of the surviving complete manuscripts of the second section of the second part, and, coming from a single library, can hardly be considered representative. As a check on the Leonine edition, then, I have also used the edition prepared by a team of Dominicans working in Canada (Ottawa, 1941–1945). The volumes from Ottawa reprint the text of the great Piana edition of Thomas's works—an edition made at the behest of Pope Pius V (Rome, 1570–1571). That too was partly critical, in that it attempted to gather at least some of the alternate readings. But it is just like the Leonine edition in being a small slice across a large textual history. The Dominican team added extremely useful notes, and their text remains the most serviceable of the modern editions.

In what follows, I have indicated significant differences between the Leonine and Piana editions, as well as among the manuscripts that the Leonine Commission used. I have thoroughly revised their proposed notations on the authorities for Thomas's discussion, trying where possible to cite a critical Latin version and preferably one close to the version that Thomas would have used. Where other intermediate sources are immediately identifiable, I have also listed them, but I have not attempted to identify all intermediaries. In other ways, too, I have tried to remain close to the manuscripts' evidence. Question and article headings have been put in brackets, for example, because they cannot be attributed with any certainty to Thomas. But in all of this we should not fool ourselves. The standardization implicit in any modern critical edition, whether of Thomas or his sources, already makes the text something very different from a medieval text. Moreover, the experience of "reading" a printed book is entirely different from that of "reading" a manuscript. For example, the speed with which we can run through print makes our reading less careful, less reflective, and less attentive to style than Thomas's reading. A modern translation can go some way towards recreating a medieval approach to Thomas's original, but its failures must always outweigh its successes.

Expository notes have been kept to a minimum. To remark even on the major points would have meant writing a running commentary at the bottom of each page. I have only added exposition where it seemed necessary to prevent a likely misunderstanding. Beyond that, Thomas himself will have to teach, however hobbled by the manacles of my English.

ABBREVIATIONS FOR WORKS CITED

Buytaert: John Damascene. *De Fide Orthodoxa* [= *On the Orthodox Faith*]. Ed. E. M. Buytaert. St. Bonaventure, N. Y.: Franciscan Institute Press, 1955.

CCL: *Corpus Christianorum, Series Latina.* [A series of patristic and medieval texts in Latin.] Turnhout: Brepols, 1953-.

Chevallier: *Dionysiaca.* Ed. Philippe Chevallier. Paris and Bruges: Desclée de Brouwer, 1937-.

CSEL: *Corpus Scriptorum Ecclesiasticorum Latinorum.* [A series of editions of patristic and medieval texts in Latin.] Vienna, 1866-.

De Boor: *Theophanis Chronographia.* Ed. Carolus De Boor. Leipzig: Teubner, 1883-1885. [The Latin version of this work was widely circulated under the title, *Historia Tripertita.*]

Grottaferrata: Peter Lombard. *Sententiae in IV Libris Distinctae.* 3rd ed. Grottaferrata: Collegium S. Bonaventurae, 1971-1981.

Lindsay: Isidore of Seville. *Isidori Hispalensis Episcopi Etymologiarum sive Originum.* Ed. W. M. Lindsay. Oxford: Clarendon Press, 1911.

Mansi: *Sacrorum Conciliorum Nova et Amplissima Collectio . . . .* Ed. I. D. Mansi. Reprint. Paris and Leipzig: H. Welter, 1901-1927.

PG: *Patrologiae Cursus Completus, Series Graeca.* Ed. J.-P. Migne. [A series of editions of patristic and medieval texts in Greek.] Paris,1857-1866.

PL: *Patrologiae Cursus Completus, Series Latina.* Ed. J.-P. Migne. [A series of patristic and medieval texts in Latin.] Paris, 1841-1864.

Quaracchi: Alexander of Hales [actually Alexander and his students]. *Summa Theologica* [= *Summa Halensis*]. Quaracchi: Collegium S. Bonaventurae, 1924-1948.

Richter-Friedberg: *Corpus Iuris Canonici.* Ed. Richter and Friedberg. Reprint. Leipzig: B. Tachnitz, 1922.

Strasbourg: *Glossa Ordinaria* and *Glossa Interlinearis.* From the version in *Biblia latina cum glossa ordinaris Walafridi Strabonis et interlineari Anselmi Laudinensis.* 4 vols. Strasbourg: Adolf Rusch, c. 1480. [This edition offers good testimony to the content and arrangement of twelfth-and thirteenth-century manuscripts of the glosses. Because the edition is unpaginated, it is cited by volume and then by biblical verse, with a final indication of the column for the marginal gloss.]

Summa theologiae, Part 2-2, Questions 1-16: On Faith

Prologue to the Second Part of the Second Part

After the consideration in general of virtues and vices and of the other things belonging to moral matter, it is necessary to consider single things specially. Universal moral discourses are less useful, in that actions are about particular things. Something can be considered specially about moral things in two ways. In one way, on the part of the moral matter, as when one considers this virtue or this vice. In another way, in regard to the special states of man, as when one considers subordinates and rulers, those who are active and those who are contemplative, or any other differences among men.[1] So we shall first consider specially the things that belong to the states of all men, then, second, specially the things that belong to determinate states.

One should consider in the first [way] that if we were to decide about virtues, gifts, vices, and precepts sequentially, it would be necessary to say the same thing many times over. Whoever wants to treat sufficiently of the precept, "You shall not commit adultery," must necessarily inquire about adultery, which is a certain sin, the apprehension of which depends on the apprehension of the opposed virtue. A more concise and rapid path (*via*) of

[1] The reader is reminded that "man" and "men" are being used to translate *homo* and *homines*, which Thomas uses to refer equally to both women and men. For the reasons behind the English translation, see the remarks in the introduction.

consideration would be to have the consideration take up simultaneously, as part of the same treatment, the virtue and the gift corresponding to it, and the opposed vices, and the affirmative or negative precepts. Furthermore, this way of consideration would appropriately take up the vices themselves according to their proper species. It was shown above that vices and sins are differentiated in species according to the matter or object, not according to other differences in the sinners, such as [sins] of the heart, mouth, and work, or [sins] according to weakness, ignorance, and malice, and other differences of this kind.[2] The virtue works rightly and the opposed vices withdraw from rightness in regard to one and the same matter.

In this way, once the whole moral matter has been traced back to the consideration of the virtues, all the virtues are further to be traced back to seven, of which three are theological and four are cardinal—the latter are taken up afterwards. As for the intellectual virtues, one of them is prudence, which is contained by the cardinal virtues and numbered among them. Art does not belong to moral knowledge, which concerns things to be done (*agibilia*), since art is right reason about things to be made (*factibilia*), as was said above.[3] The other three intellectual virtues, namely wisdom, understanding, and knowledge, share their names with certain gifts of the Holy Spirit. They will be considered at the same time as are the gifts corresponding to the virtues. All the other moral virtues are traced back in some way to the cardinal virtues, as is clear from what has been said.[4] So that in the consideration of any cardinal virtue there will also be considered all the virtues belonging to it in any way and all theopposed vices. And in this way nothing of the moral will be passed over.

---

[2] *Summa* 1–2 q.72.
[3] *Summa* 1–2 q.57 aa.3–4.
[4] *Summa* 1–2 q.61 a.3.

Question 1

[On the Object of Faith]

As regards the theological virtues, then, one should go on to consider, first, faith; second, hope; third, charity. As regards faith, there is a fourfold consideration: first, about faith itself; second, about the gifts of understanding and knowledge corresponding to it; third, about the opposed vices; fourth, about the precepts belonging to this virtue. As regards faith, one should go on to consider, first, its object; second, its act; third, the habit itself.

As regards the first point, ten queries are raised: (1) Whether the object of faith is the first truth. (2) Whether the object of faith is something complex or not complex, that is, a signified thing (*res*) or a truth-bearing statement (*enuntiabile*).[1] (3) Whether something false can come under faith. (4) Whether the object of faith can be something seen. (5) Whether it can be something known (*scitum*). (6) Whether things believed ought to be distinguished into fixed articles. (7) Whether the same articles come under faith throughout all time. (8) On the number of articles. (9) On the way of handing down the articles in a creed. (10) To whom does it belong to compose the creed for faith.

---

[1] Note that the enumeration proceeds according to the rhetorical figure called *chiasmus*: a, b//b, a. A signified thing is simple; a truth-bearing statement is complex.

Article 1. [Whether the object of faith is the first truth.]

One proceeds in this way to the first query. IT SEEMS that the object of faith is not the first truth.

[1] The object of faith seems to be what is proposed to us for believing. But what concerns the divinity, which is the first truth, is not the only thing proposed to us for believing. There are also the things that belong to the humanity of Christ, the sacraments of the Church, and the condition of creatures. Therefore the first truth alone is not the object of faith.

[2] Furthermore, faith and unfaithfulness are about the same thing, since they are opposites. But there can be unfaithfulness about all the things contained in sacred Scripture. If a man denies any one of these, he is considered to be unfaithful. Therefore faith too is about all things contained in sacred Scripture. But many things are contained there about man and about other created things. Therefore the object of faith is not only the first truth, but also created truth.

[3] Furthermore, in dividing, faith is grouped together with charity, as was said above.[2] By charity we love not only God, who is the highest good, but we also love our neighbor. Therefore the object of faith is not only the first truth.

BUT TO THE CONTRARY there is what Dionysius says, *Divine Names*, chapter 7, "faith concerns the simple and always existing truth."[3] This truth is the first truth. Therefore the object of faith is the first truth.

I ANSWER THAT IT SHOULD BE SAID that the object of every habit of apprehending (*habitus cognoscitivus*) has two aspects: namely, what is apprehended

[2] *Summa* 1–2 q.62 a.2.

[3] Ps-Dionysius, *Divine Names* chap.7 sect.4 (PG 3:872C; Chevallier 1:409). For the abbreviations used in the notes, see above, Abbreviations of Works Cited.

materially, which is like the material object; and that by which it is apprehended, which is the formal account of the object (*formalis ratio obiecti*). In the body of knowledge of geometry, the conclusions are the things known materially, while the middle terms of demonstration, by which the conclusions are apprehended, are the formal account of the knowing. So it is in faith. If we consider the formal account of the object, it is nothing else than the first truth, because the faith of which we speak assents to nothing except as it is revealed by God. Faith begins from the divine truth as from a middle term. If we consider materially the things to which faith assents, its object is not only God, but many other things. Yet these do not fall within the assent of faith except as they are ordered in some way to God—namely, so far as man is helped by certain effects[4] of divinity in tending towards divine fulfillment. And the object of faith even considered materially is in some way the first truth, so far as nothing falls within faith except as ordered to God. Just so the object of medicine is health, since medicine considers nothing except as ordered to health.

[1] TO THE FIRST ARGUMENT, THEREFORE, IT SHOULD BE SAID that what things belong to the humanity of Christ and to the sacraments of the Church or to any creature whatever fall within faith so far as we are ordered by them to God. And we also assent to them because of the divine truth.

[2] And the same should be said to the second argument, about all the things that are handed down in sacred Scripture.

[3] To the third, it should be said that charity too loves (*diligit*) a neighbor because of God, and so its proper object is God, as will be said below.[5]

---

[4] Some other versions read "affects."

[5] *Summa* 2-2 q.25 a.1.

Article 2. [Whether the object of faith is something complex in the way that a truth-bearing statement is.]

One proceeds in this way to the second query. IT SEEMS that the object of faith is not something complex in the way that a truth-bearing statement is.

[1] The object of faith is the first truth, as has been said.[6] But the first truth is something not complex. Therefore the object of faith is not something complex.

[2] Furthermore, the exposition of the faith is contained in the creed. But things are put in the creed, not truth-bearing statements. It does not say there that God is omnipotent, but "I believe in God omnipotent."[7] Therefore the object of faith is not a truth-bearing statement, but a thing.

[3] Furthermore, faith is replaced by vision, according to 1 Corinthians 13: "Now we see through a mirror in obscurity, but then face to face."[8] But the vision in the homeland is of what is not complex, since it is of the very divine essence. So also the faith of the journey.[9]

BUT TO THE CONTRARY faith is a middle between knowledge and opinion. The middle and the extremes belong to the same genus. Since knowledge and opinion concern truth-bearing statements, however, it would seem that faith too would concern truth-bearing statements. And in this

---

[6] In article 1 of this question, above.

[7] I here ignore a technical distinction that will become crucial later in Thomas's discussion of the act of faith. (See below, q.2 a.2.) In that discussion, *credere in Deum* will be rendered as "to believe for the sake of God." Here, nothing is lost if the Latin preposition *in* takes its more familiar English cognate.

[8] 1 Corinthians 13.12.

[9] One of the oldest Christian metaphors compares the present life to a journey homeward to heaven. Following this metaphor, which he learns principally from Augustine, Thomas describes this life as being "on the road" or "on the journey" (*in via*) and the next life as being "in the homeland" (*in patria*).

way the object of faith, since faith concerns truth-bearing statements, is something complex.

I ANSWER THAT IT SHOULD BE SAID that things apprehended are in the one who apprehends them according to the way of the one who apprehends. The way proper to the human intellect is that it apprehend the truth by combining and dividing, as was said in the first part.[10] And so the human intellect apprehends things that are simple in themselves according to a certain complexity, just as conversely the divine intellect apprehends without complexity the things that are complex in themselves. Thus the object of faith can be considered in two ways. In one way, on the part of the thing believed itself, and thus the object of faith is something not complex, namely the thing itself about which faith is had. In another way, [it can be considered] on the part of the believer, and in this way the object of faith is something complex in the manner of a truth-bearing statement. And so it was that both opinions were truly held among the ancients (*antiqui*),[11] and each is true in a certain way.

[1] TO THE FIRST, THEREFORE, IT SHOULD BE SAID that this reasoning proceeds from the object of faith [considered] on the part of the thing believed.

[2] To the second it should be said that the creed touches on the things of which there is faith so far as the act of the believer reaches its end in them. This is apparent from its very way of speaking. The act of the believer does not reach its end in a statement, but in the thing: we do not form statements except so that we may have apprehension of things through them. As it is in knowledge, so also in faith.

---

[10] *Summa* 1 q.85 a.5.

[11] In this context, Thomas seems to use *antiqui* to refer to medieval Latin theologians two or three generations before him (say, 1170 to 1230). But he can also use it to speak of the Jews of the Old Testament or of the Church Fathers.

[3] To the third it should be said that the vision of the homeland will be of the first truth as it is in itself, according to 1 John 3, "When he will appear, we will be like him and we will see him as he is."[12] And so that vision will not be in the manner of a statement, but in the manner of simple understanding (*simplex intelligentia*). But by faith we do not apprehend the first truth as it is in itself. So they cannot be reasoned about in the same way.

Article 3. [Whether what is false can come under faith.]

One proceeds in this way to the third query. IT SEEMS that what is false can come under faith.

[1] In dividing, faith is grouped together with hope and charity. But something false can come under hope. Many hope that they will have eternal life, which they will not have. Similarly with charity: many love as good those who are not good. So also what is false can come under faith.

[2] Furthermore, Abraham believed that Christ would be born, according to John 8: "Abraham, your father, rejoiced that he might see my day."[13] Yet, after the time of Abraham, God could still not have become incarnate. He took on flesh only by his will. And so what Abraham believed of Christ could have been false. Therefore what is false can come under faith.

[3] Furthermore, the faith of the ancients (*antiqui*) was that Christ was yet to be born, and this faith endured in many until the preaching of the gospel. But once he had already been born, and yet before preaching began, it was false that Christ was still to be born. Therefore what is false can come under faith.

[4] Furthermore, one of the things that can come under faith is that one believes that Christ's true body is con-

---

[12] 1 John 3.2.

[13] John 8.56.

tained under the sacrament of the altar.[14] It can happen, nonetheless, when it is not rightly consecrated, that the true body of Christ is not there, but only bread. Therefore what is false can come under faith.

BUT TO THE CONTRARY no virtue that completes the understanding has to do with the false so far as it is something evil for the understanding, as is clear in the Philosopher, *Ethics* 6.[15] But faith is a virtue that completes the understanding, as will be clear below.[16] Therefore nothing false can come under it.

I ANSWER THAT IT SHOULD BE SAID that nothing belongs to a power or habit, or even to an act, except by means of the formal account[17] of the object. Just so color cannot be seen except by light,[18] and a conclusion cannot be known except by the middle term of demonstration. It has been said,[19] however, that the formal account of the object of faith is the first truth. So nothing can fall under faith except so far as it stands under the first truth—under which nothing false can stand, as non-being (*non-ens*) cannot stand under being (*ens*), or evil under goodness. So it remains that nothing false can come under faith.

[1] TO THE FIRST, THEREFORE, IT SHOULD BE SAID that, since truth is the good of the understanding, it is not the good of the appetitive power.[20] Thus all virtues

---

[14] That is, in the rightly consecrated Eucharistic bread.

[15] Aristotle, *Nicomachean Ethics* bk.6 chap.2 (1139b11–12).

[16] *Summa* 2–2 q.4. a.2, a.5.

[17] Some versions read "except immediately by the formal account."

[18] Some versions read "except by the light-bearing transparent medium."

[19] In article 1 of this question, above.

[20] The notion of appetite or of the appetitive power is basic in Thomas's description of living things—indeed, by extension, in his description of all creatures. Appetite is the experience of being ordered to an end, of having a teleology. For the basic distinction between appetitive and intellectual powers in the human soul, see *Summa* 1 q.80

that complete the understanding completely exclude the false, since it is part of the account of virtue that it has to do only with the good. The virtues that complete the appetitive part do not completely exclude the false. Someone can act justly or temperately while holding a false opinion about what he does. And so, since faith completes the understanding, while hope and charity complete the appetitive part, they cannot be reasoned about in the same way.

Yet neither can something false come under hope. One does not hope that one will have eternal life by one's own power (this would be presumptuous), but with the aid of grace. If he were to persevere in grace, he would infallibly attain to eternal life.—Similarly it belongs to charity to love God in whomever he might be. So it does not matter to charity whether God is [really] in the one who is loved because of God.

[2] To the second it should be said that, considered just in itself, it was possible even after the time of Abraham that God not become incarnate. But so far as it falls under divine foreknowledge, the thing has a kind of infallible necessity, as was said in the first part.[21] And it falls under faith in this way. So far as it falls under faith, then, it cannot be false.

[3] To the third it should be said that it belonged to the faith of one who believed after Christ's birth that he should believe Christ whenever Christ might be born. But the determination of the time [of Christ's birth], in which this believer was deceived, was not from faith, but from human conjecture. It is possible for a faithful man to project something false on the basis of human conjecture. But as to what he projects by faith, this is impossible.

[4] To the fourth it should be said that the faith of the believer is not referred to these or those appearances (*species*) of bread, but to this, that the true body of Christ is

---

a.2. In us, the appetitive includes the passions and the will.

[21] *Summa* 1 q.14 a.13.

under the appearances of sensible bread when it has been rightly consecrated. So that if it was not rightly consecrated, something false would not on that account come under faith.

Article 4. [Whether the object of faith can be something seen.]

One proceeds in this way to the fourth query. IT SEEMS that the object of faith is something seen.

[1] The Lord says to Thomas, John 20, "Since you have seen me, you have believed."[22] Therefore vision and faith can be of the same thing.

[2] Furthermore, the Apostle says, 1 Corinthians 13: "Now we see through a mirror in obscurity."[23] And he speaks of the apprehension of faith. Therefore what is believed is seen.

[3] Furthermore, faith is a certain sort of spiritual light. But something is always seen by means of any kind of light. Therefore faith is of things seen.

[4] Furthermore, any sense can be called sight, as Augustine says, in *On the Word of the Lord.*[24] But faith is of things heard, according to Romans 10, "Faith comes from hearing."[25] Therefore faith is of things seen.

BUT TO THE CONTRARY there is what the Apostle says, Hebrews 11: "Faith is the argument of things that do not appear."[26]

I ANSWER THAT IT SHOULD BE SAID that faith denotes an assent of the understanding to what is believed. The understanding assents to something in two ways. In

---

[22] John 20.29.

[23] 1 Corinthians 13.12.

[24] That is, Augustine, *Serm. ad popul.* serm.112 chap.6 (PL 38:646).

[25] Romans 10.17.

[26] Hebrews 11.1.

one way, because it is moved to this by the object itself. The object is either known through itself, as is clear in first principles, of which one has understanding; or it is known through another, as is clear in conclusions, of which one has knowledge. In a second way, the understanding assents to something, not because it is sufficiently moved by the proper object, but by a choice of the will tending to one alternative rather than another. And if this occurs with doubt and hesitation about the other alternative, there is opinion. If it occurs with certainty and without any such hesitation, there is faith. Things are said to be seen that by themselves move our intellect or sense to their apprehension. And so it is manifest that neither faith nor opinion can be of things seen either by sense or by intellect.

[1] TO THE FIRST, THEREFORE, IT SHOULD BE SAID that Thomas "saw one thing and believed another. He saw a man and, believing, confessed God, when he said: My God and my lord."[27]

[2] To the second it should be said that the things that belong to faith can be considered in two ways. In one way, specially: and in this way they cannot simultaneously be seen and believed, as has been said.[28] In another way, they can be considered generally, namely, as being under the common account of the believable. And in this way they are seen by him who believes. For he would not believe if he did not see that they were to be believed, either because of the evidence of signs or because of something else of this kind.

[3] To the third it should be said that the light of faith makes one see the things that are believed. Just as by other habits of virtues a man sees what is appropriate for

[27] Compare Gregory the Great, *Hom. in Evang.* bk.2 hom.26 sect.8 (PL 76:1202A).

[28] In the body of this article.

him according to that habit, so also by the habit of faith the mind of man is inclined to assent to the things that are appropriate to right faith and not to others.

[4] To the fourth it should be said that hearing takes in words that signify the things of faith, but it does not take in the things themselves about which one has faith. And so it does not follow that things of this sort are seen.

Article 5. [Whether the things that are of faith can be known.]

One proceeds in this way to the fifth query. IT SEEMS that the things that are of faith can be known.

[1] Things that are not known would seem to be unknown, since unknowing is opposed to knowledge. But the things that are of faith are not unknown: it is unfaithful to be unknowing about them, according to 1 Timothy 1: "Unknowing I acted in my disbelief."[29] Therefore the things that are of faith can be known.

[2] Furthermore, knowledge is acquired by reasonings. But one is led to the things that are of faith by reasonings from sacred authors.[30] Therefore the things that are of faith can be known.

[3] Furthermore, things that are proved demonstratively are known, since demonstration is a syllogism making one to know. But some of the things contained in faith are proved demonstratively by the philosophers, such as that God is, that God is one, and other things of this kind. Therefore the things that are of faith can be known.

[4] Furthermore, opinion is further removed from knowledge than faith is, since faith is said to be a middle between opinion and knowledge. But opinion and knowledge can

---

[29] 1 Timothy 1.13.

[30] Some versions read "sacred teachers."

be had in some way about the same thing, as is said in *Posterior Analytics* 1.[31] So also faith and knowledge.

BUT TO THE CONTRARY there is what Gregory says, "Things that appear are not held by faith, but in acquaintance."[32] There is, then, no acquaintance with those things about which there is faith. But there is acquaintance with things that are known. Therefore there cannot be faith about the things that are known.

I ANSWER THAT IT SHOULD BE SAID that all knowledge is had by principles known through themselves, and thus seen. And so it follows that whatever things are known are seen in some way. Now it is not possible that one and the same thing be believed and seen, as was said.[33] So it is also impossible that the same thing be known and believed by one person.

It can happen, however, that what is seen or known by one is believed by another. What we believe about the Trinity, we hope to see, according to 1 Corinthians 13, "Now we see through a mirror in obscurity, but then face to face."[34] The angels already have this vision, so that they see what we believe. And similarly it can happen that what is seen or known by one man, even in the state of the journey, is believed by another, who does not know it demonstratively. What is commonly proposed to all men for believing is commonly not known. And these things belong simply to faith. And so faith and knowledge are not of the same thing.

[1] TO THE FIRST ARGUMENT, THEREFORE, IT SHOULD BE SAID that the unfaithful are unknowing of what is of faith, since they neither see nor apprehend them

[31] Aristotle, *Posterior Analytics* bk.1 chap.33 (89a23–25).

[32] Gregory the Great, *Hom. in Evang.* bk.2 hom.26 sect.8 (PL 76:1202A).

[33] *Summa* 2–2 q.1 a.4, above.

[34] 1 Corinthians 13.12.

in themselves, nor apprehend that they are believable.[35] But the faithful are aware of them in this way, not as if demonstratively, but so far as they are seen under the light of faith as things to be believed, as was said.[36]

[2] To the second it should be said that the reasonings that are brought forward by the saints[37] to prove the things of faith are not demonstrative. They are, rather, some persuasions for showing that what is proposed in faith is not impossible. Or they proceed from the principles of faith, namely from the authorities of sacred Scripture, as Dionysius says, *Divine Names*, chapter 2.[38] From these principles something is proved for the faithful in the same way that something is proved for all from naturally known principles. And so theology is also a body of knowledge, as was said in the beginning of the work.[39]

[3] To the third it should be said that things proved demonstratively can be counted among the things to be believed, but not in the sense that all should simply have faith about them. Since they are prerequisites to the things that are of faith, they ought to be presupposed all at once in faith by those who cannot demonstrate them.

[4] To the fourth it should be said that, as the Philosopher says in the same place, different men can have knowledge and opinion about the same thing, just as has now been said about knowledge and faith. One and the same person can also have faith and knowledge of something that is one in a certain respect, namely in subject, but not according to the same thing. It can be that with regard to

---

[35] Some versions read "that they may apprehend that they are to be believed."

[36] In article 4, reply [3], above.

[37] That is, the Church Fathers.

[38] Ps-Dionysius, *Divine Names* chap.2 sect.2 (PG 3:640; Chevallier 1:70–71).

[39] *Summa* 1 q.1 a.2.

one and the same thing someone knows one thing and opines something else. And similarly someone can know demonstratively that God is one, and believe that he is triune. But of the same thing in the same respect knowledge cannot exist simultaneously in one man together with opinion or with faith, though for different reasons. Knowledge cannot simultaneously be together with opinion about the same thing simply speaking, since it is part of the account of knowledge that what is known cannot possibly be otherwise. It is part of the account of opinion that what someone opines, he recognizes as possibly being in another way. But what is had by faith, because of the certainty of faith, is also recognized as not possibly being otherwise. One thing in one respect cannot simultaneously be known and believed, for the reason that the known is seen and the believed is not seen, as was said.

Article 6. [Whether believable things are to be distinguished into certain articles.]

One proceeds in this way to the sixth query. IT SEEMS that believable things are not to be distinguished into certain articles.

[1] Faith is holding all the things that are contained in sacred Scripture. But these cannot be reduced to some given number, because of their multitude. Therefore it seems superfluous to distinguish articles of faith.

[2] Furthermore, every art should avoid a material distinction, since such a distinction can go on to infinity. But the formal account of the believable object is one and indivisible, namely, the first truth, as was said above.[40] And thus believable things cannot be distinguished according to the formal account. Therefore the material distinction of believable things by objects should be avoided.

---

[40] In article 1, above.

[3] Furthermore, as is said by some,[41] an article is "an indivisible truth about God compelling us to believe." But to believe is voluntary, since, as Augustine says, "no one believes unless he wills."[42] Therefore it seems that believable things are inappropriately distinguished into articles.

BUT TO THE CONTRARY there is what Isidore says: "An article is a perception of divine truth tending towards it."[43] But the perception of divine truth properly belongs to us (*competit nobis*) according to distinction; the things that are one in God are multiplied in our understanding. Therefore believable things ought to be distinguished into articles.

I ANSWER THAT IT SHOULD BE SAID that the name "article" seems to be derived from the Greek. *Arthron* in Greek, which is called *articulus* in Latin, signifies a certain coadaptation of distinct parts. And so the small parts of the body coadapted to each other are called the "articles" of the members. And similarly in grammar the Greeks named "articles" certain parts of speech coadapted to other locutions in order to express their genus, number, or case.[44] And similarly in rhetoric the "articles" are certain coadaptations of the parts. Cicero says in the *Rhetoric*, that "an 'article' is when single words in an oration are distinguished by pauses. For example, 'By sharpness . . . voice . . . visage you have terrified your adversaries.' "[45] So also the believable things of the Chris-

---

[41] By Thomas's near predecessors, such as Philip the Chancellor and William of Auxerre.

[42] Augustine, *In Ioann.* tr.26 sect.2, on John 6.44 (PL 35:1607; CCL 36:260.14).

[43] This definition is also attributed to Isidore in Albert the Great and Bonaventure, but it appears in an earlier work by Philip the Chancellor without attribution.

[44] So too in English grammar we speak of definite and indefinite articles.

[45] Rather, the anonymous *Rhetorica ad Herennium* bk.4 chap.19

tian faith are said to be distinguished into articles in as much as they are divided into certain parts coadapted to each other.

Now the object of faith is something in the divine essence that is not seen, as was said above.[46] So wherever there is something that is not seen because of some special reason, one has a special article. Where many things are not apprehended for the same reason,[47] articles are not distinguished. Since there is one difficulty in seeing that God died, and another in seeing that he was raised from death, the article on resurrection is distinguished from the article on the passion. But since his dying, his being dead, and his being buried share in one and the same difficulty, and since having accepted one it is not difficult to accept the others, all these things belong to one article.

[1] TO THE FIRST ARGUMENT, THEREFORE, IT SHOULD BE SAID that about some believable things there is faith *per se*; about other believable things there is not faith *per se*, but only as they are ordered to other things. Just so in other bodies of knowledge some things are propounded as intended *per se*, and some for making other things clear. Because faith is principally about the things we hope to see in the homeland, according to Hebrews 11, "Faith is the substance of things to be hoped for,"[48] those things belong to faith *per se* that order us directly to eternal life, such as the three persons, the omnipotence of God, the mystery of the incarnation of Christ, and other things of this kind. And the articles of faith are distinguished according to these. Other things are pro-

---

sect.16. This work was attributed to Cicero throughout the Latin Middle Ages, and it formed one of the core texts for the teaching of rhetoric.

[46] In article 4 of this question, above.

[47] Some versions read, "apprehended or not apprehended for the same account."

[48] Hebrews 11.1.

posed for belief in sacred Scripture not as what is principally intended, but for the sake of making clear the former things, such as that Abraham had two sons, that at the touch of the bone Elijah was raised from the dead, and others of this kind, which are narrated in sacred Scripture in order to make manifest the divine majesty or the incarnation of Christ. And articles ought not to be distinguished according to such things.

[2] To the second it should be said that the formal account of the object of faith can be understood in two ways. One way, on the part of the very thing believed. And in this way the formal account of all believable things is one, namely, the first truth. And in this way articles are not distinguished. The formal account of believable things can be taken in another way, on our part. And in this way the formal account is that the believable is something not seen. And in this way the articles of faith are distinguished, as has been said.

[3] To the third it should be said that the cited definition of "article" is given more according to a particular etymology of the name, as it has a Latin derivation, than according to its true signification, as it is derived from the Greek. So the definition does not have great weight.— But it can also be said that, even though no one is compelled by force to believe, since believing is voluntary, he is bound nonetheless by the necessity of the end, for "one must believe in order to come to God," and "without faith it is impossible to please God," as the Apostle says, Hebrews 11.[49]

---

[49] Hebrews 11.6.

Article 7. [Whether the articles of faith grew with the passing of time.]

One proceeds in this way to the seventh query. IT SEEMS that the articles of faith did not grow with the passing of time.

[1] As the Apostle says, Hebrews 11, "Faith is the substance of things hoped for."[50] But the same things are to be hoped for in all times. Therefore in all times the same things are to be believed.

[2] Furthermore, in humanly ordered bodies of knowledge, there is an increase with the passing of time because there was a defect of apprehension in the first discoverers of the bodies of knowledge, as is clear in the Philosopher, in *Metaphysics* 2.[51] Yet the doctrine of faith is not humanly discovered, but handed down by God: "For it is the gift of God," as it says in Ephesians 2.[52] Since no defect of knowledge falls to God, it seems that the apprehension of believable things was complete from the beginning, and that it did not grow with the passing of time.

[3] Furthermore, the operation of grace does not proceed in a less orderly fashion than does the operation of nature. But nature always takes its beginning from complete things, as Boethius says in the *Consolation*.[53] Therefore it also seems that the operation of grace should take its beginning from complete things, so that those who at first handed down the faith apprehended it completely.

[4] Furthermore, just as faith in Christ came to us from the apostles, so in the Old Testament the apprehension of faith came from the earlier Fathers to the later ones, according to Deuteronomy 32: "Ask your father and he will

---

[50] Hebrews 11.1

[51] Aristotle, *Metaphysics* bk.2 chap.1 (993b10–19).

[52] Ephesians 2.8.

[53] Boethius, *Consolatio philosophiae* bk.3 pros.10 sect.5 (CSEL 67: 65.1–3; CCL 94:53.14–16).

announce it to you."[54] But the apostles were most fully instructed about the mysteries: they accepted them, "for just as they were the first in time, so they were more abundant than the rest," as it says in the *Gloss* on Romans 8, "we having the first fruits of the Spirit."[55] So it seems that the apprehension of believable things did not grow with the passing of time.

BUT TO THE CONTRARY there is what Gregory says, that "the knowledge of the holy Fathers grew with increments of time;" and as they were closer to the coming of the Savior, so much more plainly did they perceive the sacrament of salvation.[56]

I ANSWER THAT IT SHOULD BE SAID that the articles of faith stand in the teaching of faith as principles known through themselves stand in the teaching of what is had by natural reason. A certain order is found in these principles. Some are implicitly contained in others, just as all principles are traced back to this first principle: "It is impossible at once to affirm and to deny," as is clear from the Philosopher, *Metaphysics* 4.[57] And similarly all articles are implicitly contained in certain first believable things, namely, in its being believed that God exists and has prov-

---

[54] Deuteronomy 32.7.

[55] *Glossa Lombardi* on Romans 8.23 (PL 191:1444D).—Here and elsewhere, Thomas's references to "the Gloss" or "some gloss" can point in a number of different directions, such as the *Glossa ordinaria*, the *Glossa interlinearis*, and the *Glossa* of Peter Lombard. Sometimes, indeed, essentially the same text is repeated in two of these sources and it is impossible to determine from the citation alone just which one Thomas had in mind. But since only the Lombard's text is available in a modern edition, and since it seems more often than not to correspond to Thomas's citations, I have given it as the sole reference wherever possible. In other words, I will list the other *Glossae*, which are so much harder to consult, only as a last resort.

[56] Gregory the Great, *Hom. in Ezech.* bk.2 hom.4 sect.12 (PL 76:980; CCL 142:267.340–344).

[57] Aristotle, *Metaphysics* bk.4, e.g., chap.6 (1011b20), but Aristotle's argument advances dialectically through several chapters (bk.4 chap.3–8).

idence over the salvation of men, according to Hebrews 11: "Coming to God one must [believe] that he exists and that he rewards those who seek him."[58] Divine existence (*esse*) includes all the things that we believe exist eternally in God, in which our blessedness consists.[59] Faith about providence includes all the things dispensed by God in time for the salvation of men, which things are the way to blessedness. And in this way some of the subsequent articles[60] are contained in others. In faith about human redemption there is implicitly contained the incarnation of Christ and his passion and all such things.

Thus it is to be said that, as regards the substance of the articles of faith, there has been no increase in them with the passing of time, since whatever things the later Fathers believe were contained in the faith of the earlier, even if implicitly. But as regards explication, the number of articles grew, since some were explicitly apprehended by the later which were not explicitly apprehended by the earlier. So the Lord says to Moses, Exodus 4: "I am the God of Abraham, the God of Isaac, the God of Jacob: and I did not tell my name Adonai to them."[61] And David says, "I have understood more than the old ones."[62] And the Apostle says, Ephesians 3: "In other generations there was no acquaintance with the mystery of Christ as it is now revealed to his holy apostles and prophets."[63]

[1] TO THE FIRST ARGUMENT, THEREFORE, IT SHOULD BE SAID that the same things were always to be hoped for by all.[64] Since men would not come to the hoped-for things except through Christ, as they were more

---

[58] Hebrews 11.6.

[59] Some versions read "exists."

[60] Some versions read "the existing articles."

[61] Exodus 6.2–3, paraphrased.

[62] Psalm 118.100.

[63] Ephesians 3.5.

[64] Some versions read "hoped for from Christ by men."

remote from Christ in time, so were they farther from the attainment of what they hoped. Thus the Apostle says, Hebrews 11: "All of these died in faith, without having received what things were promised, but looking at them from afar."[65] So far as something is seen from farther off, so much less distinctly is it seen. And so the hoped for goods were more distinctly apprehended by those who were close to the coming of Christ.

[2] To the second it should be said that improvement in apprehension happens in two ways. In one way, on the part of the teacher—whether one or many—who improves in apprehension with the passing of time. And this is the reason for the increase in bodies of knowledge discovered by human reason. In another way, on the part of the learner. The master who grasps an entire art does not immediately hand it on to his student all at once, since the student would not understand, but he does so slowly, considering the student's capacity. And for this reason men improved in the apprehension of faith with the passing of time. So the Apostle, Galatians 3, compares the state of the Old Testament to childhood.[66]

[3] To the third it should be said that there are two prerequisites for natural generation, namely what is active (*agens*) and the matter. Now according to the order of the active cause, what is more complete is naturally prior, and so nature takes its beginning from complete things, since incomplete things are not led to completion except by complete, preexistent things. According to the order of the material cause, what is incomplete is prior, and so according to it nature proceeds from the incomplete to the complete. In showing forth the faith, God is like what is active, and has complete knowledge from eternity; man is like the matter, receiving the influx of the acting God. And so the apprehension of faith in men should proceed from the

[65] Hebrews 11.13.
[66] Galatians 3.24.

incomplete to the complete. And even if some men among the many act in the manner of the active cause, since they are teachers of faith, even so "the manifestation of the Spirit is given to such for the common usefulness," as 1 Corinthians 12 says.[67] And so that much was given to the Fathers, who were the instructors[68] in faith of the apprehension of faith, as was right [for them] to give to their people at the time, whether nakedly or figuratively (*in figura*).

[4] To the fourth it should be said that the last consummation of grace was made by Christ, so that his time is called the "fullness of time," Galatians 4.[69] And so those who were closer to Christ, either before him, as John the Baptist, or after, as the apostles, apprehended the mystery of faith more plainly. We also see this with regard to the state of man, that completion comes in youth, and so man has a more complete state the closer he is to youth, whether before it or after it.

Article 8. [Whether the articles of faith are appropriately counted out.]

One proceeds in this way to the eighth query. IT SEEMS that the articles of faith are inappropriately counted out.

[1] Things that can be known by demonstrative reason do not belong to faith in the sense that they are believable things for all, as was said above.[70] But that God is one can be known by demonstration. The Philosopher proves this in *Metaphysics*, 12,[71] and many other philosophers offered demonstrations of it. Therefore that God is one should not be put as one article of faith.

---

[67] 1 Corinthians 12.7, paraphrased.

[68] Some versions read "the institutors."

[69] Galatians 4.4.

[70] In article 5 of this question, reply [3], above.

[71] Aristotle, *Metaphysics* bk.12 chap.10 (1076a4).

[2] Furthermore, just as it belongs necessarily to faith that we believe in an omnipotent God, so also that we believe him to know all things and to provide for all. Concerning both of these some have erred. Therefore mention should be made of the divine wisdom and providence among the articles of faith, just as mention is made of omnipotence.

[3] Furthermore, awareness of the Father and of the Son is the same, according to John 14, "Who sees me sees also the Father."[72] Therefore there ought to be only one article about the Father and the Son—and, for the same reason, about the Holy Spirit.

[4] Furthermore, the person of the Father is not less than that of the Son or the Holy Spirit. But many articles are put about the person of the Holy Spirit, and similarly about the person of the Son. Therefore many articles ought to be put about the person of the Father.

[5] Furthermore, just as something is appropriated to the person of the Father and the person of the Holy Spirit, so also to the person of the Son according to [his] divinity. But in the articles there is put some work appropriated to the Father, namely the work of creation; and similarly some work appropriated to the Holy Spirit, namely that "he spoke through the prophets." Therefore in the articles some work should also be appropriated to the Son according to divinity.

[6] Furthermore, the sacrament of the Eucharist presents a special difficulty beyond many other articles. Therefore a special article ought to be put about it. It does not seem, therefore, that the articles are sufficiently counted out.

BUT TO THE CONTRARY there is the authority of the Church so counting them.

I ANSWER THAT IT SHOULD BE SAID that those things belong *per se* to faith in the vision of which we will

---

[72] John 14.9.

have fruition in eternal life and by which we are led to eternal life, as was said.[73] Now two things are proposed for us to see there: namely what is hidden in divinity, the vision of which will make us blessed; and the mystery of the humanity of Christ, by which "we enter into the glory of the sons of God," as is said in Romans 5.[74] So it is said in John 17, "This is eternal life, that they apprehend you, the true God, and him whom you sent, Jesus Christ."[75] And so the first distinction of believable things is that some belong to the majesty of divinity, while some belong to the mystery of the humanity of Christ, which is the "sacrament of piety," as it says in 1 Timothy 4.[76]

Now concerning the majesty of divinity three things are proposed to us for believing. First, the unity of the deity, and to this belongs the first article. Second, the trinity of persons, and for this there are three articles according to the three persons. Third, there are proposed to us the proper works of divinity. Of which the first belongs to the existence of nature, and so there is proposed to us the article of creation. The second belongs to the existence of grace, and thus there is proposed to us under one article all things belonging to human sanctification. The third belongs to the existence (*esse*) of glory, and so there is proposed another article about the resurrection of the flesh and eternal life. And so there are seven articles belonging to divinity.

Similarly seven articles are also put concerning the humanity of Christ. Of which the first is about the incarnation or conception of Christ; the second, about his birth from the Virgin; the third, about his passion and death and burial; the fourth is about the descent into hell (*ad inferos*); the fifth is about the resurrection; the sixth, about

---

[73] In article 6 of this question, reply [1], above.

[74] Romans 5.2, paraphrased.

[75] John 17.3

[76] 1 Timothy 3.16.

the ascension; the seventh, about the coming in judgment. And so altogether there are fourteen.

Some distinguish twelve articles of faith, six belonging to divinity and six belonging to humanity. They comprehend the three articles about the three persons under one, since the apprehension of the three persons is the same. They distinguish the article about the work of glorification into two parts, namely the resurrection of the flesh and the glory of the soul. Similarly they conjoin into one the article of the conception and that of the birth.

[1] TO THE FIRST ARGUMENT, THEREFORE, IT SHOULD BE SAID that we hold many things about God by faith that the philosophers could not investigate by natural reason, such as about his providence and omnipotence, and that he alone is to be worshiped. All of which are contained under the article about the unity of God.

[2] To the second it should be said that the very name "divinity" (*divinitas*) denotes a kind of providing (*provisio*), as was said in the first book [that is, in the first part].[77] In those who have understanding, however, a power does not work except according to will and apprehension. And so the omnipotence of God includes in some way all knowledge and providence: for he cannot do all the things he wills in these lower beings unless he apprehends them and has providence over them.

[3] To the third it should be said that the apprehension of the Father and the Son and the Holy Spirit is one as regards unity of essence, which belongs to the first article. As concerns the distinction of persons, which is by relations of origin, the apprehension of the Son is somehow included in the apprehension of the Father, for he would not be Father if he did not have a Son. Their connection is the Holy Spirit. And so far as this goes, those who put one article for three persons were well motivated. But since

---

[77] *Summa* 1 q.13 a.8.

there are also some things to be attended to about the single persons that give rise to error, in this respect three articles can be put for three persons. Arius believed the Father to be omnipotent and eternal, but did not believe the Son to be coequal and consubstantial with the Father. And so it was necessary to insert the article on the person of the Son in order to determine this. And for the same reason it was necessary to put the third article on the person of the Holy Spirit against Macedonius.

And similarly also Christ's conception and birth, and the resurrection and eternal life, can be comprehended under one article according to one account, so far as they are ordered to one [thing]; and according to another account they can be distinguished, so far as they have special difficulties.

[4] To the fourth it should be said that it was appropriate to send the Son and the Holy Spirit for sanctifying creatures, concerning which there are many things to be believed. And so concerning the person of the Son and of the Holy Spirit many more articles are added than concerning the person of the Father, who was never sent, as was said in the first [part].[78]

[5] To the fifth is should be said that the sanctification of the creature by grace and its consummation by glory are done both by the gift of charity, which is appropriated to the Holy Spirit, and by the gift of wisdom, which is appropriated to the Son. And so either work belongs both to the Son and to the Holy Spirit by appropriation according to different accounts.

[6] To the sixth it should be said that two things can be considered in the sacrament of the Eucharist. One being what a sacrament is, and this has the same account as the other effects of sanctifying grace. Another is that the body of Christ is miraculously contained there; this is included

---

[78] *Summa* 1 q.43 a.4.

under omnipotence, as are all other miracles, which are attributed to omnipotence.

Article 9. [Whether the articles of faith are appropriately put into a creed.]

One proceeds in this way to the ninth query. IT SEEMS that the articles of faith are not appropriately put into a creed.

[1] Sacred Scripture is the rule of faith. It is not permitted to add to it or to subtract from it, as is said in Deuteronomy 4, "You shall not add to the word that I speak to you, nor will you take away from it."[79] Therefore it was illicit to compose a creed as a rule of faith after sacred Scripture was set forth (*editam*).

[2] Furthermore, as the Apostle says, Ephesians 4, "The faith is one."[80] But the creed is a profession of faith. Therefore it is inappropriate that a creed with many parts be handed down.

[3] Furthermore, the confession of faith that is contained in the creed belongs to all the faithful. But it is not appropriate for all the faithful to believe "for the sake of God,"[81] but only those who have formed faith. Therefore it is inappropriate that the creed of faith be handed down in the form of these words, "I believe for the sake of one God" (*in unum Deum*).

[4] Furthermore, the descent into hell is one of the articles of faith, as was said above.[82] But in the Nicene creed there is no mention of the descent into hell. Therefore it seems insufficiently comprehensive.

---

[79] Deuteronomy 4.2.

[80] Ephesians 4.5, paraphrased.

[81] Thomas recognizes a technical distinction among *credere Deo, credere Deum,* and *credere in Deum.* See below, q.2 a.2. See also above, the glossary in the introduction.

[82] In article 8 of this question, above.

[5] Furthermore, as Augustine says, expounding John 14,[83] "Believe for the sake of God, and believe for my sake," we believe Peter or Paul, but we do not say that we believe for the sake of anyone except "for the sake of God." Since therefore the catholic Church is simply something created, it seems inappropriate that it should be said, "for the sake of one holy, catholic, and apostolic Church."

[6] Furthermore, the creed is handed down so that it might be the rule of faith. But a rule of faith is said to be proposed to all and publicly. Every creed should therefore be sung in the mass, as is the Nicene creed.[84] Therefore it does not seem to be appropriate to set forth the articles of faith in a creed.

BUT TO THE CONTRARY the universal Church cannot err, since it is governed by the Holy Spirit, who is the Spirit of truth. This the Lord promised to his disciples, John 16, saying, "When the Spirit of truth comes, he will teach you all truth."[85] But the creed is set forth by the authority of the universal Church. Therefore nothing inappropriate is contained in it.

I ANSWER THAT IT SHOULD BE SAID that, as the Apostle says, Hebrews 11, "coming to God one must believe."[86] But someone cannot believe unless the truth that he believes is proposed to him. And so it was necessary that the truth of faith be collected into one, so that it might be more easily proposed to all, that no one should lack the truth of faith because of ignorance. From this sort of collection of the judgments (*sententiae*) of faith the name "creed" is taken.

---

[83] Augustine, *In Ioann.* tr.29 sect.6, on John 7.17 (PL 35:1631; CCL 36:287.36–39).

[84] Literally, the "creed of the Fathers," the Fathers here being the Fathers of the Council of Nicea.

[85] John 16.13.

[86] Hebrews 11.6.

[1] TO THE FIRST ARGUMENT, THEREFORE, IT SHOULD BE SAID that the truth of faith is contained in sacred Scripture diffusely and in various ways, and in some places obscurely; so that long study and exercise are required in order to elicit the truth of faith from sacred Scripture. But all those for whom it is necessary to apprehend the truth of faith cannot arrive at this point, because many of them, occupied by other affairs, cannot pursue study. And so it was necessary that something clear be collected in summary form from the judgments of sacred Scripture, which would be proposed to all for believing. This is not something added to sacred Scripture, but rather taken from sacred Scripture.

[2] To the second it should be said that the same faith is taught in all the creeds. But where errors arise, there the people must be more diligently instructed in the faith, that the faith of the simple not be corrupted by heretics. And this was the cause for its being necessary to set forth many creeds. These differ in nothing except that in one there are more fully explained what are contained in another implicitly, as is required by the presence of heretics.

[3] To the third it should be said that the confession of faith is handed down in a creed as if by the person of the whole Church, which is united by faith. The faith of the Church is formed faith; such faith is found in all those who are of the Church in number and in merit. And so the confession of faith in the creed is handed down as appropriate to formed faith, so that if some of the faithful do not have formed faith, they may study to achieve this form.

[4] To the fourth it should be said that no error arose among heretics about the descent into hell, and so it was not necessary to make another explication about this. And so it was not reiterated in the Nicene creed, but was supposed as already predetermined in the Apostles' creed. A

subsequent creed does not abolish a preceding one, but rather expounds it, as was said.[87]

[5] To the fifth it should be said that if the creed says "for the sake of the holy catholic Church," this is to be understood according to how our faith is referred to the Holy Spirit, who sanctifies the Church, as if the meaning were, "I believe for the sake of the Holy Spirit sanctifying the Church." But it is better, and according to the more common usage, that "for the sake of" not be put here, but that it simply say "holy catholic Church," just as Pope Leo says.

[6] To the sixth it should be said that, since the Nicene creed serves to declare the Apostles' creed, it was established once the faith had been made manifest and the Church was at peace. On account of this it is publicly sung at mass. The Apostles' creed, which was set forth in the time of persecution when the faith had never been made public, is said privately at prime and compline,[88] as if against the shadows of past and future error.

Article 10. [Whether it belongs to the supreme pontiff to ordain[89] the creed of the faith.]

One proceeds in this way to the tenth query. IT SEEMS that it does not belong to the supreme pontiff to ordain the creed of faith.

---

[87] In this article, reply [2].

[88] That is, at the first prayer of the full day and at the last prayer at night. The actual hours of celebration for these offices varied considerably in Dominican houses.

[89] The verb *ordinare* means here both to give order to the creed and to establish it as legally binding. Both senses should be read into the English "ordain."

[1] A new setting forth of the creed is necessary in order to explain the articles of faith, as was said.[90] But in the Old Testament the articles of faith were explained more and more with the passing of time because the truth of faith was made more manifest with greater nearness to Christ, as was said above.[91] Since such a cause disappears with the new law, there should be no greater and greater explanation of the articles of faith. Therefore it does not seem to belong to the authority of the supreme pontiff to set forth creeds.

[2] Furthermore, what is interdicted under anathema to the universal Church cannot be within the power of any man. But a new setting forth of the creed was prohibited under anathema by the authority of the universal Church. It is said in the acts of the first Ephesian synod that, the creed of the Nicene synod having been completed, "the holy synod decreed that it was not licit for anyone to offer or write or compose another faith than the one defined by the holy Fathers who were congregated in Nicea with the Holy Spirit."[92] And it adds the penalty of anathema. The same is also reiterated in the acts of the Chalcedonian synod.[93] Therefore it seems that a new setting forth of the creed does not belong to the authority of the supreme pontiff.

[3] Furthermore, Athanasius was not the supreme pontiff, but the Alexandrian patriach. And yet he composed a creed that is sung in the Church. Therefore a setting forth of the creed does not seem to belong more to the authority of the supreme pontiff than to others.

BUT TO THE CONTRARY the setting forth of a creed takes place in a general synod. This sort of synod can

---

[90] In article 9 of this question, reply [2], above.

[91] In article 7 of this question, above.

[92] Within Act 6 of the Council of Ephesus (Mansi 4:1362D-1364A).

[93] Within Act 5 of the Council of Chalcedon (Mansi 7:109A-B).

be convoked by the authority of the supreme pontiff alone, as is had in the *Book of Decrees* dist.17.[94] Thus the setting forth of a new creed belongs to the authority of the supreme pontiff.

I ANSWER THAT IT SHOULD BE SAID that a new setting forth of the creed is necessary in order to avoid errors that arise, as was said above. The authority to issue a creed belongs to whomever has the authority to determine by judgment (*sententialiter*)[95] the things that are of faith, so that they might be held by all with an unshattered faith. This belongs to the authority of the supreme pontiff, "to whom the larger and more difficult questions of the Church are referred," as it says in the *Book of Decrees* dist.43.[96] So also the Lord, Luke 22, says to Peter, whom he constituted as supreme pontiff: "I will pray for you, Peter, that your faith does not lack: and you, being strong, will sometimes confirm your brothers."[97] And the reason for this is that there should be one faith in the whole Church, according to 1 Corinthians 1, "The same thing say to all, that there not be schisms among you."[98] This cannot be fostered unless a question of faith arising from faith be determined by him who comes before the whole Church, so that his judgment be firmly held by the whole Church. And so it belongs only to the authority of the supreme pontiff to set forth a new creed, just as do all other things that belong to the whole Church, such as to convoke a general synod and other things of this kind.

---

[94] Gratian, *Decretum* part 1 dist.17 can.4 Nec licuit (Richter-Friedberg 1:51).

[95] Some versions read "finally" (*finaliter*).

[96] Gratian, *Decretum* part 1 dist.17 can.5 Multis denuo (Richter-Friedberg 1:51).

[97] Luke 22.32. Some versions read "when he constituted him as supreme pontiff."

[98] 1 Corinthians 1.10.

[1] TO THE FIRST ARGUMENT, THEREFORE, IT SHOULD BE SAID that in the teaching of Christ and the apostles the truth of faith is sufficiently explained. But because perverse men "perverted to their own perdition" the apostolic doctrine and the other Scriptures, as is said at the end of 2 Peter,[99] the explanation of faith against errors that arise is necessary as time goes on.

[2] To the second it should be said that the prohibition and judgment of the synod extend to private persons, who are not to determine about faith. The general synod did not by this kind of judgment take away the power of a subsequent synod to set forth the creed anew—not in the sense of containing another faith, but rather as better explaining the faith. For any synod has proceeded in this way, that a later synod can expound something beyond what a previous synod expounded, because of the necessity of some heresy that arises. Hence it belongs to the supreme pontiff, by whose authority the synod is convoked and by whom its judgment is confirmed.

[3] To the third it should be said that St. Athanasius did not compose a manifestation of faith in the way of a creed, but rather in the way of a teaching, as appears from his way of speaking. But since its teaching briefly contained the whole truth of faith, it was received by the authority of the supreme pontiff, that it should be held as if it were a rule of faith.

---

[99] 2 Peter 3.16

Question 2

[On the Inward Act of Faith]

One should next consider the act of faith. And first, the inward act; second, the outward act.

Ten queries are raised with regard to the first point. (1) What is believing, which is the inward act of faith? (2) In how many ways is the word "believe" used? (3) Whether believing something beyond natural reason is necessary to salvation. (4) Whether believing the things at which natural reason cannot arrive is necessary. (5) Whether it is necessary for salvation to believe something explicitly. (6) Whether all are held equally to believe something explicitly. (7) Whether it is always necessary for salvation to have explicit faith about Christ. (8) Whether it is necessary for salvation to believe something explicitly about the Trinity. (9) Whether the act of faith is meritorious. (10) Whether human reason diminishes the merit of faith.

Article 1. [Whether to believe is "to think with assent."]

One proceeds in this way to the first query. IT SEEMS that to believe is not "to think with assent."[1]

[1] Thinking implies some inquiry. In Latin, *cogitare,* "to think," seems to come from *simul agitare,* "to treat simultaneously." But the Damascene says, in book 4, that

[1] This phrase comes from Augustine, as will be made clear below in the argument "But to the contrary."

faith is consent without inquiry.[2] Therefore thinking does not belong to the act of faith.

[2] Furthermore, faith is placed in reason, as will be said below.[3] But to think is an act of the cogitative power (*virtus cogitativa*),[4] which belongs to the sensitive part, as is said in the first [part].[5] Therefore thinking does not belong to faith.

[3] Furthermore, believing is an act of the understanding, since its object is the truth. Yet to assent does not seem to be an act of the understanding, but of the will, just as consenting is, as was said above.[6] Therefore believing is not to think with assent.

BUT TO THE CONTRARY Augustine defines believing in this way in *On the Predestination of the Saints.*[7]

I ANSWER THAT IT SHOULD BE SAID that "thinking" can be taken in three ways. In one way, it is taken commonly and as applying to any actual consideration of the understanding, as Augustine says, *On the Trinity* 14: "I now call understanding that by which we understand when thinking."[8] In another way, "thinking" is said more properly of the consideration of the understanding that takes place with inquiry, before one comes to the completion of understanding in the certainty of vision. And according to this sense, Augustine says, in *On*

---

[2] John Damascene, *On the Orthodox Faith* bk.4 sect.11 (PG 94:1128D; Buytaert chap.84 sect.1, 300.20–21).

[3] *Summa* 2–2 q.4 a.2.

[4] This objection equivocates on the words *cogitatio* and *cogitativa*. *Cogitatio* means something like what we ordinarily mean by "thinking," and *cogitativa* would ordinarily mean something like "of thinking." But *virtus cogitativa* is a technical name for a subintellectual power of collating sense images.

[5] *Summa* 1 q.78 a.4.

[6] *Summa* 1–2 q.15 a.1.

[7] Augustine, *De praedest. sanct.* chap.2 sect.5 (PL 44:963).

[8] Augustine, *De Trinitate* bk.14 chap.7 sect.10 (PL 42:1044; CCL 50A:435.53–54).

the Trinity 15, that "the Son of God is not called the thinking, but the Word of God. Thinking is obviously our coming to what we know, and when formed from it our word is true. And so the Word of God should be understood without thinking, but not as having something formable in it, which could be unformed."[9] And in this way, thinking is properly said of a motion of the deliberating soul that is not yet completed by the full vision of truth. But because such a motion can be either of the soul deliberating about a universal intention, which belongs to the understanding part; or of the soul deliberating about particular intentions, which belongs to the sensitive part; so "thinking" in the second sense is taken for the act of the understanding deliberating; in the third way, for the act of the cogitative power.

If "thinking" be taken commonly, therefore, and according to the first sense, "to think with assent" does not capture the whole account of what it is to believe. For in this sense even one who considers things he knows or understands thinks with assent. If "thinking" be taken in the second sense, one can understand in this phrase the whole account of the act that is believing. Some of the acts belonging to the understanding have firm assent without such thinking, as when one considers what one knows or understands; this sort of consideration is already formed. Other acts of understanding have a certain unformed thinking without firm assent: whether tending to neither alternative, as happens when one doubts; or tending more to one alternative, but holding it lightly, as happens in one who suspects; or adhering to one alternative, but with hesitation about the other, which happens in one who opines.

But the act of believing has firm adherence to one alternative, in which the believer agrees with the knower and the one who understands. Yet its apprehension is not com-

---

[9] Augustine, *De Trinitate* bk.15 chap.16 sect.25 (PL 42:1079; CCL 50A:500.9–14).

pleted by manifest vision,[10] in which the believer agrees with the doubter, the suspecter, and the opiner. And so it is proper to the believer to think with assent. Because of this the act of believing is distinguished from all other acts of the understanding that are about the true and the false.

[1] TO THE FIRST ARGUMENT, THEREFORE, IT SHOULD BE SAID that faith does not have the inquiry of natural reason, which demonstrates what it believes. But it has some inquiry into the things by which a man is led to believe, namely that they are said by God and confirmed by miracles.

[2] To the second it should be said that "to think" (*cogitare*) is not taken here so far as it is an act of the cogitative power (*virtus cogitativa*), but so far as it belongs to the understanding, as was said.

[3] To the third it should be said that the understanding of the believer is determined to one alternative not by reason, but by the will. And so "assent" is here taken as an act of the understanding so far as it is determined to one alternative by the will.

Article 2. [Whether the act of faith is appropriately distinguished into "believing God" (*credere Deo*), "believing about God" (*credere Deum*), and "believing for the sake of God" (*credere in Deum*).]

One proceeds in this way to the second query. IT SEEMS that the act of faith is inappropriately distinguished into believing about God, believing God, and believing for the sake of God.

[1] There is one act for one habit. But faith is one habit, since it is one virtue. Therefore many acts are inappropriately put for it.

---

[10] Some versions read "by the greatest vision."

[2] Furthermore, what is common to every act of faith should not be put as a particular act of faith. But believing God is found commonly in every act of faith, since faith begins from the first truth. Therefore it seems that this is inappropriately distinguished from every other act of faith.

[3] Furthermore, what belongs even to those who are not faithful cannot be put as an act of faith. But believing about God does belong even to those who are not faithful. Therefore it ought not be put as an act of faith.

[4] Furthermore, to be moved to an end belongs to the will, the object of which is the good and the end. But to believe is not an act of the will, but of understanding. Therefore believing for the sake of God ought not to be put as one difference of faith, since it implies motion to an end.

BUT TO THE CONTRARY Augustine put this distinction in *On the Word of the Lord* and *On John.*[11]

I ANSWER THAT IT SHOULD BE SAID that the act of any power or habit is taken according to the order (*ordo*) of the power or habit to its object. Now the object of faith can be considered in three ways. Since believing belongs to the understanding so far as it is moved by the will to assenting, as was said,[12] the object[13] of faith can be taken on the part of the understanding itself, or on the part of the will moving the understanding. If it is taken on the part of the understanding, two things can be considered in the object of faith, as was said above.[14] One is the

---

[11] Rather, Augustine, *Serm. ad popul.* serm.144 chap.2 sect.2 (PL 38:788) and *In Ioann.* tr.29 sect.6, on John 7:19 (PL 35:1631; CCL 36:287.33–41).

[12] Preceding article, reply [3].

[13] Some versions read "the subject."

[14] In question 1, article 1, above. The reader is reminded that the translations proposed in what follows are, at best, unidiomatic English renderings of a technical distinction in Latin. "Believing about God" (*credere Deum*) means believing things that have to do with God or

material object of faith. And thus the act of faith is put as "believing about God," since, as was said above,[15] nothing is proposed to us for believing except as it belongs to God. The other consideration is the formal account of the object, which serves as a middle through which one assents to such a believable thing. And in this way the act of faith is put as "believing God," since, as was said above,[16] the formal object of faith is the first truth, in which man inheres so that through it he might assent to what is believed. If the object of faith is considered in the third way, according as the understanding is moved by the will, in this way the act of faith is put as "believing for the sake of God." The first truth is referred to the will according as it has the account of an end.

[1] TO THE FIRST ARGUMENT, THEREFORE, IT SHOULD BE SAID that these three do not designate diverse acts of faith, but one and the same act in diverse relations to the object of faith.

[2] And this makes clear the answer to the second argument.

[3] To the third it should be said that believing about God does not belong to those without faith according to the same account by which it is put as an act of faith. They do not believe that God exists under the conditions that faith determines. And so they do not truly believe about God, since, as the Philosopher says, *Metaphysics* 9, in simple things a defect of apprehension just by itself makes for not grasping them entirely.[17]

---

with what God does. "Believing God" (*credere Deo*) means believing what God says because God says it. "Believing for the sake of God" (*credere in Deum*) means believing for the sake of attaining God as one's last end, as the goal of one's willing.

[15] In question 1, article 1, above. Note that Thomas reverses the order of the terms in the traditional list.

[16] In question 1, article 1, above.

[17] *Metaphysics* bk.9 chap.10 (1051b23–27).

[4] To the fourth it should be said that, as was said above,[18] the will moves the understanding and the other powers of the soul to the end. And according to this the act of faith is put as believing for the sake of God.

Article 3. [Whether believing something beyond natural reason is necessary for salvation.][19]

One proceeds in this way to the third query. IT SEEMS that believing is not necessary to salvation.

[1] The salvation and completion of anything is sufficiently provided for by the things that belong to it according to its nature. But the things that are of faith exceed the natural reason of man, since they are of what does not appear, as was said above.[20] Therefore believing does not seem to be necessary for salvation.

[2] Furthermore, it is dangerous for a man to assent to things when he cannot judge whether what is proposed is true or false, according to Job 12, "Does he not judge words by the ear?"[21] But a man cannot make such a judgment about the things that are of faith, since a man cannot trace them back to first principles, by which we judge all things. Therefore it is dangerous to give faith to such things. Therefore believing is not necessary for salvation.

[3] Furthermore, the salvation of man lies in God, according to Psalms, "The salvation of the just is from the

---

[18] *Summa* 1 q.82 a.4.

[19] The Latin term *salus*, which we ordinarily translate as "salvation" in theological contexts, means more simply well-being. That is why Thomas is perfectly comfortable speaking about the "salvation . . . of anything." He does not mean that inanimate objects can be saved in the theological sense, but that they can attain to a level of well-being appropriate to their kind. I have chosen to retain the customary translation, even though it will conceal certain analogies, because it alone can bear the theological senses required.

[20] In question 1, article 4, above.

[21] Job 12.11.

Lord."[22] Yet "the invisible things of God are disclosed, being understood by the things that are made, his sempiternal power and divinity," as Romans 1 says.[23] Things conceived by the understanding are not believed. Therefore it is not necessary to salvation that man believe some things.

BUT TO THE CONTRARY Hebrews 11 says, "Without faith it is impossible to please God."[24]

I ANSWER THAT IT SHOULD BE SAID that in all ordered natures it is found that two things concur in completing the lower nature: one according to its proper motion; another according to the motion of the higher nature. Just so water moves by its proper motion to the center; by the motion of the moon it is moved around the center in flux and reflux.[25] Similarly the spheres of the planets are moved with a proper motion from west to east, then by the motion of the first sphere from east to west.[26] Only the created rational nature has an immediate ordering to God. Other creatures do not attain to something universal, but to something particular alone, participating only in the divine goodness or in being (*in essendo*), such as do inanimate things, or also in living and in apprehending singulars, such as do plants and animals. But the rational nature, in as much as it apprehends the universal of the good and the account of being (*entis ratio*), has an immediate ordering to the universal principle of being (*essendi*). The completion of the

---

[22] Psalm 36.39.

[23] Romans 1.20.

[24] Hebrews 11.6.

[25] In Aristotelian physics, water by itself or properly tends downwards, to the center of the cosmos, which is the center of the earth. The tidal motion of the oceans is not natural or proper to water, but is caused by the moon.

[26] In Ptolemaic astronomy, as Thomas understands it, the particular or proper motion of a planet is along its unique path from west to east. The daily rotation of the whole of the heavens around the earth is caused by the separate motion of the whole celestial sphere.

rational creature thus does not consist only in what belongs to it according to its nature, but also in what is attributed to it by a certain supernatural participation[27] of divine goodness. So it was said above that the last blessedness of man lies in a certain supernatural vision of God.[28] To which vision man cannot attain except in the way of one who learns from God as teacher, according to John 6, "Whoever listens to the Father and learns comes to me."[29] But this kind of learning does not make man a participant all at once, but successively, as is the way of his nature. It follows that every such learner must believe, so that he might come to complete knowledge, as even the Philosopher says, that the learner ought to believe.[30] Hence in order that man come to the complete vision of blessedness it is required beforehand that he believe God, just as a student must believe a master who teaches him.

[1] TO THE FIRST ARGUMENT, THEREFORE, IT SHOULD BE SAID that, since the nature of man depends upon a higher nature, natural apprehension is not sufficient for his completion, as was said above.[31]

[2] To the second it should be said that, just as man assents to principles by the natural light of understanding, so the man who is virtuous with the habit of faith has right judgment about the things appropriate to that virtue. And in this way also, by the light of faith divinely infused in him, man assents to what things are of faith, but not to their contraries. And so "nothing" dangerous or "of damnation is for those who are in Jesus Christ,"[32] illuminated by him through faith.

---

[27] Some versions read "completion."

[28] *Summa* 1 q.21 a.1, 1–2 q.3 a.8.

[29] John 6.45.

[30] Aristotle, *On Sophistical Refutations* bk.1 chap.2 (165b3).

[31] In the body of this article.

[32] Romans 8.1.

[3] To the third it should be said that faith perceives the invisible things of God in a higher mode, as regards most, than the natural reason proceeding from the creature towards God. So Sirach 3 says: "Many things above the sense of man were shown to you."[33]

Article 4. [Whether it is necessary to believe things that natural reason can prove.]

One proceeds in this way to the fourth query. IT SEEMS that it is not necessary to believe things that can be proved by natural reason.

[1] Nothing superfluous is found in the works of God, much less than in the works of nature. But it is superfluous to add another thing to what can be done by one thing. Therefore it would be superfluous to accept by faith the things that can be apprehended by natural reason.

[2] Furthermore, it is necessary to believe the things about which there is faith. But knowledge and faith are not of the same thing, as was had above.[34] Since knowledge is of all those things that can be known by natural reason, it seems that one ought not to believe the things that can be proved by natural reason.

[3] Furthermore, all knowable things seem to share in one account. If then some of them were proposed to man as things to be believed, by the same account it would be necessary to believe all such things. But this is false. Therefore it is not necessary to believe the things that can be known by natural reason.

BUT TO THE CONTRARY it is necessary to believe that God is one and not bodily, things that are proved by the philosophers by natural reason.

---

[33] Sirach 3.25.

[34] In question 1, article 5, above.

I ANSWER THAT IT SHOULD BE SAID that it is necessary for man to accept in the way of faith not only the things that are above reason, but also the things that can be known by reason. And this for three reasons. First, so that man might come more quickly to the apprehension of divine truth. The body of knowledge that has the task of proving that God exists and other such things about God, is proposed to men for learning last, many other sciences being presupposed. And so man could not come to the apprehension of God during his life except after a long time. Second, so that the apprehension of God be more common. Many cannot make progress in the study of knowledge, either because of dullness of wit; or because of other occupations and the necessities of temporal life; or even because of laziness in learning. All of them would be entirely cheated of the apprehension of God unless divine things were proposed to them in the manner of faith. Third, on account of certainty. Human reason is much deficient in divine things. A sign of this is that the philosophers, investigating human things naturally, erred in many things and held opinions (*senserunt*) contrary to themselves. Divine things had to be handed down to them in the manner of faith, as being said by God, who cannot lie, so that there might be indubitable and certain apprehension of God among men.

[1] TO THE FIRST ARGUMENT, THEREFORE, IT SHOULD BE SAID that the investigation of natural reason does not suffice to humankind for the apprehension even of the divine things that can be shown by reason. And so it is not superfluous that such things be believed.

[2] To the second it should be said that knowledge and faith cannot be about the same thing in the same individual. But what is known by one can be believed by another, as was said above.[35]

---

[35] In question 1, article 5, above.

[3] To the third it should be said that, if all knowable things agree in [sharing] the account of knowledge, they do not agree in being equally ordered to blessedness. And so all things are not equally proposed as things to be believed.

Article 5. [Whether man is held to believe something explicitly.]

One proceeds in this way to the fifth query. IT SEEMS that man is not held to believe something explicitly.

[1] No one is held to what is not in his power. But to believe something explicitly is not in man's power. It is said in Romans 10, "How will they believe him whom they have not heard? How will they hear without a preacher? How will they preach if they are not sent?"[36] Therefore man is not held to believe something explicitly.

[2] Furthermore, just as we are ordered by faith to God, so also by charity. But man is not held to follow the precepts of charity. Preparation of the soul [for charitable acts] suffices by itself, as is clear in the precept of the Lord, Matthew 5, "If someone strikes you on one cheek, lend to him also the other,"[37] and in other similar [texts], which Augustine expounds, in the *Lord's Sermon on the Mount*.[38] Therefore man is also not held to believe something explicitly, but it is enough that he have a soul prepared to believe what things are proposed by God.

[3] Furthermore, the good of faith lies in a certain obedience, according to Romans 1, "to the obedience of faith in all the gentiles."[39] But it is not required for the virtue of

---

[36] Romans 10.14–15.

[37] Matthew 5.39.

[38] Augustine, *De serm. Dom. in monte* bk.1 chap.19 sect.58–59 (PL 34:1260; CCL 35:66–69).

[39] Romans 1.5.

obedience that man observe some determinate precept. It suffices that he have a soul prompt in obeying,[40] according to the psalm, "I am prepared and I am not troubled, that I might observe your commandment."[41] Therefore it seems that also for faith it suffices that man have a soul prompt in believing the things that can be divinely proposed to him, without his having to believe something explicitly.

BUT TO THE CONTRARY there is what is said in Hebrews 11, "Coming to God, one must believe that he exists, and that he rewards those who seek him."[42]

I ANSWER THAT IT SHOULD BE SAID that the precepts of the law that man is held to fulfill concern the acts of virtue, which are the path for coming to salvation. But acts of virtue, as was said above,[43] are taken according to their standing towards the virtue's object. In the object of any virtue whatever two things can be considered, namely, what is properly and *per se* the object of the virtue, which is necessary in every act of the virtue; and again what stands *per accidens* or in consequence to the proper account of the object. So it belongs properly and *per se* to the object of fortitude to bear up under the danger of death and to attack enemies, even if there is danger, for the sake of the good. But that a man should be armed or should strike with a sword in a just war, or do something of this sort, is traced back in some way to the object of fortitude, but *per accidens*. Thus the determination of virtuous acts to the proper and *per se* object of virtue comes under the necessity of precept, just as does the very act of virtue. But the determination of the virtuous act to the things that stand accidentally or secondarily in relation to the proper and *per se* object of virtue does not fall

[40] Some versions read "believing," others "observing."

[41] Psalm 118.60.

[42] Hebrews 11.6.

[43] In article 2 of this question, above.

under the necessity of the precept, except as regards a certain time and place.

Therefore it is to be said that the *per se* object of faith is that by which man is made blessed, as was said above.[44] All those other things that are contained in divinely revealed Scripture stand either *per accidens* or secondarily to the object of virtue: such as that Abraham had two sons, that David was the son of Isaac, and others of this kind. As regards the first believable things, which are the articles of faith, man is held to believe them explicitly, just as he is also held to have faith. As regards the rest of the believable things, man is not held explicitly to believe, but only implicitly or by preparation of soul, so far as he is prepared to believe whatever is contained in divine Scripture. But then he is held explicitly to believe only when something becomes present to him as being contained in the doctrine of faith.

[1] TO THE FIRST ARGUMENT, THEREFORE, IT SHOULD BE SAID that if we speak of what is in man's power without the help of grace, then man is held to do many things that he cannot do without restoring grace,[45] such as loving God and neighbor. He is similarly held to believe the articles of faith. But man can do this with the help of grace. This help is given mercifully to whomever it is given. To whom it is not given, it is justly denied in punishment for preceding sin, especially original sin, as Augustine says, in *On Correction and Grace*.[46]

[2] To the second it should be said that man is held to love determinately those lovable things which are properly and *per se* the objects of charity, namely God and neighbor. But the objection proceeds from those precepts of

---

[44] In question 1, article 6, reply [1], above.

[45] Some versions read "preparing grace."

[46] Rather, Augustine, *Epist.* ep.190 chap.3 sect.9 (PL 33:860; CSEL 57:144.15–145.2); and *De praedest. sanct.* chap.8 (PL 44:971).

charity that belong to the object of charity as if consequently.

[3] To the third it should be said that the virtue of obedience lies properly in the will. And so promptness of will towards the commanding subject suffices for the act of obedience, which is properly and *per se* the object of obedience. But this or that [particular] precept stands either *per accidens* or consequently to the proper and *per se* object of obedience.

Article 6. [Whether all are equally held to have explicit faith.]

One proceeds in this way to the sixth query. IT SEEMS that all are equally held to have explicit faith.

[1] All are held to the things that are necessary to salvation, as is clear in the precepts of charity. But making things to be believed explicit is necessary to salvation, as was said.[47] Therefore all are equally held to believing explicitly.

[2] Furthermore, no one should be examined about what he is not held to believe explicitly. But sometimes even simple people are examined about the smallest articles of faith. Therefore all are held explicitly to believe all.

[3] Furthermore, if the lesser are not held to have explicit faith, but only implicit faith, it follows that they have implicit faith in the faith of the greater. But this seems to be dangerous, because it may happen that those greater ones err. Therefore it seems that the lesser ought also to have explicit faith. Therefore all are equally held to believe explicitly.[48]

---

[47] In article 5 of this question, above.

[48] Here and in many passages following, Thomas uses a variety of metaphors to describe the hierarchy of believers. He contrasts the greater with the lesser (*maior, minor*) and the higher with the lower (*superior,*

BUT TO THE CONTRARY there is what is said in Job 1, that "the oxen were watered and the asses were put to pasture next to them."[49] The lesser, who are signified by the asses, should adhere in things to be believed to the greater, who are signified by the oxen, as Gregory explains, *Moralia* 2.[50]

I ANSWER THAT IT SHOULD BE SAID that the making explicit of things to be believed is done by divine revelation, since believable things exceed natural reason. But divine revelation comes in a certain order from the higher to the lower, from angels to man, and from the higher angels to the lower, as is clear in Dionysius, *Celestial Hierarchy*.[51] And so, by the same reason, it follows that the making explicit of faith comes to lower men from greater. And so just as the higher angels, who illuminate the lower, have a fuller awareness of divine things than the lower, as Dionysius says,[52] so also higher men, to whom it belongs to teach others, are held to have a fuller awareness of things to be believed and are held to believe more explicitly.

[1] TO THE FIRST ARGUMENT, THEREFORE, IT SHOULD BE SAID that the making explicit of things to be believed is not necessary for salvation equally with respect to all, since the greater, who have the office of teaching others, are held to believe explicitly more than the others.

[2] To the second it should be said that the simple are not to be examined about the subtleties of faith except

---

inferior), but also mixes the pairs of terms. The hierarchy of believers represents degrees of explicitness or "formation" in faith, not degrees of actual virtue or of actual sanctity.

49 Job 1.14.

50 Gregory the Great, *Moralia* bk.2 chap.30 sect.49 (PL 75:578; CCL 143:88.5–89.11).

51 Ps-Dionysius, *Celestial Hierarchy* chap.4 sect.3 (PG 3:180C–182D; Chevallier 2:812).

52 Ps-Dionysius, *Celestial Hierarchy* chap.12 sect.2 (PG 3:292C-294A; Chevallier 2:935-937).

when there is suspicion that they have been depraved by heretics, who are accustomed to deprave the faith of the simple in what things belong to the subtlety of faith. If however they are found not to adhere to perverse doctrine stubbornly—if they are deficient in such things from simplicity—it is not imputed to them.

[3] To the third it should be said that the lesser do not have implicit faith in the faith of the greater except so far as the greater adhere to divine teaching. So the Apostle says, 1 Corinthians 11, "Be imitators of me, as I of Christ."[53] Human apprehension is not the rule of faith; divine truth is. If some of the greater are deficient in this, it does not prejudice the faith of the simple, since they believe them to have right faith, unless they stubbornly adhere to errors in a particular point against the faith of the universal Church, which cannot be deficient, since the Lord says, Luke 22, "I pray for you, Peter, that your faith not be deficient."[54]

Article 7. [Whether explicitly believing the mystery of Christ is necessary for salvation among all.]

One proceeds in this way to the seventh query. IT SEEMS that to believe explicitly in the mystery of Christ is not necessary for salvation among all.

[1] Man is not held to believe explicitly what the angels did not know; faith is made explicit by divine revelation, which comes to men by the mediation of angels, as was said.[55] But even the angels did not know the mystery of the incarnation, so that they asked in the psalm, "Who is this king of glory?"[56] and in Isaiah 63, "Who is this

[53] 1 Corinthians 11.1.

[54] Luke 22.32.

[55] In article 6 of this question, above.

[56] Psalm 23.8.

who comes from Edom?"[57] as Dionysius explains, *Celestial Hierarchy* 7.[58] Therefore men were not held explicitly to believe the mystery of the incarnation.

[2] Furthermore, it happens that blessed John the Baptist was among the greater and that he was closest to Christ. Of him, the Lord says, Matthew 11, that "among those born of woman no one arose greater than him."[59] But John the Baptist does not seem explicitly to have known the mystery of Christ, since he asks Christ, "Are you the one who is to come, or should we expect another?" as is had in Matthew 11.[60] Therefore even the greater were not held to explicit faith about Christ.

[3] Furthermore, many gentiles were enabled to attain salvation through the ministry of the angels, as Dionysius says, *Celestial Hierarchy* 9.[61] But the gentiles did not have either explicit or implicit faith about Christ, as it seems, since no revelation was made to them. Therefore it seems that to believe explicitly in the mystery of Christ was not necessary for salvation among all.

BUT TO THE CONTRARY there is what Augustine says, in *On Correction and Grace:* "That faith is healthy [or saving] faith by which we believe that no man, whether of greater or of lesser age, is freed from the contagion of death and the obligation of sin except by the mediator of God and men, Jesus Christ."[62]

I ANSWER THAT IT SHOULD BE SAID that what belongs properly and *per se* to the object of faith is that

---

[57] Isaiah 63.1.

[58] Ps-Dionysius, *Celestial Hierarchy* chap.7 sect.3 (PG 3:209B-C; Chevallier 2:855–857).

[59] Matthew 11.11.

[60] Matthew 11.3.

[61] Ps-Dionysius, *Celestial Hierarchy* chap.9 sect.4 (PG 3:261B; Chevallier 2:909–911).

[62] Rather, Augustine, *Epist.* ep.190 chap.2 sect.5 (PL 33:858; CSEL 57:141.10–15), with an allusion to 1 Timothy 2.5.

by which man acquires blessedness, as was said above.[63] The path for men to come to blessedness is the mystery of the incarnation and passion of Christ. It is said in Acts 4, "There is no other name given to men in which we ought to be saved."[64] And so it follows that the mystery of the incarnation of Christ is somehow to be believed by all in every time, but in different ways according to the diversity of times and persons.

Before the state of sin, man had explicit faith about the incarnation of Christ, so far as it was ordered to the consummation of glory, but not as ordered to liberation from sin by passion and death, since man did not have foreknowledge of future sin. It seems, however, that he did have foreknowledge of the future incarnation of Christ, since it is said: "On account of this a man leaves father and mother and clings to his wife," as in Genesis 2.[65] The Apostle says, Ephesians 5, that this "is a great sacrament in Christ and the Church."[66] It is not believable that the first man should be ignorant of this great sacrament.

After sin, the mystery of Christ was explicitly believed not only as regards the incarnation, but also as regards the passion and resurrection, by which humankind is liberated from sin and death. Otherwise they would not have prefigured the passion of Christ by certain sacrifices both before the law and under the law. The greater knew explicitly the significance of these sacrifices; the lesser, however, in a certain way had a veiled apprehension through the veils of the sacrifices, believing the sacrifices to be divinely disposed towards the coming Christ. And, just as is said above, they apprehended more distinctly the things that belong to the mysteries of Christ the nearer they were to Christ.

---

[63] In article 5 of this question, above.

[64] Acts 4.12.

[65] Genesis 2.24.

[66] Ephesians 5.32, condensed.

After the time of the revelation of grace, both the greater and the lesser are held to have explicit faith about the mysteries of Christ, principally as regards those which are commonly made customary in the Church and publicly proposed, such as are the articles of the incarnation, about which something was said above.[67] But they are held to other, subtle considerations concerning the articles of the incarnation as befits the state and office of each one.

[1] TO THE FIRST ARGUMENT, THEREFORE, IT SHOULD BE SAID that "the mystery of the kingdom of God was not entirely hidden from the angels," as Augustine says, *On Genesis to the Letter* 5.[68] But they apprehended more completely the reasons for this kind of mystery when Christ revealed them.

[2] To the second it should be said that John the Baptist did not ask about the coming of Christ in the flesh as if he did not know of it. He himself expressly confessed it, saying, "I saw, and gave testimony that this was the son of God," as is had in John 1.[69] So he does not say, "Are you he who came?" but, "Are you he who is to come?" asking about the future, not the past. Similarly it is not to be believed that John did not know of the passion that was to come, for he himself had said, "Behold the Lamb of God, who takes away the sins of the world,"[70] announcing his future immolation. Other prophets had predicted this before, as is clear principally in Isaiah 53.

It can be said, as Gregory says,[71] that John asked because he did not know whether he would descend to hell in his own person. He did know that the power of his pas-

---

[67] In question 1, article 8, above.

[68] Augustine, *De Genesi ad litt.* bk.5 chap.19 sect.38 (PL 34:334; CSEL 28:162.1–7).

[69] John 1.34.

[70] John 1.29.

[71] Gregory the Great, *Hom. in Evang.* bk.1 hom.6 sect.1 (PL 76:1095D-1096A).

sion would be extended even to those who were detained in limbo, according to Zechariah 9, "You also, in the blood of your testament, set free the captives of the lake in which there is no water."[72] John was not held to believe this explicitly, before it was fulfilled, that Christ himself should descend.

Or it can be said, as Ambrose says, *On Luke*,[73] that John did not ask out of doubt or ignorance, but rather out of piety.—Or it can be said, as Chrysostom says,[74] that John did not ask as if he did not know him, but so that his disciples might be satisfied through Christ. So that Christ too answered in order to instruct the disciples, showing the signs of works.

[3] To the third it should be said that the revelation of Christ was made to many of the gentiles, as is clear by what they predicted. It is said in Job 19, "I know that my Redeemer lives."[75] The Sibyl also announced certain things about Christ, as Augustine says.[76] There is also found in the histories of the Romans[77] that in the time of Constantine Augustus and Irene, his mother, there was discovered a certain tomb in which there lay a man who had a golden plate on his chest. On it was written, "Christ is to be born of a Virgin and I believe in him. O Sun, in the times of Irene and Constantine you will see me again."

---

[72] Zechariah 9.11.

[73] Ambrose, *In Luc.* bk.5 sect.98, on Luke 7.19 (PL 15:1662; CCL 14:167.1039–1044).

[74] John Chrysostom, *On Matt.* hom.36 (PG 57:418).

[75] Job 19.25.

[76] Augustine, *Contra Faustum* bk.13 chap.15 (PL 42:290, CCL 25:394.17–20).

[77] The original Latin source for the story is Anastasius's translation of the *Chronographia* of Theophanes for the Byzantine year corresponding to AD 780–781 ("Annus Mundi 6273"; De Boor 2:302). Changes of detail suggest that Thomas has the story from an intermediate source. The emperor is Constantine VI and Irene is Irene the Athenian, his mother and coruler. Most versions confuse Constantine VI with Constantine the Great, and so change "Irene" to "Helen."

If some were saved to whom a revelation was not made, they were still not saved without faith in a mediator. So that even if they did not have explicit faith, they nonetheless had implicit faith in divine providence, believing that God would be the liberator of men, in ways pleasing to him and according as he would reveal the truth to some who would know it, according to Job 35, "Who teaches us above the beasts of the earth."[78]

Article 8. [Whether believing explicitly in the Trinity is necessary to salvation]

One proceeds in this way to the eighth query. IT SEEMS that believing explicitly in the Trinity was not necessary to salvation.

[1] The Apostle says, Hebrews 11, "Coming to God one must believe that God exists and that he rewards those who seek him."[79] But this can be believed without faith in the Trinity. Therefore one did not have to have faith in the Trinity explicitly.

[2] Furthermore, the Lord says, John 17, "Father, I have made your name known among men."[80] Expounding this, Augustine says, "Not your name by which you are called 'God,' but that by which you are called 'my Father.' "[81] And he adds later: "So far as God made this world, he was known to all the gentiles; so far as he is not to be worshipped with false gods, God was known in Judaea; so far as he is the Father of Christ, by whom he takes away the sin of the world—this name of his, hidden beforehand, he now makes manifest to them." Before the

---

[78] Job 35.11.

[79] Hebrews 11.6.

[80] John 17.6

[81] Augustine, *In Ioann.* tr.106 sect.4, on John 17.6 (PL 35:1909; CCL 36:610.7–9).

coming of Christ, therefore, it was not known that there was fatherhood and sonhood in the deity. Therefore the Trinity was not explicitly believed.

[3] Furthermore, we are held explicitly to believe whatever in God is the object of blessedness. But the object of blessedness is the highest goodness, which can be understood in God even without the distinction of persons. Therefore it was not necessary to believe explicitly in the Trinity.

BUT TO THE CONTRARY in the Old Testament the Trinity of persons is expressed in many ways. Immediately at the beginning of Genesis it is said, in order to express the Trinity, "Let us make man in our image and likeness."[82] Therefore from the beginning it was necessary for salvation to believe in the Trinity.

I ANSWER THAT IT SHOULD BE SAID that the mystery of Christ cannot be believed explicitly without faith in the Trinity, since in the mystery of Christ this much is contained, that the Son of God assumed flesh, that he will renew the world by the grace of the Holy Spirit, and again that he was conceived of the Holy Spirit. And so in the same way that the mystery of Christ was explicitly believed by the greater before Christ, implicitly and as if darkly by the lower, so also was the mystery of the Trinity. And thus, after the time that grace was given out, all are held to believe explicitly the mystery of the Trinity. And all who are reborn in Christ are brought to it by invocation of the Trinity, according to the end of Matthew, "Go forth, teach all people, baptizing them in the name of the Father and of the Son and of the Holy Spirit."[83]

[1] TO THE FIRST ARGUMENT, THEREFORE, IT SHOULD BE SAID that it was necessary to believe those

---

[82] Genesis 1.26.

[83] Matthew 28.19.

two things about God explicitly in every time and for all. It is not sufficient, however, in every time and for all.

[2] To the second it should be said that before the coming of Christ, faith in the Trinity was hidden in the faith of the greater. But through Christ it was made manifest to the world by the apostles.

[3] To the third it should be said that the highest goodness of God as highest good can be understood in the way it is now understood, by its effects, without the trinity of persons. But according as it is understood in itself, as it is seen by the blessed, it cannot be understood without the trinity of persons. And again this seeing[84] of the divine persons leads us to blessedness.

Article 9. [Whether it is meritorious to believe.]

One proceeds in this way to the ninth query. IT SEEMS that it is not meritorious to believe.

[1] The principle of meriting is charity, as was said above.[85] But faith is a preamble to charity, as nature is. Therefore, just as the act of nature is not meritorious (since we do not merit by natural things), so also neither is the act of faith.

[2] Furthermore, believing is a middle [term] between opining and knowing or considering things known. But the consideration of bodies of knowledge is not meritorious; similarly neither is opinion. Therefore neither is believing meritorious.

[3] Furthermore, he who assents to something in believing either has a cause sufficiently inducing him to believe or [he does] not. If he does have something sufficient inducing him to believe, this does not seem to be meritorious for him, because he is no longer free to believe or not to

[84] Other versions read "sending."

[85] *Summa* 1–2 q.114 a.4.

believe. If he does not have something sufficient inducing him to believe, believing is frivolous, according to Sirach 19, "He who believes quickly is not serious of heart."[86] And so it does not seem to be meritorious. Therefore to believe is in no way meritorious.

BUT TO THE CONTRARY there is what is said in Hebrews 11, that the saints "are enabled by faith to obtain the fulfillment of promises."[87] This would not happen unless they merited by believing. Therefore believing itself is meritorious.

I ANSWER THAT IT SHOULD BE SAID that our acts are meritorious so far as they proceed from free decision moved by God in grace, as was said above.[88] So every human act that comes under free decision can be meritorious, if it is related to God. Believing itself is an act of understanding assenting to divine truth by command of the will, moved by God in grace, and so it lies under free decision as ordered to God. So the act of faith can be meritorious.

[1] TO THE FIRST ARGUMENT, THEREFORE, IT SHOULD BE SAID that nature is compared to charity, which is the principle for meriting, as matter to form. Faith, however, is compared to charity as a disposition preceding the last form. It is manifest that a subject or matter or even a preceding disposition cannot act through the power of the form before the form comes. But once the form has come, both the subject and the preceding disposition act in virtue of the form, which is the chief principle of acting. So fire's heat acts in the power of the substantial form. Therefore neither nature nor faith without charity can produce a meritorious act. But once charity has supervened, the act of faith is made meritorious by

---

[86] Sirach 19.4.

[87] Hebrews 11.33, condensed.

[88] *Summa* 1–2 q.114 aa.3–4.

charity, as are the acts of nature and of natural free decision.

[2] To the second it should be said that two things can be considered in knowledge, namely, the assent of the one knowing to the thing known, and the consideration of the thing known. The assent of knowledge does not come under free choice, since the one knowing is led to assent by the force of demonstration. And so the assent of knowledge is not meritorious. But the actual consideration of a thing known does come under free choice; it is within the power of man to consider or not to consider. And so the consideration of knowledge can be meritorious, if it refer to the end of charity, that is, to the honor of God or to neighbor's use. And so, as regards both of these, the act of faith can be meritorious. But opinion does not have firm assent: it is something weak and infirm, according to the Philosopher in *Posterior Analytics* 1.[89] So it does not seem to proceed from a complete will. And so on the part of assent it does not much seem to have the account of merit. But on the part of actual consideration it can be meritorious.

[3] To the third it should be said that he who believes does have something sufficient inducing him to believe. He is induced by the authority of divine teaching confirmed by miracles, and, what is more, by an inward impulse towards God, who invites him. So he does not believe lightly. But he does not have something sufficient inducing to knowledge.[90] And so the account of merit is not taken away.

---

[89] Aristotle, *Posterior Analytics* bk.1 chap.33 (89a5).

[90] Some versions read "since he has something sufficient inducing him to believe."

Article 10. [Whether a reason[91] induced in support of what things are of faith diminishes the merit of faith.]

One proceeds in this way to the tenth query. IT SEEMS that a reason induced in support of what things are of faith would diminish the merit of faith.

[1] Gregory says, in some homily, that "the faith to which human reason lends experience does not have merit."[92] If therefore human reason by sufficiently lending experience entirely excludes the merit of faith, it would seem that any human reason whatever induced in support of what are of faith would diminish the merit of faith.

[2] Furthermore, whatever diminishes the account of virtue diminishes the account of merit, since "happiness is the reward of virtue," as the Philosopher says in *Ethics* 1.[93] But human reason would seem to diminish the account of the virtue of faith itself, since it is part of the account of faith that it be of things not appearing, as was said above.[94] The more reasons are induced for something, the less it does not appear. Therefore a human reason induced in support of what things are of faith diminishes the merit of faith.

[3] Furthermore, contraries are causes of contraries. But what is induced as contrary to faith increases the merit of faith, whether it be a persecution leading to withdrawal from faith or some reason persuading to this. Therefore a reason helping faith diminishes the merit of faith.

BUT TO THE CONTRARY there is what is said in 1 Peter 3: "Be always prepared to satisfy anyone asking you for a reason for the things that you hold in faith and

---

[91] Or a piece of reasoning or even the power of reason.

[92] Gregory the Great, *Hom. in Evang.* bk.2 hom.26 sect.1, on John 20.19–31 (PL 76:1197C).

[93] Aristotle, *Nicomachean Ethics* bk.1 chap.9 (1099b13–18).

[94] In question 1, articles 4 and 5, above.

hope."[95] But the Apostle would not induce to this if it would diminish the merit of faith. Therefore reason does not diminish the merit of faith.

I ANSWER THAT IT SHOULD BE SAID that the act of faith can be meritorious so far as it lies under the will, not only as regards use, but also as regards assent, as was said.[96] A human reason induced in support of what things are of faith can stand in two ways with regard to the will of the believer. In one way, as preceding it; for example, if someone either did not have any will, or did not have a will prompt in believing, unless some human reason were to be induced. And in this way an induced human reason does diminish the merit of faith. It was also said above that a passion that precedes choice in moral virtues diminishes the praise for virtuous acts.[97] Just as a man ought to exercise moral virtue because of the judgment of reason, not because of passion, so a man ought to believe the things that are of faith not because of human reason, but because of divine authority.

In another way human reason can stand as consequence to the will of the believer. When a man has a will prompt in believing, he loves the believed truth, and thinks about it, and he embraces reasons for it if he can find them. And in this respect a human reason does not exclude the merit of faith, but is a sign of greater merit: just so a passion following on moral virtues is a sign of more prompt will, as was said above.[98]—And this is signified in John 4, where the Samaritans say to the woman, by whom human reason is figured, "Now we do not believe because of what you said."[99]

---

[95] 1 Peter 3.15.
[96] In article 9 of this question, reply [2], above.
[97] *Summa* 1–2 q.24 a.3 ao.1.
[98] *Summa* 1–2 q.24 a.3 ao.1.
[99] John 4.42.

[1] TO THE FIRST ARGUMENT, THEREFORE, IT SHOULD BE SAID that Gregory speaks of the case when a man does not have the will to believe except because of the induced reason. When, however, a man has the will to believe the things that are of faith on divine authority alone, even if he has a demonstrative reason for some of them, for example that God exists, the merit of faith is not taken away or lessened because of this.

[2] To the second it should be said that the reasons that are introduced for the authority of faith are not demonstrations that can be traced back to human understanding's intelligible vision. And so they do not cease being things that do not appear. But reasons do remove impediments to faith, showing how what is proposed in faith is not impossible. By such reasons neither the merit of faith nor the account of faith is diminished. But demonstrative reasons induced for what things are of faith (though still as preambles to the articles), while they do diminish what belongs to the account of faith by making what is proposed appear, do not however diminish what belongs to the account of charity, by which the will is prompt in believing those things even if they do not appear. And so the account of merit is not diminished.

[3] To the third it should be said that things that attack faith, either in man's consideration or in external persecution, increase the merit of faith so far as they show a will more prompt and firm in faith. And so the martyrs had greater merit of faith in not drawing back from faith under persecutions; and the wise had more merit of faith in not drawing back from faith despite the reasons of the philosophers or heretics induced against faith. But reasons that agree with faith do not always diminish the promptness of the will in believing. And so they do not always diminish the merit of faith.

Question 3

[On the Confession of Faith]

One should next consider the outward act of faith, which is confession. Two queries are raised concerning it: (1) Whether confession is an act of faith. (2) Whether confession is necessary to salvation.

Article 1. [Whether confession is an act of faith.]

One proceeds in this way to the first query. IT SEEMS that confession is not an act of faith.

[1] The same act does not belong to different virtues. But confession belongs to penitence, of which it is put as a part. Therefore it is not an act of faith.

[2] Furthermore, man is sometimes drawn back from confessing faith by fear or even by some confusion, so that the Apostle, in the last chapter of Ephesians, asks them to pray for him, that it be given him "to make known the mystery of the gospel with faithfulness."[1] But not drawing back from a good because of confusion or fear belongs to fortitude, which moderates audacity and fear. Therefore it seems that confession is not an act of faith, but rather of fortitude or of constancy.

[3] Furthermore, just as someone is induced to the outward confession of faith by faith's fervor, so also one is led to the doing of other good outward acts. It is said in

[1] Ephesians 6.19.

Galatians 5 that "faith works by love."[2] But other outward works are not put as the act of faith. Therefore neither should confession.

BUT TO THE CONTRARY there is what the Gloss says on 2 Thessalonians 1,[3] "and the work of faith in virtue." The Gloss says, "that is, confession, which properly is said to be the work of faith."[4]

I ANSWER THAT IT SHOULD BE SAID that outward acts are properly the act of that virtue to which their ends are referred according to their species. Fasting is referred according to its species to the end of abstinence, which is controlling the flesh, and so it is an act of abstinence. Now confession of the things that are of faith is ordered to what is of faith as to an end according to its species, according to 2 Corinthians 4, "Having the same spirit we believe by faith, by which we also speak."[5] Outward speech is ordered to signifying what is conceived in the heart. So that just as the inward concept of the things of faith belongs properly to the act of faith, so also does outward confession.

[1] TO THE FIRST ARGUMENT, THEREFORE, IT SHOULD BE SAID that confession is mentioned in the Scriptures in three ways. One is the confession of the things that are of faith. And this is what is proper to the act of faith, namely as it is related to the end of faith, as has been said.[6] Another is the confession of thanksgiving or praise. And this is the act of worship (*latria*). It is ordered to exhibiting outwardly the honor of God, which is the end of worship. The third is the confession of sins. And this is ordered to taking away sins, which is the end of penance. So that it belongs to penance.

---

[2] Galatians 5.6.

[3] 2 Thessalonians 1.11.

[4] *Glossa Lombardi* on 2 Thessalonians 1.11 (PL 192:315B).

[5] 2 Corinthians 4.13, condensed.

[6] In the body of this article.

[2] To the second it should be said that removing something that prohibits something else is not a cause *per se*, only *per accidens*, as is clear in the Philosopher, *Physics* 8.[7] So fortitude, which removes the impediment to the confession of faith, namely fear or shame, is not properly and *per se* the cause of confession, but as if *per accidens*.

[3] To the third it should be said that interior faith causes, by means of love (*dilectio*), all the outward acts of the virtues. It does so by means of the virtues, but as ruling, not as eliciting. Yet it produces confession as its proper act, without the mediation of any other virtue.

Article 2. [Whether the confession of faith is necessary to salvation.]

One proceeds in this way to the second query. IT SEEMS that the confession of faith is not necessary to salvation.

[1] That by which man attains the end of virtue would seem to be sufficient for salvation. But the proper end of faith is the conjoining of the human mind to the divine truth, which can take place without exterior confession. Therefore confession of faith is not necessary to salvation.

[2] Furthermore, by exterior confession of faith a man makes his faith clear to other men. But this is not necessary except for those to whom it belongs to instruct others in the faith. Therefore it seems that the lower [believers] are not held to the confession of faith.

[3] Furthermore, whatever can lead to scandal and the troubling of others is not necessary to salvation. The Apostle says, 1 Corinthians 10, "Be without offense to the Jews and the gentiles and the Church of God."[8] But the unfaithful are sometimes provoked to disturbance by the

---

[7] Aristotle, *Physics* bk.8 chap.4 (255b23–27).

[8] 1 Corinthians 10.32.

confession of faith. Therefore the confession of faith is not necessary for salvation.

BUT TO THE CONTRARY there is what the Apostle says, Romans 10: "It is believed in the heart for justice, and confessed by the mouth for salvation."[9]

I ANSWER THAT IT SHOULD BE SAID that the things that are necessary for salvation fall under the precept of divine law. Now the confession of faith, since it is something affirmative, cannot fall anywhere except under an affirmative precept. So it is one of the things necessary to salvation so far as it can fall under the affirmative precept of divine law. Now the affirmative precepts, as was said above,[10] do not oblige for every time, even if they always oblige: they oblige for a place and a time, according to other due circumstances by which a human act is delimited as an act of virtue. So confessing faith is not necessary to salvation always and in every place, but in some place and time. It is necessary, namely, when the omission of this sort of confession would take away from God some due honor, or from one's neighbor something useful. For example, if someone on being asked about the faith were to keep silent, and from this it were to be believed that he did not have faith, or that the faith were not true, or from his keeping silent others were to be turned away from faith. In cases of this kind, the confession of faith is necessary to salvation.

[1] TO THE FIRST ARGUMENT, THEREFORE, IT SHOULD BE SAID that the end of faith, as of the other virtues, should be referred to the end of charity, which is love of God and neighbor. And so when the honor of God or being useful to one's neighbor demands this, a man should not be content that he is joined to the divine truth itself by his faith. He should confess faith outwardly.

---

[9] Romans 10.10.

[10] In question 2, article 5, above.

[2] To the second it should be said that in case of necessity, where faith is endangered, everyone is held to set forth his faith before others, either for the instruction or confirmation of the other faithful, or to resist the scoffing of the unfaithful. But in other times it does not belong to all the faithful to instruct men about faith.

[3] To the third it should be said that, if the unfaithful should be troubled by the manifest confession of faith, without [there being] any usefulness to the faith or the faithful, then in such a case it is not praiseworthy to confess the faith publicly. So the Lord says, Matthew 7, "Do not give holy things to the dogs, nor cast your pearls before pigs, who turning around will trample you."[11] But if there is hope for some usefulness to the faith, or if there is some necessity, a man should publicly confess the faith without regard for any troubling of the unfaithful. So in Matthew 15, it is said that, when the disciples told the Lord that the Pharisees were scandalized by hearing his word, the Lord replied, "Leave them," that is, to be troubled, "they are blind and the leaders of the blind."[12]

---

[11] Matthew 7.6.
[12] Matthew 15.14.

Question 4
[On the Virtue of Faith]

One should consider next the virtue of faith. And first, faith itself; second, those who have faith; third, the cause of faith; fourth, its effects.

Eight queries are raised about the first point. (1) What faith is. (2) In what power of the soul it is as in a subject. (3) Whether its form is charity. (4) Whether formed faith and unformed faith are the same in number. (5) Whether faith is a virtue. (6) Whether it is one virtue. (7) Its ordering to the other virtues. (8) The comparison of its certainty to the certainty of the intellectual virtues.

Article 1. [Whether this is a suitable definition of faith: "Faith is the substance of things to be hoped for, the argument of things that do not appear."]

One proceeds in this way to the first query. IT SEEMS that what the Apostle puts in Hebrews 11 is an unsuitable definition of faith, when he says: "It is the substance of things to be hoped for, the argument of things that do not appear."[1] No quality is a substance. But faith is a quality, since it is a theological virtue, as was said above.[2] Therefore it is not a substance.

[2] Furthermore, the objects of different virtues are different. But a thing to be hoped for is the object of hope.

---

[1] Hebrews 11.1.

[2] *Summa* 1-2 q.62 a.3.

Therefore it should not be put in the definition of faith as its object.

[3] Furthermore, faith is completed more by charity than by hope, since charity is the form of faith, as will be said below.[3] Therefore the thing to be loved ought to be put in the definition of faith rather than the thing to be hoped for.

[4] Furthermore, the same thing should not be put in different genera. But substance and argument are in different genera that are not subordinated one to another. Therefore faith is inappropriately said to be substance and argument.

[5] Furthermore, an argument makes manifest the truth of what it leads to. But a thing whose truth is apparent is said to be manifest. Therefore there would seem to be an opposition implied in saying "the argument of what does not appear." Therefore faith is inappropriately so described.

BUT TO THE CONTRARY there suffices the authority of the Apostle.

I ANSWER THAT IT SHOULD BE SAID that some say that the aforementioned words of the Apostle are not a definition of faith.[4] Still, if one considers rightly, everything from which faith can be defined is touched on in the foregoing description, even if the words are not ordered in the form of a definition. So also among the philosophers the principal forms of the syllogisms are treated without using syllogisms.

In order that this become evident, it should be considered that, since habits are known by acts and acts by objects, faith, since it is a habit, should be defined by a proper act in relation to a proper object. The act of faith

---

[3] In article 3 of this question, below.

[4] Some versions add "since a definition indicates the thing's whatness [*quidditas*] and essence [*essentia*], as is had in *Metaphysics* 7." See, for example, Aristotle, *Metaphysics* bk.7 chap.4 (1030a6–18). The reference seems to be to Hugh of St.-Victor and Alexander of Hales.

is believing, which, as was said above, is the act of understanding determined to one alternative by the command (*imperium*) of will.[5] So the act of faith is ordered both to the object of will, which is the good and end; and to the object of understanding, which is the true. Since it is a theological virtue, as was said above,[6] faith has the same thing for object and end. So it is necessary that the object of faith and the end correspond to each other proportionally. It was said above[7] that the first truth is the object of faith so far as it is not seen, together with the things in which it inheres through itself. And so the very first truth should stand to the act of faith as an end under the account of the thing not seen. This belongs to the account of something hoped for, according to the Apostle, Romans 8, "What we do not see we hope for."[8] To see the truth is to have it. One does not hope for what one already has; hope is rather of what one does not have, as was said above.[9]

So the standing of the act of faith to the end, which is the object of will, is signified by saying "faith is the substance of things to be hoped for." The first beginning of anything is often called substance, and most of all when the whole of anything following is contained virtually in the first principle. So we could say that first indemonstrable principles are the substance of a body of knowledge, because the first things that are in us of a body of knowledge are principles of this sort, and in them is virtually contained the whole body of knowledge. In this way faith is said to be the substance of things to be hoped for, namely since the first beginning in us of things to be hoped for comes with the assent of faith, which virtually contains all things to be hoped for. In faith we hope to be

[5] In question 2, article 1, reply [3], above.
[6] *Summa* 1–2 q.62 a.3.
[7] *Summa* 2–2 q.1 a.1, a.4.
[8] Romans 8.25.
[9] *Summa* 1–2 q.67 a.4.

made blessed, that we might see with plain vision the truth to which we adhere by faith, as is clear in the things that were said above about happiness.[10]

The standing of the act of faith to the object of understanding, so far as it is the object of faith, is designated in saying "the argument of things that do not appear." "Argument" is taken for the effect of argument; by argument the understanding is induced to adhere to some truth; so that the firm adhesion of the understanding to the truth of faith that does not appear is here called "argument." So also another text has "conviction," namely since by divine authority the understanding of the believer is convinced to assent to what it does not see.

If therefore someone wanted to reduce words of this kind to the form of a definition, it could be said that "faith is a habit of mind, by which eternal life begins in us, making the understanding assent to what does not appear." Faith is distinguished by this from all other things that belong to the understanding. By saying "argument," faith is distinguished from opinion, suspicion, and doubt, by which there is no first, firm adhesion of the understanding to something. By saying "of things that do not appear," faith is distinguished from knowledge and understanding, by which something is made to appear. By saying "the substance of things to be hoped for," the virtue of faith is distinguished from faith in the ordinary sense, which is not ordered to a hoped-for blessedness.

All other definitions whatever that are given of faith make explicit the kinds of things the Apostle puts. Augustine says, "Faith is the virtue by which are believed what things are not seen."[11] Damascene says that faith is consent not [produced] by inquiry.[12] Others say that faith is

---

[10] *Summa* 1–2 q.3 a.8.

[11] Augustine, *In Ioann.* tr.40 sect.9, on John 8.32 and tr.79 sect.1, on John 14.29 (PL 35:1690, 1837; CCL 36:355.8–9, 525.9–10).

[12] John Damascene, *On the Orthodox Faith* bk.4 chap.11 (PG

"some certainty of the soul about absent things that is above opinion and below knowledge."[13] All of these are the same as what the Apostle says, "the argument of things that do not appear." What Dionysius says, in *Divine Names* 7, that faith is "the persisting foundation of believers, placing them in truth and truth in them," is the same as saying, "the substance of things to be hoped for."[14]

[1] TO THE FIRST ARGUMENT, THEREFORE, IT SHOULD BE SAID that "substance" is not taken here as the most general genus divided against other genera. It is taken rather so far as there is found in any genus whatever some likeness to substance—namely so far as the first thing in any genus, containing the others virtually in itself, is said to be their substance.

[2] To the second it should be said that, since faith belongs to the understanding so far as it is commanded by the will, it follows that it is ordered as to an end to the objects of those virtues by which the will is completed. Among which is hope, as will be clear below.[15] And so the object of hope is put in the definition of faith.

[3] To the third it should be said that love can be of things both seen and not seen, of things present and absent. And so the thing to be loved is not so properly adapted to faith as is the thing to be hoped for, since hope is always of things absent and not seen.

[4] To the fourth it should be said that substance and argument, so far as they are put in the definition of faith, do not imply different genera of faith, nor different acts, but different standings of the one act to different objects, as is clear from what has been said.[16]

94.1128D; Buytaert chap.84 sect.1, 300.20–21).

[13] The reference seems to be to Hugh of St.-Victor.

[14] Ps-Dionysius, *Divine Names* chap.7 sect.4 (PG 3:872C; Chevallier 1:409).

[15] *Summa* 2–2 q.18 a.1.

[16] In the body of this article, above.

[5] To the fifth it should be said that an argument that is taken from the proper principles of a thing makes the thing apparent. But an argument that is taken from divine authority does not make the thing in itself apparent. And such argument is what is put in the definition of faith.

Article 2. [Whether faith is in the understanding as in a subject.]

One proceeds in this way to the second query. IT SEEMS that faith is not in the understanding as in a subject.

[1] Augustine says, in *On the Predestination of the Saints*, that faith lies in the will of the believers.[17] But the will is another power than the understanding. Therefore faith is not in the understanding as in a subject.

[2] Furthermore, the assent of faith to something to be believed comes from the will to obey God. Therefore the whole of what is praiseworthy in faith would seem to come from obedience. But obedience is in the will. Therefore faith is too. It is, therefore, not in the intellect.

[3] Furthermore, understanding is either speculative or practical. But faith is not in the speculative intellect. The speculative intellect, since "it says nothing about what is to be imitated[18] or avoided," as it says in *On the Soul* 3,[19] is not a principle of action. But faith is what "works by love," as Galatians 5 says.[20] Similarly faith is not in the practical intellect, the object of which is the contingent truth of what is made or done. The object of faith is eternal truth, as is clear from what has been said above.[21] Therefore faith is not in the understanding as in a subject.

---

[17] Augustine, *De praedest. sanct.* chap.5 sect.10 (PL 44:968).

[18] Some versions read "what is evitable."

[19] Aristotle, *On the Soul* bk.3 chap.9 (432b28).

[20] Galatians 5.6.

[21] In question 1, article 1, "But to the contrary," above.

BUT TO THE CONTRARY faith is succeeded by the vision of the homeland, according to 1 Corinthians 13: "We see now through a mirror in obscurity, but then face to face."[22] But vision is in the intellect. Therefore faith is too.

I ANSWER THAT IT SHOULD BE SAID that, since faith is a virtue, its act ought to be complete. For the completion of an act that proceeds from two principles, it is required that both of the active principles be complete. One cannot saw well unless he has skill and the saw is well disposed to sawing. Habit is a disposition to do well in those powers of the soul that stand in relation to opposites,[23] as was said above.[24] And an act proceeding from two such powers ought to be complete when it comes from some habit preexisting in both powers. It was said above[25] that believing is an act of the understanding so far as the will moves it to assent. This kind of act proceeds, then, from both the will and the understanding. Each of these is so made as to be completed by habit, according to what was said before.[26] And so it follows that some habit must be as much in the will as in the intellect, if the act of faith would be complete. Just so it is necessary for a complete act of desire that there be the habit of prudence in reason and the habit of temperance in the desiring power (*in concupiscibili*). Believing is immediately an act of understanding, since the object of this act is truth, which belongs properly to understanding. And so it is necessary that faith, which is the proper principle of this act, be in the understanding as in a subject.

[1] TO THE FIRST ARGUMENT, THEREFORE, IT SHOULD BE SAID that Augustine takes faith for the act

---

[22] 1 Corinthians 13.12.

[23] Some versions read "to objects."

[24] *Summa* 1-2 q.49 a.4 ao.1, 2, 3.

[25] In the preceding article of this question, above.

[26] *Summa* 1-2 q.50 aa.4-5.

of faith, which is said to be constituted by the will of believers so far as the understanding assents to believable things under the will's rule.

[2] To the second it should be said that not only should the will be prompt in obedience, but also that the understanding should be well disposed to follow the will's command. Just so the desiring power ought to be well disposed to follow the command of reason. And so not only should there be a habit of virtue in the commanding will, but also in the assenting understanding.

[3] To the third it should be said that faith is in the speculative understanding as in a subject, as is most clear from the object of faith. But since the first truth, which is the object of faith, is the end of all our desires and actions, as is clear in Augustine, *On the Trinity* 1,[27] so it is that faith works by love. So also the speculative understanding is made practical in extension, as is said in *On the Soul* 3.[28]

Article 3. [Whether charity is the form of faith.]

One proceeds in this way to the third query. IT SEEMS that charity is not the form of faith.

[1] Every single thing takes its species from its form. In things that are divided against each other as different species of one genus, one cannot be the form of another. But faith and charity are divided against each other as different species of virtue, 1 Corinthians 13.[29] Therefore charity cannot be the form of faith.

[2] Furthermore, form and that of which it is the form are in the same thing, since one thing simply speaking

---

[27] Augustine, *De Trinitate* bk.1 chap.8 sect.17, chap.10 sect.20 (PL 42:831, 834; CCL 50:50.80–81, 56.4–5).

[28] Aristotle, *On the Soul* bk.3 chap.10 (433a15).

[29] 1 Corinthians 13.3.

results from them. But faith is in the understanding, charity in the will. Therefore charity is not the form of faith.

[3] Furthermore, form is the principle of a thing. But the principle of believing on the part of the will would seem rather to be obedience than charity, according to Romans 1, "to the obedience of faith in all the gentiles."[30] Therefore obedience is more the form of faith than is charity.

BUT TO THE CONTRARY each single thing works by its form. Faith "works by love."[31] Therefore the love of charity is the form of faith.

I ANSWER THAT IT SHOULD BE SAID that acts of will receive their species from the end, which is the object of will, as is clear from the above.[32] That from which a thing takes its form stands as the form in natural things. And so the form of every act of the will is in some way the end to which it is ordered, as much because it receives its species[33] from it, as also because the manner of its action makes it that it should respond proportionately to the end. It is manifest from what has been said[34] that the act of faith is ordered to the object of the will as to an end, which is the good. This good which is the end of faith, namely the divine good, is the proper object of charity. And so charity is called the form of faith, inasmuch as the act of faith is completed and formed by charity.

[1] TO THE FIRST ARGUMENT, THEREFORE, IT SHOULD BE SAID that charity is said to be the form of faith inasmuch as it informs its act. Nothing prohibits one act from being informed by diverse habits. Accordingly it can be traced back to different species in some

---

[30] Romans 1.5.

[31] Galatians 5.6.

[32] *Summa* 1–2 q.1 a.3.

[33] Some versions read "form."

[34] In article 1 of this question, above.

order, as was said above, when dealing with human acts in common.[35]

[2] To the second it should be said that this objection proceeds from intrinsic form. In this sense, charity is not the form of faith, but only so far as it informs its act, as was said above.[36]

[3] To the third it should be said that even obedience itself—and similarly hope and any other virtue that can precede the act of faith—is formed[37] by charity, as will be clear below.[38] And so charity itself is put as the form of faith.

Article 4. [Whether unformed faith can be formed, or conversely.]

One proceeds in this way to the fourth query. IT SEEMS that unformed faith does not become formed, nor conversely.

[1] As is said in 1 Corinthians 13, "when what is complete comes, what is partial is taken away."[39] But unformed faith is incomplete with respect to form. Therefore, when formed faith comes, unformed faith is excluded, so that the two are not a habit one in number.

[2] Furthermore, what is dead is not brought to life. But unformed faith is dead, according to James 2, "Faith without works is dead."[40] Therefore unformed faith cannot be made into formed faith.

[3] Furthermore, when the grace of God comes, it has no less effect in the man of faith than in the unfaithful. But coming to the unfaithful man, it causes in him the

---

[35] *Summa* 1–2 q.18 a.7 ao.1.
[36] In the body of this article, above.
[37] Some versions read "rationally formed."
[38] *Summa* 2–2 q.23 a.8.
[39] 1 Corinthians 13.10.
[40] James 2.20.

habit of faith. Therefore coming to the faithful man who previously had the habit of unformed faith, it causes in him another [new] habit of faith.

[4] Furthermore, as Boethius says, accidents cannot be altered.[41] Faith is an accident. Therefore the same faith cannot be sometimes formed and sometimes unformed.

BUT TO THE CONTRARY, with regard to James 2, "Faith without works is dead," the Gloss says, "by which it is revived."[42] Therefore faith that was previously dead and unformed is made formed and living.

I ANSWER THAT IT SHOULD BE SAID that there were different opinions on this. Some said[43] that the habit of formed faith is other than the habit of unformed faith; when formed faith comes, it takes away unformed faith. And so when a man sins mortally after having formed faith, there succeeds another habit of formed faith infused by God.—But it is not appropriate that faith's coming to a man should exclude another gift of God, nor that God should infuse a gift in a man because of mortal sin.

And so others said[44] that while there are different habits of formed faith and unformed faith, the coming of formed faith does not take away the habit of unformed faith, but remains in the same [subject] with the habit of formed faith.—But this also seems inappropriate, since the habit of unformed faith in the one having formed faith would be redundant.

And so it should rather be said that the habit of formed faith is the same as that of unformed faith. The reason is that a habit is differentiated according to what belongs to the habit *per se*. Since faith is a completion of understanding, what belongs to the understanding is what belongs *per se* to faith. What belongs to the will does not belong

---

[41] Boethius, *In categor. Arist.* bk.1 De substantia (PL 64:198A).

[42] *Glossa interlin.* on James 2.17 (Strasbourg 4).

[43] The reference seems to be to William of Auxerre.

[44] The reference seems to be to the *Summa Halensis*.

per se to the understanding, such that the habit of faith could be differentiated by it. The distinction between formed and unformed faith is according to what belongs to the will, that is, according to charity. It is not according to what belongs to the understanding. So formed faith and unformed faith are not different habits.

[1] TO THE FIRST ARGUMENT, THEREFORE, IT SHOULD BE SAID that the Apostle's word is to be understood as holding when the incompleteness belongs to the account of what is incomplete. From this it follows that, when the complete comes, the incomplete is excluded. So when plain vision comes, faith is excluded, since it belongs to the account of faith that it be of things that do not appear. When the incompleteness is not part of the account of the incomplete thing, then the numerically one thing that was incomplete is made complete. Since childhood is not part of the account of man, the thing one in number that was a boy becomes a man. The unformedness of faith is not part of the account of faith,[45] but stands to it *per accidens*, as has been said.[46] So the very same unformed faith is made into formed faith.

[2] To the second it should be said that what gives life to an animal is part of the account of it, since it belongs to its essential form, the soul. And so what is dead cannot be brought to life; rather what is dead is different in species from what is alive. But what makes faith to be formed or alive is not of the essence of faith. And so [the case] is not similar.

[3] To the third it should be said that grace makes faith not only when faith begins to be anew in a man, but also so long as faith lasts. It was said above that God always works the justification of man, just as the sun always works the illumination of the air.[47] So grace does nothing

---

[45] Some versions read "of the complete thing."

[46] In the body of this article, above.

[47] *Summa* 1 q.104 a.1, 1–2 q.109 a.9.

less in coming to the faithful man than to the unfaithful, since it works faith in both, confirming and completing in the one, creating anew in the other.—Or it can be said that it is *per accidens*, because of the subject's disposition, that grace does not cause faith in the one who has it. So, on the contrary, God does not take away grace according to mortal sin from him who [already] casts it away by the preceding mortal sin.

[4] To the fourth it should be said that faith is not changed in going from formed faith to unformed faith, but rather the subject of faith, which is the soul, is changed. For it sometimes has faith without charity, sometimes with charity.

Article 5. [Whether faith is a virtue.]

One proceeds in this way to the fifth query. IT SEEMS that faith is not a virtue.

[1] A virtue is ordered to the good, since virtue is what makes the one having it good, as the Philosopher says, *Ethics* 2.[48] But faith is ordered to the truth. Therefore faith is not a virtue.

[2] Furthermore, an infused virtue is more complete than an acquired virtue. But faith, because of its incompleteness, is not placed among the acquired intellectual virtues, as is clear from the Philosopher, *Ethics* 6.[49] Therefore much less can it be put as an infused virtue.

[3] Furthermore, formed and unformed faith are of the same species, as was said. But unformed faith is not a virtue, since it has no connection with the other virtues. Therefore neither is formed faith a virtue.

---

[48] Aristotle, *Nicomachean Ethics* bk.2 chap.6 (1106a15–17).
[49] Aristotle, *Nicomachean Ethics* bk.6 chap.2 (1139b15–18).

[4] Furthermore, freely given graces and fruits are distinguished from virtues.[50] But faith is enumerated among the freely given graces, 1 Corinthians 12.[51] And similarly among the fruits, Galatians 5.[52] Therefore faith is not a virtue.

BUT TO THE CONTRARY man is justified by virtues, for justice is every virtue, as it is said in *Ethics* 5.[53] But man is justified by faith, according to Romans 5, "Therefore justified by faith we have peace," and so on.[54] Therefore faith is a virtue.

I ANSWER THAT IT SHOULD BE SAID that human virtue is that by which the human act is rendered good, as is clear from what has been said.[55] So that when a habit is always the principle of good acts, it can be called human virtue. Such a habit is formed faith. Since believing is the act of the understanding assenting under the will's command, two things are required for completing this act. One is that the understanding infallibly tends to its good, which is the truth; the other is that it infallibly be ordered to the last end, because of which the will assents. And both of these are found in the act of formed faith. It is part of the very account of faith that it always carry the understanding to the truth, since the false cannot come under faith, as was had above.[56] From charity, which forms

---

[50] The history of the terminology of grace is very complicated, and to explain its evolution even within Thomas's works would require much. A "freely given grace" (*gratia gratis data*) is, most simply, a grace for doing some special act or activity, given (as it were) in addition to saving grace, the "grace that makes one pleasing" (*gratia gratum faciens*). The list of "fruits" is drawn from Isaiah 11.2–3.

[51] 1 Corinthians 12.9.

[52] Galatians 5.23.

[53] Aristotle, *Nicomachean Ethics* bk.5 chap.1 (1130a9–10).

[54] Romans 5.1.

[55] *Summa* 1–2 q.56 a.3.

[56] In question 1, article 3, above.

faith, the soul has it that it is infallibly ordered to the good end. And so all formed faith is a virtue.

Unformed faith is not a virtue. Even if the act of unformed faith were to have the required completeness on the part of the understanding, it does not have the required completeness on the part of the will. So if temperance were in the desiring power, but prudence were not in the rational power, temperance would not be a virtue, as was said above.[57] Just as the act of temperance requires both the act of reason and the act of desire, so the act of faith requires both the act of will and the act of understanding.

[1] TO THE FIRST ARGUMENT, THEREFORE, IT SHOULD BE SAID that the good itself is the good of the understanding, since it is its completeness. And so far as the understanding is determined to the truth by faith, faith is ordered to some good. But, furthermore, so far as faith is formed by charity, it is ordered to the good according as it is the object of the will.

[2] To the second it should be said that the faith of which the Philosopher speaks begins from a human reason without any necessary conclusion. Something false can come under it. And so such faith is not a virtue. But the faith of which we speak begins from the divine truth, which is infallible, and so the false cannot come under it. And so such faith can be a virtue.

[3] To the third it should be said that formed and unformed faith do not differ in species as though they existed in different species. They differ rather as complete and incomplete in the same species. So unformed faith, since it is incomplete, does not attain to the complete account of virtue, since "virtue is a perfection," as is said in *Physics* 7.[58]

[4] To the fourth it should be said that some say that the faith enumerated among the freely given graces is

---

[57] *Summa* 1–2 q.65 a.1.

[58] Aristotle, *Physics* bk.7 chap.3 (246a13).

unformed faith. But this is not said appropriately. The freely given graces there enumerated are not common to all members of the Church. So the Apostle says in that passage, "There are divisions of graces,"[59] and again, "This is given to some, that to others." Unformed faith, however, is common to all members of the Church, since unformedness is not part of its substance, so far as it is a gratuitous gift.

So it is to be said that faith is taken in that passage for some excellence of faith—for "constancy of faith," as the Gloss says, or for "the speaking (*sermo*) of faith."[60]—Faith is put among the fruits according as it has something delightful in its act, on account of certainty. So in Galatians 5,[61] where the fruits are enumerated, faith is explained as "certainty about invisible things."

Article 6. [Whether faith is one.]

One proceeds in this way to the sixth query. IT SEEMS that faith is not one.

[1] Just as faith "is the gift of God," as Ephesians says,[62] so also wisdom and knowledge are counted among the gifts of God, as is clear in Isaiah 11.[63] But wisdom and knowledge differ in this, that while wisdom is of the eternal, knowledge is of the temporal, as is clear in Augustine, *On the Trinity* 12.[64] Since faith is both of the eternal and of some temporal things, it seems that there is not one faith, but that it is distinguished into parts.

---

[59] 1 Corinthians 12.4.

[60] *Glossa Lombardi* on 1 Corinthians 12.9 (PL 191:1653A).

[61] *Glossa Lombardi* on Galatians 5.22 (PL 192:160B).

[62] Ephesians 2.8.

[63] Isaiah 11.2.

[64] Augustine, *De Trinitate* bk.12 chap.14 sect.22 (PL 42:1009; CCL 50:375.7–9), and bk.12 chap.15 sect.25 (PL 42:1012; CCL 50:379.41–44).

[2] Furthermore, confession is the act of faith, as was said above.[65] But there is not one and the same confession of faith among all, for what we confess as accomplished, the ancient Fathers confessed as future. This is clear in Isaiah 7, "Behold a virgin shall conceive."[66] Therefore there is not one faith.

[3] Furthermore, faith is common to all the faithful in Christ. But one accident cannot be in different subjects. Therefore there cannot be one faith for all.

BUT TO THE CONTRARY the Apostle says, Ephesians 4, "One Lord, one faith."[67]

I ANSWER THAT IT SHOULD BE SAID that faith, if it is taken as a habit, can be considered in two ways. In one way, on the part of the object. And so considered there is one faith. The formal object of faith is the first truth, by inhering in which we believe whatever is contained in faith. In another way, on the part of the subject. And thus considered faith is differentiated according as it is in different [subjects]. It is clear that faith, as any other habit, has its species from the formal account of the object, but is individuated by subject. And so, if faith is taken as the habit by which we believe, then faith is one in species, and different in number in different [subjects].—If it is taken as what is believed, so also there is one faith. What is believed by all is the same. And if there are different believable things that are commonly believed by all, still they are traced back to one.

[1] TO THE FIRST ARGUMENT, THEREFORE, IT SHOULD BE SAID that the temporal things that are propounded in faith do not belong to the object of faith except as ordered to something eternal, which is the first truth, as was said above.[68] And so there is one faith of

---

[65] In question 3, article 1, above.

[66] Isaiah 7.14.

[67] Ephesians 4.5

[68] In question 1, article 1, above.

temporal and eternal things. The argument about wisdom and knowledge is pointless (*secus*), since these consider temporal and eternal things according to the proper accounts of each.

[2] To the second it should be said that the difference between past and future does not occur because of some difference in what is believed, but because of the different standing of believers to the one thing believed, as was had above.[69]

[3] To the third it should be said that the reasoning proceeds from the difference of faith according to number.

Article 7. [Whether faith is first among the virtues.]

One proceeds in this way to the seventh query. IT SEEMS that faith is not first among the virtues.

[1] The Gloss on Luke 12, "I call you my friends,"[70] says that "fortitude is the foundation of faith."[71] But the foundation is prior to that of which it is the foundation. Therefore faith is not the first virtue.

[2] Further, some gloss says, on the psalm, "Do not imitate,"[72] that hope leads to faith.[73] But hope is a virtue, as will be said below.[74] Therefore faith is not the first of the virtues.

[3] Furthermore, it was said above that the understanding of the believer is inclined to assent to the things that are of faith by obedience to God.[75] But obedience is also

---

[69] *Summa* 1–2 q.103 a.4.

[70] Luke 12.4.

[71] *Glossa ordinaria* on Luke 12.4 (Strasbourg 4, "Dico autem vobis," col. a, with variation in word order).

[72] Psalm 36.1.

[73] *Glossa Lombardi* on Psalm 36.1 (PL 191:368B), after Cassiodorus.

[74] *Summa* 2–2 q.17 a.1.

[75] In article 2 of this question, reply [2], above.

a virtue. Therefore faith is not the first virtue.

[4] Furthermore, unformed faith is not the foundation. Formed faith is, as the Gloss says on 1 Corinthians 3.[76] Faith is formed by charity, as was said above.[77] Therefore faith is a foundation because of charity. Therefore charity is more the foundation than faith, since the foundation is the first part of the building. And so it seems that it is prior to faith.

[5] Furthermore, the order of habits is understood according to the order of acts. But in the act of faith the act of the will, which charity completes, precedes the act of the intellect, which faith completes, as a cause precedes its effect. Therefore charity precedes faith. Therefore faith is not the first of the virtues.

BUT TO THE CONTRARY there is what the Apostle says, Hebrews 11, that "faith is the substance of things to be hoped for."[78] But substance has the account of the first thing. Therefore faith is first among the virtues.

I ANSWER THAT IT SHOULD BE SAID that something can be prior to another in two ways: in one way, *per se*; in another way, *per accidens*. *Per se* faith is first among all the virtues. Since in things that can be done the end is the principle, as was said above,[79] it is necessary that the theological virtues, of which the object is the last end, be prior to the other virtues. Now the last end itself must be in the understanding before it is in the will, since the will is not carried towards something except insofar as that thing is apprehended by the understanding. Since the last end is in the will by hope and charity, in the understanding by faith, it is necessary that faith be first among all the virtues, since natural apprehension cannot attain to God

---

[76] *Glossa Lombardi* on 1 Corinthians 3.10 (PL 191:1556B).

[77] In article 3 of this question, above.

[78] Hebrews 11.1.

[79] *Summa* 1–2 q.13 a.3.

as the object of blessedness so far as hope and charity tend towards him.

But *per accidens* another virtue can be prior to faith. A *per accidens* cause is prior *per accidens*. Removing an obstacle belongs to a *per accidens* cause, as is clear in the Philosopher, *Physics* 8.[80] And in this way other virtues can be said to be prior to faith, inasmuch as they remove impediments to believing. So fortitude removes the inordinate fear that impedes faith; humility removes pride, by which the understanding refuses to submit to the truth of faith. And the same thing can be said of many other virtues, however much they are not true virtues unless faith is presupposed, as is clear in Augustine, *Against Julian*.[81]

[1] The answer TO THE FIRST ARGUMENT is clear.

[2] To the second it should be said that hope cannot lead universally to faith. There cannot be hope in eternal blessedness unless it is believed in as something possible, since what is impossible does not fall under faith, as is clear from what has been said.[82] But hope can lead someone to persevere in faith, or to adhere more firmly to faith. And in this way hope is said to lead to faith.

[3] To the third it should be said that "obedience" is said in two ways. Sometimes it implies an inclination of the will towards fulfilling the divine commandments. And in this way it is not a special virtue, but is generally included in every virtue, since all acts of virtue fall under the precept of divine law, as was said above.[83] And in this way obedience is required for faith. — In another way it can be taken as implying a certain inclination towards fulfilling the commandments so far as they share in the account of what is due. And in this way obedience is a special virtue, and is a part of justice, for it gives back to the higher

---

[80] Aristotle, *Physics* bk.8 chap.4 (255b23–24).
[81] Augustine, *Contra Julianum* bk.4 chap.3 sect.23–24 (PL 44:750).
[82] *Summa* 1–2 q.40 a.1.
[83] *Summa* 1–2 q.100 a.2.

what is his due in obeying him. And in this way obedience follows faith, by which it is made clear to man that God is someone higher, whom one duly obeys.

[4] To the fourth is should be said that in the account of a foundation there is required not only that it be first, but also that it be connected to the other parts of the building. It would not be a foundation if the other parts of the building did not cohere with it. The connection of the spiritual building is by charity, according to Colossians 3, "Above all have charity, which is the bond of completion."[84] And so faith cannot be a foundation without charity; but it does not follow that charity is prior to faith.

[5] To the fifth it should be said that an act of the will is prerequisite for faith, but not an act of the will informed by charity. But this kind of act presupposes faith, since the will cannot tend to God with complete love unless the understanding has right faith about him.

Article 8. [Whether faith is more certain than knowledge and the other intellectual virtues.]

One proceeds in this way to the eighth query. IT SEEMS that faith is not more certain than knowledge and the other intellectual virtues.

[1] Doubt is opposed to certainty. What has less of doubt would seem to be more certain, just as what is whiter is less mixed with blackness. But understanding and knowledge, and wisdom as well, do not have doubt about the things they concern. But the believer can sometimes suffer a motion of doubt and so doubt the things that are of faith. Therefore faith is not more certain than the intellectual virtues.

---

[84] Colossians 3.14, paraphrased.

[2] Furthermore, vision is more certain than hearing. But "faith comes from hearing," as Romans says.[85] Some intellectual vision is contained in understanding, knowledge, and wisdom. Therefore knowledge and understanding are more certain than faith.

[3] Furthermore, in what belongs to the understanding, the more complete something is, the more certain it is. But understanding is more complete than faith, since one comes to understanding by faith, according to Isaiah 7, "If you do not believe, you will not understand," according to another version [of the text](*littera*).[86] And Augustine says about knowledge, in *On the Trinity* 14, that faith will be strengthened by knowledge.[87] Therefore it seems that knowledge or understanding is more certain than faith.

BUT TO THE CONTRARY there is what the Apostle says, 1 Thessalonians 2: "When you accepted the word heard from us," namely by faith, "you accepted it not as a human word, but as the word of God, which it truly is."[88] But nothing is more certain than the word of God. Therefore knowledge is not more certain than faith, nor is anything else.

I ANSWER THAT IT SHOULD BE SAID that two of the intellectual virtues, namely prudence and art, concern contingent things, as was said above.[89] Faith is to be preferred to these in certainty, by reason of its matter, since it is about eternal things, which cannot happen otherwise. – The three remaining intellectual virtues, namely wisdom, knowledge, and understanding, are about necessary things, as was said above.[90] But it should be known that

---

[85] Romans 10.17.

[86] Isaiah 7.9, according to the Septuagint.

[87] Augustine, *De Trinitate* bk.14 chap.1 sect.3 (PL 42:1037; CCL 50A:424.60–61).

[88] 1 Thessalonians 2.13.

[89] *Summa* 1–2 q.57 a.4 ao.2, a.5 ao.3.

[90] *Summa* 1–2 q.57 a.5 ao.3.

knowledge, wisdom and understanding are said in two ways: in one way, as the Philosopher considers them intellectual virtues, *Ethics* 6;[91] in another way, as they are considered gifts of the Holy Spirit. In the first way, it should be said that certainty can be considered in two ways. In one way, from the cause of certainty, and in this way a thing is said to be more certain as it has the more certain cause. And in this way faith is more certain than the three others mentioned, since faith begins from the divine truth, while the three others mentioned begin from human reason. In another way, certainty can be considered on the part of the subject, and in this way something is said to be more certain as it appears more fully to man's understanding. And in this way, since the things that are of faith are above the understanding of man, but not the things that fall under the other three mentioned, faith is less certain. But since each thing is judged simply speaking according to its cause, and is judged with some qualification (*secundum quid*) according to a disposition on the part of the subject, so it is that faith is simply more certain, but the others are more certain with some qualification, namely with respect to us. — Similarly even if the three others mentioned are taken so far as they are (infused) gifts in the present life, they are compared to[92] faith as to a principle that they presuppose. And so even in this way faith is more certain.

[1] TO THE FIRST ARGUMENT, THEREFORE, IT SHOULD BE SAID that this doubt does not arise with respect to the cause of faith, but with respect to us, so far as we do not fully gain by understanding the things that are of faith.

[2] To the second it should be said that, other things being equal, vision is more certain than hearing. But if the thing that is heard for exceeds the vision of the seer, in

---

[91] Aristotle, *Nicomachean Ethics* bk.6 chap.3 (1139b15–18).

[92] Some versions read "they cooperate in."

this way what is heard is more certain than what is seen. Just so someone with little knowledge might be more certain of what he hears from another, who is most learned, than of what might seem to him according to his own reason. And much more is a man more certain of what he hears from God, who cannot fail, than of what he sees with his own reason, which can fail.

[3] To the third it should be said that the completeness of understanding and knowledge exceeds the apprehension of faith as regards greater manifestness, not as regards a more certain inhering [in the truth had]. The whole certainty of understanding or knowledge so far as they are gifts proceeds from the certainty of faith, just as the certainty of the apprehension of conclusions proceeds from the certainty of principles. So far as knowledge and wisdom and understanding are intellectual virtues, they begin from the natural light of reason, which falls short of the certainty of the word of God, from which faith begins.

Question 5
[On Those Who Have Faith]

One should next consider those who have faith. Four queries are raised with regard to this: (1) Whether an angel or a man in his first condition had faith. (2) Whether demons have faith. (3) Whether heretics erring about one article of faith have faith about the other articles. (4) Whether one of those who have faith has greater faith than another.

Article 1. [Whether an angel or a man in his first condition had faith.]

One proceeds in this way to the first query. IT SEEMS that an angel or a man in his first condition did not have faith.

[1] Hugh of St.-Victor says, "Since man does not have the eye of contemplation, he cannot see God and the things that are in God."[1] But an angel in the state of its first condition, before confirmation or fall,[2] did have the eye of contemplation. It saw things in the Word, as Augustine says, *On Genesis to the Letter* 2.[3] And similarly the first

[1] Hugh of St.-Victor, *De sacramentis* bk.1 part.10 chap.2 (PL 176:330A).

[2] "Confirmation" is here a technical term that refers to the hardening of the angel's will in its turning from God.

[3] Augustine, *De Genesi ad litt.* bk.2 chap.8 sect.17 (PL 34:270; CSEL 28/1:44.7).

man in the state of innocence seems to have had open the eye of contemplation. Hugh of St.-Victor says, in his *Sentences*, that "man" in the first state "knew his Creator not with the apprehension that perceives only outward things by hearing, but with the one that is ministered inwardly by inspiration; not with the apprehension by which God is sought a little by believers in the absence of faith, but with the one by which he is most clearly discerned through presence in contemplation."[4] Therefore neither man nor angels in the state of the first condition had faith.

[2] Furthermore, the apprehension of faith is enigmatic and obscure, according to 1 Corinthians 13, "We see now though a mirror in obscurity."[5] But in the state of the first condition there was no obscurity either in man or in angel, since darkness is the punishment of sin. Therefore there could be no faith in the state of the first condition either in man or angel.

[3] Furthermore, the Apostle says, Romans 10, that "faith is from hearing."[6] But this does not apply to the first state of the angelic or human condition. For there was then no hearing from another. Therefore there was no faith in that state for either angel or man.

BUT TO THE CONTRARY the Apostle says, Hebrews 11, "Coming to God one must to believe."[7] But angel and man in the first condition were in the state of one who comes to God. Therefore they needed faith.

I ANSWER THAT IT SHOULD BE SAID that some say[8] that there was no faith in the angels before confirmation and fall, and in man before sin, because of the clear

---

[4] That is, Hugh of St.-Victor, *De sacramentis* bk.1 part.6 chap.14 (PL 176:271C).

[5] 1 Corinthians 13.12.

[6] Romans 10.17.

[7] Hebrews 11.6.

[8] The reference may be to Hugh of St.-Victor, the *Summa Halensis*, or Bonaventure.

contemplation of divine things that there then was. But since faith is the "argument of things that do not appear," according to the Apostle,[9] and "by faith those things are believed that are not seen," as Augustine says,[10] the only clarity that excludes the account of faith is one that renders apparent or seen the things about which principally there is faith. The principal object of faith is the first truth, the vision of which makes [us] blessed and replaces faith. Since an angel before confirmation and a man before sin did not have that blessedness by which God is seen in his essence, it is clear that they did not have such a clear apprehension that the account of faith would be excluded. So that if they did not have faith, this could only be because they almost did not know what faith is about. And if man and angel were created in pure nature [that is, without grace], as some say,[11] perhaps it could be held that there was no faith in an angel before confirmation or in a man before sin. The apprehension of faith is above the natural apprehension of God not only for man, but also for angel. But since we already said in the first [part] that man and angel were created with the gift of grace,[12] it is necessary to say that, by the grace they accepted and never consummated, there was in them a beginning (*inchoatio*) of the hoped-for blessedness. This is begun in the will by hope and charity, but in the intellect by faith, as was said above.[13] And so it is necessary to say that the angel before confirmation had faith, and similarly man before sin.

---

[9] Hebrews 11.1.

[10] Augustine, *In Ioann.* tr.40 sect.9, on John 8.32, and tr.79 sect.1, on John 14.29 (PL 35:1690, 1837; CCL 36:335.8–9, 525.9–10); *Quaest. Evang.* bk.2 q.39, on Luke 17.5–10 (PL 35:1352; CCL 44B:93.3–4).

[11] The reference seems to be to Bonaventure.

[12] *Summa* 1 q.62 a.3, q.95 a.1.

[13] In question 4, article 7, above.

But it is also to be considered that in the object of faith there is something formal, namely the first truth existing above all natural apprehension of the creature; and something material, that to which we assent when inhering in the first truth. As regards the first of these, faith is commonly in all those who apprehend God, in a way not yet adapted to future blessedness, by inhering in the first truth. But as regards the things that are materially proposed for believing, some are believed by one that are manifestly known by the other, even in the present state, as was said above.[14] And in this way it can be said that an angel before confirmation and a man before sin apprehended by a clear apprehension of the divine mysteries what we cannot now apprehend except in believing.

[1] TO THE FIRST ARGUMENT, THEREFORE, IT SHOULD BE SAID that the sayings of Hugh of St.-Victor are academic opinions (*magistralia*) and do not have the force of authority. But even so it can be said that the contemplation that takes away the necessity of faith is the contemplation of the homeland, by which the supernatural truth is seen in its essence. The angel before confirmation and man before sin did not have this contemplation. But their contemplation was higher than ours. Coming much nearer to God, they could clearly apprehend by contemplation more of the divine effects and mysteries than we can. So there was not in them the faith by which God is sought as he is sought by us. He was more present to them by the light of wisdom than he is to us, though he was not so present to them as he is to the blessed by the light of glory.

[2] To the second it should be said that in the state of the first condition of man or angel there was no obscurity of sin or punishment. Yet there was in the intellect of man and angel a certain natural obscurity, however, according

[14] In question 1, article 5, above.

to which every creature is darkness in comparison with the immensity of the divine light. And such obscurity suffices for the account of faith.

[3] To the third it should be said that in the state of the first condition there was no hearing of a man speaking outwardly, but rather God inspiring inwardly. So the prophet heard [God], according to that psalm, "Let me hear what the Lord God says in me."[15]

Article 2. [Whether there is faith in demons.]

One proceeds in this way to the second query. IT SEEMS that there is no faith in demons.

[1] Augustine says, in *On the Predestination of the Saints*, that faith is constituted by the will of the believers.[16] That will by which one wants to believe in God is good. Since there is no deliberated good will in demons, as was said in the first [part],[17] it seems that there is no faith in them.

[2] Furthermore, faith is a certain gift of divine grace, according to Ephesians, "You will be saved by grace through faith: it is a gift of God."[18] But the demons put away graced gifts by sin, as it says in the gloss on Hosea 3, "They respect foreign gods, and loved the vines of grapes."[19] Therefore faith cannot remain in demons after sin.

[3] Furthermore, infidelity seems to be one of the more serious of sins, as is clear in Augustine on John 15: "If I had not come, and had not spoken to them, they would not have sin: but now they have no excuse from their

---

[15] Psalm 84.9, paraphrased.

[16] Augustine, *De praedest. sanct.* chap.5 sect.10 (PL 44:968).

[17] *Summa* 1 q.64 a.2 ao.5.

[18] Ephesians 2.8.

[19] Paraphrase of *Glossa ordinaria* on Hosea 3.1 (Strasbourg 3, "Vinacia uvarum," col. b).

sin."[20] But in some men there is the sin of infidelity. If then there were faith in demons, the sin of some men would be more serious than the sin of demons. This seems to be inappropriate. Therefore there is no faith in demons.

BUT TO THE CONTRARY it is said in James 2, "The demons believe and tremble."[21]

I ANSWER THAT IT SHOULD BE SAID that the believer's understanding assents to the thing believed not because he sees it, whether by itself or by resolution to first principles seen by themselves, but because of the will's rule,[22] as was said above.[23] The will can move the intellect in two ways. First, from the ordering of the will to the good; in this way believing is a praiseworthy act. In another way, because the intellect is convinced in judging that there is something to be believed in what is said, even if it is not convinced by the evidence of the thing. Just so some prophet might predict some future thing with the word of the Lord, and add to it the sign of raising the dead, and might convince by this sign the understanding of an observer, so that the observer might clearly apprehend that the things said were said by God, who does not lie. Even so the predicted future thing would not be evident in itself, so that the account of faith would not be taken away. It should be said, therefore, that faith in the first sense is praised in those who are Christ's faithful. And in this way it is not in demons, but only in the second way. Demons see many clear indications from which they perceive that the doctrine of the Church is from God, even if they do not see the things that the Church teaches, for

---

[20] Augustine, *In Ioann.* tr.89 sect.1, on John 15.22 (PL 35:1856; CCL 36:549.25–29).

[21] James 2.19.

[22] Other versions read "but because he is convinced by divine authority to assent to what he does not see and because of the rule of the will moving the intellect and obeying God."

[23] In question 1, article 4, and question 2, article 1, reply [3], above.

example, that God is three and one or something else of this kind.

[1] TO THE FIRST ARGUMENT, THEREFORE, IT SHOULD BE SAID that demons have faith when they are in a certain way coerced by the evidence of signs. And so their believing is nothing praiseworthy in their will.

[2] To the second it should be said that the faith that is a gift of grace inclines man to believe by some affect of the good, even if the faith is unformed. So that the demons' faith is not a gift of grace. They are led to believe, rather, from the perspicacity of natural intellect.

[3] To the third it should be said that it displeases the demons that the signs of faith are so evident that they are compelled to believe by them. And so their malice is in no way diminished by their believing.

Article 3. [Whether a heretic who disbelieves one article of faith can still have unformed faith about the other articles.]

One proceeds in this way to the third query. IT SEEMS that a heretic who disbelieves one article of faith can still have unformed faith of the other articles.

[1] The natural intellect of a heretic is not more powerful than the intellect of a catholic. But the intellect of a catholic needs to be helped by the gift of faith in believing any article of faith. Therefore it seems that neither can the heretic believe other articles without the gift of unformed faith.

[2] Furthermore, just as many articles of faith are contained under faith, so also many conclusions are contained under one body of knowledge—for example, under geometry. But a man can have knowledge of geometry concerning some geometrical conclusions while not knowing others. Therefore a man can have faith in some articles of faith while not believing the others.

[3] Furthermore, just as man obeys God in believing the articles of faith, so also he obeys in following the commandments of the law. But a man can be obedient to some commandments and not to others. Therefore he can have faith concerning some articles and not others.

BUT TO THE CONTRARY, just as mortal sin is contrary to charity, so to disbelieve one article is contrary to faith. But charity does not remain in a man after one mortal sin. Therefore neither does faith remain after he disbelieves one article of faith.

I ANSWER THAT IT SHOULD BE SAID that the heretic who disbelieves one article of faith does not have the habit of faith, neither formed nor unformed. The reason for this is that the species of any habit depends on the formal account of its object. When this is removed, the species of the habit cannot remain. The formal object of faith is the first truth as it is manifested in sacred Scripture and the doctrine of the Church. So that whoever does not inhere, as in an infallible and divine rule, in the teaching of the Church, which proceeds from the first truth made clear in sacred Scripture, does not have the habit of faith. He holds the things that are of faith in some way other than by faith. Just so if someone were to have in mind a conclusion without apprehending the middle term of its demonstration, it is clear that he would not have knowledge about it, but only opinion.

It is clear that someone who inheres in the doctrine of the Church, as in an infallible rule, assents to all that the Church teaches. If he holds and does not hold whatever he wants from among what the Church teaches, he does not inhere in the teaching of the Church as in an infallible rule, but rather by his own will. And so it is clear that the heretic who stubbornly disbelieves one article of faith is not ready to follow the teaching of the Church in everything. (If he does not do so stubbornly, he is not yet a heretic, but only someone in error). So it is also clear that a heretic in one article does not have faith about the other articles, but only a certain opinion by means of his own will.

[1] TO THE FIRST ARGUMENT, THEREFORE, IT SHOULD BE SAID that a heretic does not hold the other articles of faith, about which he does not err, in the way that the faithful man holds them—namely, simply by inhering in the first truth, to which a man must be helped by the habit of faith. Rather the heretic holds the things that are of faith by his own will and judgment.

[2] To the second it should be said that the different conclusions of one body of knowledge are proved by different middle terms, one of which can be apprehended without another. And so a man can know certain conclusions of one body of knowledge without knowing the others. But faith inheres in all the articles of faith through one middle term, namely, through the first truth proposed to us in Scripture according to the teaching of the Church healthily understood. And so someone who falls away from this middle term lacks faith.

[3] To the third it should be said that the different precepts of the law can be referred either to different proximate motives, and in this way one can be followed without another; or to one first motive, which is to obey God completely. Anyone who transgresses against one precept in the second sense falls away from obedience to God, according to James 2, "Who offends in one thing done is guilty of all."[24]

Article 4. [Whether faith can be greater in one than in another.]

One proceeds in this way to the fourth query. IT SEEMS that faith cannot be greater in one than in another.

---

[24] James 2.10.

[1] One looks for the quantity of a habit according to its objects. Yet whoever has faith believes all things that are of faith, since he who falls away from one [of these things] completely rejects faith, as was said above.[25] Therefore it seems that faith cannot be greater in one than in another.

[2] Furthermore, the things that are in the highest admit neither greater nor less. But the account of faith is in the highest. It is required for faith that a man inhere in the first truth above all. Therefore faith does not admit of greater or less.

[3] Furthermore, faith stands in graced apprehension as the understanding of principles does in natural apprehension: the articles of faith are the first principles of graced apprehensions, as is clear from what has been said.[26] But the understanding of principles is found equally in all men. Therefore faith is found equally in all the faithful.

BUT TO THE CONTRARY wherever there is found something small and something great, there is also found more and less. But in faith there is found a great and a small, for the Lord says to Peter, Matthew 14, "O you of little faith, why did you doubt?"[27] And to the woman he said, Matthew 15, "Woman, your faith is great."[28] Therefore faith can be greater in one than in another.

I ANSWER THAT IT SHOULD BE SAID that the quantity of a habit can be looked for in two ways, as was said above.[29] In one way, from the object; in another way, according to the participation of the subject. Now the object of faith can be considered in two ways: in one way, according to its formal account; in another, according to the things that are materially proposed for believing. Now

---

[25] In article 3 of this question, above.

[26] In question 1, article 7, above.

[27] Matthew 14.31

[28] Matthew 15.28.

[29] *Summa* 1-2 q.52 aa.1-2, q.112 a.4.

the formal object of faith is one and simple, namely the first truth, as was said above.[30] So that faith is not differentiated among believers in this respect, but is of one species in all, as was said.[31] But the things that are materially proposed for believing are many, and can be taken more or less explicitly. And in this way one man can believe explicitly more things than another. And so there can be more faith in one because the faith has been made more explicit.

If faith then be considered according to the subject's participation, this happens in two ways. For the act of faith proceeds from the intellect and from the will, as was said above.[32] Faith can be said to be greater in someone in one way on the part of the intellect, because of greater certainty and firmness; in another way, on the part of the will, because of greater promptness or devotion or confidence.

[1] TO THE FIRST ARGUMENT, THEREFORE, IT SHOULD BE SAID that anyone who stubbornly disbelieves some of the things contained under faith does not have the habit of faith. The one who does not explicitly believe all, but is ready to believe all, does have it. And in this way one has greater faith than another on the part of the object, so far as he explicitly believes more things, as was said.[33]

[2] To the second argument it should be said that it belongs to the account of faith that the first truth be placed before all. Still, of those who place it before all, some submit themselves to it more certainly and devoutly than others.

---

[30] In question 1, article 1, above.

[31] In question 4, article 6, above.

[32] In article 2 of this question, above. See also question 1, article 4, and question 2, article 1, reply [3], above.

[33] In the body of this article, above.

[3] To the third argument it should be said that the understanding of principles follows upon human nature itself, which is found equally in all. But faith follows from a gift of grace, which is not equally in all, as was said above.[34] So there is not the same reasoning [about the two cases].—And even so, according to a greater capacity for understanding, one can apprehend the virtue of principles more than another.[35]

---

[34] *Summa* 1–2 q.112 a.4.

[35] Some versions read "more of the power of principles than another."

Question 6

[On the Cause of Faith]

One should next consider the cause of faith. About this two queries are raised: (1) Whether faith is infused in man by God. (2) Whether unformed faith is a gift.

Article 1. [Whether faith is infused in man by God.]

One proceeds in this way to the first query. IT SEEMS that faith is not infused in man by God.

[1] Augustine says, *On the Trinity* 14, that by knowledge "faith is begotten in us by knowledge, and nourished, defended, and strengthened."[1] But things begotten in us by knowledge seem more to be acquired than to be infused. Therefore faith does not seem to be in us by divine infusion.

[2] Furthermore, what a man comes to by hearing and seeing seems to be acquired by the man. But a man comes to believing by seeing miracles and hearing the teaching of the faith, as it is said in John 4: "The father apprehended that it was in that hour in which Jesus had said to him, 'Your son lives.' And he believed, together with his whole house."[2] And it is said in Romans 10 that "faith is from

[1] Augustine, *De Trinitate* bk.14 chap.1 sect.3 (PL 42:1037; CCL 50A:424.60–61).

[2] John 4.53.

hearing."[3] Therefore man has faith as it is acquired.

[3] Furthermore, what is constituted by man's will can be acquired by man. But "faith is constituted by the will of the believers," as Augustine says, *On the Predestination of the Saints.*[4] Therefore faith is acquired by man.

BUT TO THE CONTRARY it is said in Ephesians 2, "You will be saved by grace through faith, and not from yourselves, that no one may glory: for it is a gift of God."[5]

I ANSWER THAT IT SHOULD BE SAID that two things are required for faith. One is that believable things be proposed to a man, which is required in order for man to believe something explicitly. The other thing that is required for faith is the assent of the one believing to the things that are proposed. As regards the first of these, it is necessary that faith be from God. The things that are of faith exceed human reason; they do not fall under man's contemplation except when God reveals them. But to some they are revealed immediately by God, as they were revealed to the apostles and the prophets. To others they are proposed by God's sending preachers of faith, according to Romans 10, "How will they preach if they have not been sent?"[6]

As regards the second, namely man's assent to the things that are of faith, the cause can be considered in two ways. In one way, as an outward inducement, such as a miracle seen or a human persuasion inducing one to faith. Neither of which is a sufficient cause. Among those seeing one and the same miracle, and those hearing the same preaching, some believe and some do not believe. And so another inward cause must be recognized, which moves man inwardly to assent to the things that are of faith. This

---

[3] Romans 10.17.

[4] Augustine, *De praedest. sanct.* chap.5 (PL 44:968).

[5] Ephesians 2.8.

[6] Romans 10.15.

cause the Pelagians put as nothing more than man's free choice. Because of this they said that the beginning of faith was from us, namely so far as we are prepared in ourselves to assent to the things that are of faith; but the consummation of faith is from God, by whom are proposed to us the things that we ought to believe. But this is false. Since man, in assenting to the things that are of faith, is raised above his nature, this must happen in him by a supernatural principle moving inwardly, which is God. And so as regards assent, which is the principal act of faith, faith is from God moving inwardly by grace.

[1] TO THE FIRST ARGUMENT, THEREFORE, IT SHOULD BE SAID that faith is begotten by knowledge and nourished by it in the way of an outward persuasion, which is done by another knowledge. But the principal and proper cause of faith is what moves to assent inwardly.

[2] To the second it should be said that this reasoning also proceeds from an outward cause proposing the things that are of faith, or persuading to believe by word or by deed.

[3] To the third it should be said that believing does lie in the will of the believer. But it is required that the will of man be prepared by God through grace in order to be elevated to the things that are above nature, as was said above.[7]

Article 2. [Whether unformed faith is a gift of God.]

One proceeds in this way to the second query. IT SEEMS that unformed faith is not a gift of God.

[1] It is said in Deuteronomy 32 that "the works of God are complete."[8] Unformed faith is something incomplete. Therefore unformed faith is not the work of God.

---

[7] In the body of this article, above.

[8] Deuteronomy 32.4.

[2] Furthermore, just as an act is said to be deformed because it lacks due form, so also faith is said to be unformed because it lacks due form. But the deformed act of sin is not from God, as was said above.[9] Therefore neither is unformed faith from God.

[3] Furthermore, whatever God heals, he heals completely. It is said in John 7, "A man may accept circumcision on the sabbath so that the law of Moses be not held in suspense, but you become indignant with me because I make the whole man healthy on the sabbath."[10] But by health man is healed from unfaithfulness. Therefore whoever accepts the gift of faith from God is at the same time healed from all sins. But this does not occur except by formed faith. Therefore only formed faith is the gift of God. Therefore unformed faith is not.

BUT TO THE CONTRARY some gloss says of 1 Corinthians 13 that "faith without charity is a gift of God."[11] But faith without charity is unformed faith. Therefore unformed faith is the gift of God.

I ANSWER THAT IT SHOULD BE SAID that unformedness is a privation. It should be considered that a privation sometimes belongs to the account of the species. Sometimes it does not, but rather comes on top of a thing already having its own species. So privation of the due balance of humors is part of the account of the very species of sickness; darkness is not part of the account of the very species of the transparent, but comes on top of it. Now when the cause of any thing is assigned, its cause is understood to be assigned according as it exists (*existit*) in its proper species. What is not the cause of privation cannot be said to be the cause of the thing to which the pri-

---

[9] *Summa* 1–2 q.79 a.2.

[10] John 7.23.

[11] Rather, Peter Lombard, *Sent.* bk.3 dist.23 chap.4 (Grottaferrata 2:657). Compare *Glossa Lombardi* on 1 Corinthians 13.2 (PL 191: 1659A).

vation belongs as existing in the account of the species. What is not the cause of the distemper of the humors cannot be said to be the cause of sickness. Still, something can be said to be the cause of transparency, however much it is not the cause of obscurity, because obscurity is not part of the account of the species of the transparent. Unformed faith does not belong to the account of the species of faith; since faith is said to be unformed on account of a defect of some outward form, as was said.[12] And the cause of unformed faith is the cause of faith said simply. This is God, as was said.[13] So it remains that unformed faith is the gift of God.

[1] TO THE FIRST ARGUMENT, THEREFORE, IT SHOULD BE SAID that unformed faith, even if it is not simply complete with the completeness of a virtue, is nonetheless complete with a certain completeness that satisfies the account of faith.

[2] To the second it should be said that the deformity of the act is part of the account of the species of act so far as it is a moral act, as was said above.[14] An act is said to be deformed by the privation of intrinsic form, which is the due balance of the act's circumstances. And so God cannot be said to be the cause of the deformed act, since he is not the cause of deformity, even if he is the cause of the act as act.

Or it should be said that deformity not only implies privation of due form, but also the contrary disposition. So that deformity stands to act as falsity to faith. And just as the act of deformity is not from God, so neither is a false faith. And just as unformed faith is from God, so also are acts good in kind, however much they are not formed by charity, as often happens in sinners.

---

[12] In question 4, article 4, above.

[13] In article 1 of this question, above.

[14] *Summa* 1 q.48 a.1 ao.2, 1–2 q.18 a.5.

[3] To the third it should be said that anyone who accepts faith from God without charity is not simply speaking healed from unfaithfulness, since the fault of his preceding unfaithfulness is not removed. But he is healed in a certain respect, namely as he ceases from such sinning. This frequently happens, that someone desists from some act of sin, even by God's act, who nonetheless does not desist from another act of sin, which is suggested by his own iniquity. And in this way God sometimes gives it to a man that he believe, but does not give him the gift of charity. Just so to some without charity there is given the gift of prophecy or of something similar.

Question 7

[On the Effects of Faith, Which Are Fear and Purification of Heart]

One should next consider the effects of faith. And about this two queries are raised. (1) Whether fear is an effect of faith. (2) Whether purification of heart is an effect of faith.

Article 1. [Whether fear is an effect of faith.]

One proceeds in this way to the first query. IT SEEMS that fear is not an effect of faith.

[1] An effect does not precede a cause. But fear precedes faith, as it says in Sirach 2, "You who fear God, believe him."[1] Therefore fear is not an effect of faith.

[2] Furthermore, the same thing is not the cause of contraries. But fear and hope are contraries, as was said above.[2] Faith generates hope, as it is said in the Gloss on Matthew 1.[3] Therefore it is not the cause of fear.

[3] Furthermore, a contrary is not the cause of contraries. But the object of faith is something good, the first truth. The object of fear is evil, as was said above.[4] Acts

---

[1] Sirach 2.8.

[2] *Summa* 1–2 q.23 a.2, q.40 a.4 ao.1.

[3] Paraphrase of *Glossa ordinaria* on Matthew 1.2 (Strasbourg 4, "Abraham genuit," col.b).

[4] *Summa* 1–2 q.42 a.1.

have species from their objects, according to what was already said.[5] Therefore faith is not the cause of fear.

BUT TO THE CONTRARY there is what is said in James 2, "The demons believe and tremble."[6]

I ANSWER THAT IT SHOULD BE SAID that fear is a certain motion of the appetitive power, as was said above.[7] The principle of all appetitive motions is an apprehended good or evil. So it follows that the principle of fear and of all appetitive motions is some apprehension. Faith produces in us an apprehension of certain punitive evils that are assigned because of divine judgment. And in this way faith is the cause of the fear by which someone fears to be punished by God, which is servile fear. It is also the cause of filial fear, by which someone fears to be separated from God, or by which someone avoids comparing himself to God in revering him—so far as we have by faith this idea (*existimatio*) of God, that he is an immense and highest good, separation from which is most grievous, and wishing to be equal with which is evil. Unformed faith is the cause of the first fear, namely servile fear. Formed faith is the cause of the second fear, namely filial fear, since formed faith makes man inhere in God by charity and be subjected to him.

[1] TO THE FIRST ARGUMENT, THEREFORE, IT SHOULD BE SAID that the fear of God cannot universally precede faith, since if we were not to know at all of the rewards or punishments about which faith instructs us, we would in no way fear God. But if faith is supposed about other articles of faith, for example divine excellence, there follows the fear of reverence, from which it further follows that man should subject his understanding to God in believing all things promised by God. So

---

[5] *Summa* 1–2 q.18 a.2.

[6] James 2.19.

[7] *Summa* 1–2 q.41 a.1, q.42 a.1.

that it follows in the passage cited: "and your mercy be not taken away."[8]

[2] To the second it should be said that the same thing can be the cause of contraries according to contraries, but the same according to the same cannot be. Faith generates hope by producing in us an idea of the rewards that God bestows on the just. It is the cause of fear by producing in us an idea of the punishments that he inflicts on sinners.

[3] To the third it should be said that the first and formal object of faith is the good that is the first truth. But among the things that belong materially to faith, there are also proposed for believing some evil things: for example, that it is evil not to be subjected to God or to be separated from him, and that sinners suffer punitive evils from God. And in this way God is the cause of fear.

Article 2. [Whether purification of heart is an effect of faith.]

One proceeds in this way to the second query. IT SEEMS that purification of heart is not an effect of faith.

[1] Purity of heart is principally constituted in the affective part (*in affectu*). But faith is in the intellect. Therefore faith does not cause purification of heart.

[2] Furthermore what causes purification of heart cannot exist at the same time as impurity. But faith can exist at the same time as the impurity of sin, as is clear in those who have unformed faith. Therefore faith does not purify the heart.

[3] Furthermore, if faith were to purify the human heart in some way, it would purify the intellect of man most of all. But it does not purify the intellect from obscurity, since it is an enigmatic apprehension. Therefore faith in no way purifies the heart.

---

[8] Sirach 2.8.

BUT TO THE CONTRARY Peter says, Acts 15, "By faith purifying their hearts."[9]

I ANSWER THAT IT SHOULD BE SAID that the impurity of anything is constituted by its being mixed with vile things. Silver is not said to be impure from mixture with gold, by which it is rendered better, but from mixture with lead or tin. It is manifest that the rational creature is more dignified than all temporal things and all bodily creatures. And so it is rendered impure by subjugating itself in love to temporal things. It is purified from this impurity by a contrary motion, namely, when it tends towards what is above it, to God. In this motion the first principle is faith: "Coming to God one must believe," as is said in Hebrews 11.[10] And so faith is the first principle of purification of heart.[11] If faith be completed by formed charity, it causes complete purification.

[1] TO THE FIRST ARGUMENT, THEREFORE, IT SHOULD BE SAID that the things that are in the understanding are the principles of the things that are in the affective part, namely, so far as an understood good moves the affective part.

[2] To the second it should be said that even unformed faith excludes a certain impurity opposed to itself, namely, the impurity of error. This impurity happens when the human understanding inordinately inheres in things below it, namely, when it wills to measure[12] divine things according to the accounts of sensible things. But when it is formed by charity, it admits no impurity within itself, since "charity covers all faults," as it is said in Proverbs 10.[13]

---

[9] Acts 15.9.

[10] Hebrews 11.6.

[11] Some versions add "by which it is purified of the impurity of error."

[12] Some versions read "to merit."

[13] Proverbs 10.12.

[3] To the third it should be said that the obscurity of faith does not belong to the impurity of fault, but rather to the natural defect of human understanding in the state of the present life.

Question 8
[On the Gift of Understanding]

One should next consider the gift of understanding and of knowledge, which answers to the virtue of faith.

Eight queries are raised concerning the gift of understanding. (1) Whether understanding is a gift of the Holy Spirit. (2) Whether it can be together with faith at the same time in the same person. (3) Whether the understanding that is a gift is speculative only or also practical. (4) Whether all those who are in grace also have the gift of understanding. (5) Whether this gift is found in some who are without grace. (6) How the gift of understanding stands to the other gifts. (7) Of what answers to this gift among the beatitudes.[1] (8) Of what answers to it in the fruits.

Article 1. [Whether understanding is a gift of the Holy Spirit.]

One proceeds in this way to the first query. IT SEEMS that understanding is not a gift of the Holy Spirit.

[1] The gifts given in grace are distinguished from the natural gifts, for they are superadded to them. But under-

---

[1] The term *beatitudo* refers both to blessedness and to the particular blessings pronounced by Christ in the Sermon on the Mount. When it appears with the former sense, the translation adopted continues to be "blessedness." When it has the latter sense, the English is the technical term "beatitude." The careful reader will note the interplay of the two senses, as well as Thomas's reiteration of the point that Christ's beatitudes are about our final blessedness.

standing is a certain natural habit in the soul, by which are apprehended the naturally known principles, as is clear in *Ethics* 6.[2] Therefore it should not be put as a gift of the Holy Spirit.

[2] Furthermore, according to their proportion and way, creatures participate in the divine gifts, as is clear in Dionysius, *On the Divine Names.*[3] But the way of human nature is not that it should apprehend the truth simply, which belongs to the notion of understanding, but [rather do so] discursively, which is proper to reason, as is clear in Dionysius, *Divine Names* chapter 7.[4] Therefore the divine apprehension that is given to men ought more to be called the gift of reason than of understanding.

[3] Furthermore, among the powers of the soul the intellect is divided from the will, as is clear in *On the Soul* 3.[5] But no gift of the Holy Spirit is called will. Therefore also no gift of the Holy Spirit should be called understanding.

BUT TO THE CONTRARY there is what is said in Isaiah 11: "There rests on him the Spirit of the Lord, the Spirit of wisdom and understanding."[6]

I ANSWER THAT IT SHOULD BE SAID that the name "understanding" implies a certain intimate apprehension. We say *intelligere* (to understand) as if we meant *intus legere* (to read inwardly). And this is clear most manifestly to those considering the difference of understanding and sense. Sensitive apprehension is occupied with outward sensible qualities. Understanding apprehension penetrates to the essence of the thing, for the object of intel-

---

[2] Aristotle, *Nicomachean Ethics* bk.6 chap.6 (1140b31–32).

[3] Ps-Dionysius, *Divine Names* chap.4 sect.20 (PG 3:720A; Chevallier 1:247–249).

[4] Ps-Dionysius, *Divine Names* chap.7 sect.2 (PG 3:869B-[C]; Chevallier 1:388–389).

[5] Aristotle, *On the Soul* bk.3 chap.9 (432b5–6), bk.3 chap.10 (433a21–25).

[6] Isaiah 11.2.

lect is "what it is," as is said in *On the Soul* 3.[7] There are many kinds of things that hide inwardly and that the apprehension of man must penetrate as if intrinsically. For the substantial nature of things lies hidden under accident; the meanings of words lie hidden under words; figured truth lies hidden under similitudes and figures. And intelligible things are in a certain way inward with respect to sensible things that are sensed outwardly, and effects are hidden in causes and conversely. So understanding can be said with respect to all of these. But since the apprehension of man begins from sense, as if from the outward, it is manifest that as the light of intellect is stronger, so much more can it penetrate into inner things. The natural light of our intellect is of finite power, so that it can attain [only] to a determinate something. Man needs supernatural light that he might penetrate further towards apprehending the things that cannot be apprehended by the natural light. And this supernatural light given to man is called the gift of understanding.

[1] TO THE FIRST ARGUMENT, THEREFORE, IT SHOULD BE SAID that by the natural light endowed in us there are apprehended at once certain common principles that are naturally known. But since man is ordered to supernatural blessedness, as was said above,[8] it is necessary that man reach further to higher things. And for this is required the gift of understanding.

[2] To the second it should be said that the discourse of reason always begins from understanding and terminates in understanding. For we reason by proceeding from certain understood things, and the discourse of reason is completed when we come to this: that we understand what we earlier did not know. What we reason out proceeds, then, from something previously understood. The gift of grace

---

[7] Aristotle, *On the Soul* bk.3 chap.6 (430b27–28).

[8] This very general reference seems to point back to the series of arguments in *Summa* 1–2 qq.1–5.

does not proceed from the natural light, but is superadded to it, as if completing it. And so this superaddition is not called reason, but rather understanding, since the superadded light has to do with what we know naturally, just as the natural light has to do with what we primordially apprehend.

[3] To the third it should be said that "will" simply names an appetitive motion, without the determination of any excellence. But "understanding" names a certain excellence of apprehension penetrating to inner things. And so the supernatural gift is better named by the name of "understanding" than by the name of "will."

Article 2. [Whether the gift of understanding can exist at the same time as faith.]

One proceeds in this way to the second query. IT SEEMS that the gift of understanding is not had at the same time as faith.

[1] Augustine says, in the *Book of 83 Questions*,[9] that what is understood ends with the comprehension of the one understanding. But what is believed is not understood, according to the Apostle, Philippians 3, "Not that I am now comprehended or complete."[10] Therefore it seems that faith and understanding cannot exist in the same one.

[2] Furthermore, everything that is understood is seen by the understanding.[11] But faith is of what does not appear, as was said above.[12] Therefore faith cannot be at the same time in the same one as understanding.

[3] Furthermore, understanding is more certain than knowledge. But knowledge and faith cannot be about the

---

[9]Compare Augustine, *De divers. quaest. lxxxiii* q.15 (PL 40:14; CCL 44A:48.13–14).

[10]Philippians 3.12, paraphrase.

[11]Some versions read "is seen naturally by the understanding."

[12]In question 1, article 4, above.

same things, as is had above.[13] Much less therefore understanding and faith.

BUT TO THE CONTRARY there is what Gregory says, *Moral Remarks*,[14] that understanding illumines the mind about what is heard. But one who has faith can be illumined in the mind about things heard, so that it is said at the end of Luke that the Lord "opened the sense of his disciples, that they might understand the Scriptures."[15] Therefore understanding can exist at the same time as faith.

I ANSWER THAT IT SHOULD BE SAID that here a double distinction is needed: one on the part of faith, another on the part of understanding. On the part of faith, one should distinguish the things that fall under faith *per se* and directly, and exclude natural reason, such as that God is three and one or that the Son of God was incarnated. Others fall under faith as if ordered to faith in some way, such as all that is contained in holy Scripture.

On the part of understanding, one should distinguish two ways in which what we say can be understood. In one way, completely, namely when we reach apprehending the essence of the understood thing, and the very truth of the understood truth-bearing statement, as it is in itself. And in this way we cannot understand the things that fall directly under faith while we are in the the state of faith. But certain other things ordered to faith can be understood in this way.

In another way it happens that something is understood incompletely, namely when there is not apprehended what or how the essence of a thing or the truth of a proposition is, but only that the outward appearances of truth are not contradicted [by the incomplete understanding]. In other

---

[13] In question 1, article 5, above.

[14] Gregory the Great, *Moralia* bk.1 chap.32 sect.44 (PL 75:547; CCL 143:48.13–14).

[15] Luke 24.45.

words, so far as a man understood that on account of outward appearances one should not retreat from the things that are of faith. And according to this sense nothing prohibits that one also understand the things that *per se* fall under faith, even while the state of faith remains.

And from this the answer TO WHAT THINGS WERE OBJECTED is clear. For the first three reasonings proceed according as something is completely understood. The last reasoning proceeds from the understanding of the things that are ordered to faith.

Article 3. [Whether the understanding that is a gift is speculative alone or also practical.]

One proceeds in this way to the third query. IT SEEMS that the understanding which is put as a gift of the Holy Spirit is not practical, but speculative alone.

[1] For understanding, as Gregory says in *Moral Remarks* 1, penetrates certain higher things.[16] But the things that belong to the practical intellect are not high things, but low things, namely singulars, about which there are acts. Therefore the understanding that is posited as a gift is not practical understanding.

[2] Furthermore, the understanding that is a gift is worthier than the understanding that is an intellectual virtue. But the understanding that is an intellectual virtue is only about necessary things, as it clear in the Philosopher, *Ethics* 6.[17] Therefore even more is the understanding that is a gift only about necessary things. Practical understanding is not about necessary things, however, but about contingents that can be otherwise—about what can be done by human action. Therefore the understanding that is a gift is not practical understanding.

---

[16] Gregory the Great, *Moralia* bk.1 chap.32 sect.45 (PL 75:547; CCL 143:49.28–29).

[17] Aristotle, *Nicomachean Ethics* bk.6 chap.6 (1140b31).

[3] Furthermore, the gift of understanding illuminates the mind about the things that exceed natural reason. But the things that human action can do, about which there is practical understanding, do not exceed natural reason, which directs in things to be done, as is clear from what was said before.[18] Therefore the understanding that is a gift is not practical understanding.

BUT TO THE CONTRARY there is what is said in the Psalms, "A good understanding to all who do it."[19]

I ANSWER THAT IT SHOULD BE SAID that, as was said,[20] the gift of understanding not only has to do with the things that fall primarily and principally under faith, but also with all things that are ordered to faith. Good actions have a certain ordering to faith, since "faith acts by love," as the Apostle says, Galatians 5.[21] And so the gift of understanding also extends to certain actions, not as if it concerned them principally, but so far as in things to be done we are ruled "by eternal reasons, by contemplating and consulting which the higher reason inheres [in them]," as Augustine says, *On the Trinity* 12.[22] This completes the gift of understanding.

[1] TO THE FIRST ARGUMENT, THEREFORE, IT SHOULD BE SAID that the things of human work, so far as they are considered in themselves, do not have any excellence of high rank (*altitudo*). But so far as they are referred to the rule of eternal law and the end of divine blessedness,[23] they do have high rank, and there can be understanding about them.

---

[18] *Summa* 1–2 q.58 a.2.

[19] Psalm 110.10.

[20] In article 2 of this question, above.

[21] Galatians 5.6.

[22] Augustine, *De Trinitate* bk.12 chap.7 sect.12 (PL 42:1005; CCL 50:367.105–106).

[23] Some versions read "to the faith of divine blessedness."

[2] To the second it should be said that this itself belongs to the dignity of the gift that is understanding, that it considers the eternal or necessary intelligibles not only according as they are in themselves, but also according as they are certain rules of human acts, since the more an apprehensive power extends itself to many things, the more noble it is.

[3] To the third it should be said that the rule of human acts is both human reason and the eternal law, as was said above.[24] The eternal law exceeds natural reason. And so the apprehension of human acts according as they are regulated by eternal law exceeds human reason and needs the supernatural light of the gift of the Holy Spirit.

Article 4. [Whether the gift of understanding is in all those who have grace.]

One proceeds in this way to the fourth query. IT SEEMS that the gift of understanding is not in all those who have grace.

[1] Gregory says, *Moral Remarks* 2, that the gift of understanding is given against dullness of mind.[25] But many who have grace still suffer dullness of mind. Therefore the gift of understanding is not in all those who have grace.

[2] Furthermore, among the things that belong to apprehension, only faith would seem to be necessary for salvation, since "by faith Christ dwells in our hearts," as is said in Ephesians 3.[26] But not all those who have faith have the gift of understanding. Rather those who believe should pray that they might understand, as Augustine says, *On*

---

[24] *Summa* 1-2 q.71 a.6.

[25] Gregory the Great, *Moralia* bk.2 chap.49 sect.77 (PL 75:592D; CCL 143:106.42).

[26] Ephesians 3.17.

the Trinity.[27] Therefore the gift of understanding is not necessary to salvation. Therefore it is not in all those who have grace.

[3] Furthermore, the things that are common to all who have grace are never taken away from those who have grace. But the grace of understanding and of the other gifts "is sometimes usefully taken away, when" namely, "while the soul raises itself in elation to the understanding of sublime things, it becomes sluggish in lower and vile things because of a heavy dullness," as Gregory says, *Moral Remarks* 2.[28] Therefore the gift of understanding is not in all those who have grace.

BUT TO THE CONTRARY there is what is said in Psalms: "They did not know, neither did they understand, they walk in darkness."[29] But no one who has grace walks in darkness, according to John 8, "He who follows me does not walk in darkness."[30] Therefore no one who has grace lacks the gift of understanding.

I ANSWER THAT IT SHOULD BE SAID that in all those who have grace there must necessarily be rightness of will, since "by grace the will of man is prepared for the good," as Augustine says.[31] The will cannot be rightly ordered to the good unless there preexist some apprehension of truth, since the object of the will is an understood good, as is said in *On the Soul* 3.[32] Just as by the gift of charity the Holy Spirit orders the will of man that it be directly moved to some supernatural good, so also by the gift of understanding he illuminates the mind of man that

---

[27] Augustine, *De Trinitate* bk.15 chap.27 sect.49 (PL 42:1096; CCL 50A:531.46–47).

[28] Gregory the Great, *Moralia*, bk.2 chap.49 sect.78 (PL 75:593B; CCL 143:106.60–62).

[29] Psalm 81.5.

[30] John 8.12.

[31] Augustine, *Contra Julianum* bk.4 chap.3 sect.5 (PL 44:744).

[32] Aristotle, *On the Soul* bk.3 chap.10 (433a20–21, b12–13).

it apprehend a certain supernatural truth, to which the right will must tend. And so, just as the gift of charity is in all those who have the grace that makes one pleasing, so also is the gift of understanding.

[1] TO THE FIRST ARGUMENT, THEREFORE, IT SHOULD BE SAID that some who have the grace that makes one pleasing can suffer dullness about certain things that are outside what is necessary to salvation. But about the things that are necessary to salvation they are sufficiently instructed by the Holy Spirit, according to 1 John 2, "Unction teaches you about all things."[33]

[2] To the second it should be said that even if all those who have faith do not fully understand what is proposed for believing, they nonetheless understand that these things are to be believed, and that they are not to be deviated from for anything.

[3] To the third it should be said that the gift of understanding about what things are necessary for salvation is never taken away from the holy. But about other things it is taken away from time to time, so that they cannot penetrate all things fluently by understanding, in order that occasion for pride be taken away.

Article 5. [Whether the gift of understanding is found also in those who do not have the grace that makes one pleasing.]

One proceeds in this way to the fifth query. IT SEEMS that the gift of understanding is also found in those who do not have the grace that makes one pleasing.

[1] Augustine, expounding that psalm, "My soul wanted to desire your justifications," says that "the understanding flies before, the affective power follows tardily or not at

---

[33] 1 John 2.27, condensed.

all."[34] But in all those who have the grace that makes one pleasing there is a prompt affective power, on account of charity. Therefore the gift of understanding can also be in those who do not have the grace that makes one pleasing.

[2] Furthermore, it is said in Daniel 10 that "understanding is required in" prophetic "vision,"[35] and so it seems that prophecy is not without the gift of understanding. But prophecy can be without the grace that makes one pleasing, as is clear in Matthew 7. To those saying "we prophesied in your name," it is there answered, "I never knew you."[36] Therefore the gift of understanding can be without the grace that makes one pleasing.

[3] Furthermore, the gift of understanding answers to the virtue of faith, according to another version of Isaiah 7, "If you do not believe, you will not understand."[37] But faith can be without the grace that makes one pleasing. Therefore also the gift of understanding.

BUT TO THE CONTRARY there is what the Lord says, John 6: "Everyone who has heard the Father and learned, comes to me."[38] But by a heard understanding we learn or we penetrate, as is clear in Gregory, *Moral Remarks* 1.[39] Therefore whoever has the gift of understanding comes to Christ. But this cannot happen without the grace that makes one pleasing. Therefore the gift of understanding is not without the grace that makes one pleasing.

I ANSWER THAT IT SHOULD BE SAID that the gifts of the Holy Spirit complete the soul according as it is easily movable (*bene movibilis*) by the Holy Spirit, as was

---

[34] Augustine, *Enarr. in Ps.* ps.118 serm.8 sect.4, on Psalm 118.20 (PL 37:1522; CCL 40:1689.59–61).

[35] Daniel 10.1.

[36] Matthew 7.22–23.

[37] Isaiah 7.9, alternate version.

[38] John 6.45.

[39] Gregory the Great, *Moralia* bk.1 chap.32 sect.44 (PL 75:547A; CCL 143:48.13–14).

said above.[40] The intellectual light of grace is put as a gift of understanding, so far as the understanding of man is easily movable by the Holy Spirit. The consideration of this kind of motion in this case is that man apprehend the truth about the end.[41] So that unless the human intellect is moved by the Holy Spirit to have a idea of the end, the gift of understanding has not been attained, however many other preambles it apprehends by the Holy Spirit's illumination. It does not have a right idea of the last end unless it does not err about the things that are of the end. Instead, it must firmly inhere in it as in the best thing, which can only be in one having the grace that makes one pleasing. Just so in morals a man has a right idea of the end by the habit of virtue. So no one has the gift of understanding without the grace that makes one pleasing.

[1] TO THE FIRST ARGUMENT, THEREFORE, IT SHOULD BE SAID that Augustine calls any intellectual illumination "understanding." Nonetheless illumination does not attain the complete account of the gift unless the mind of man is led to have a right idea about the end.

[2] To the second it should be said that the intelligence that is necessary to prophecy is an illumination of the mind about the things revealed to prophets. It is not, however, an illumination of the mind about the right idea of the last end, which belongs to the gift of understanding.

[3] To the third it should be said that faith implies only assent to the things that are proposed. But understanding implies some perception of the truth, which cannot be about the end except in him who has the grace that makes one pleasing, as was said. And so there is no similar reasoning about understanding and faith.

---

[40] *Summa* 1–2 q.68 aa.1–3.

[41] Some versions read "about the faith."

Article 6. [Whether the gift of understanding is distinguished from other gifts.]

One proceeds in this way to the sixth query. IT SEEMS that the gift of understanding is not distinguished from other gifts.

[1] Things that have the same opposites are the same. But wisdom is opposed to stupidity, dullness to understanding, hastiness to counsel, ignorance to knowledge, as is clear in Gregory, *Moral Remarks* 2.[42] But stupidity, dullness, ignorance, and hastiness do not seem to differ. Therefore neither is understanding distinguished from the other gifts.

[2] Furthermore, the understanding that is put as an intellectual virtue differs from the other intellectual virtues by what is proper to it, that it is about principles known *per se*. But the gift of understanding is not about other principles known *per se*, since the natural habit of first principles suffices for those that are naturally apprehended *per se*. To those that are supernatural, faith suffices, since the articles of faith are as the first principles in supernatural apprehension, as was said.[43] Therefore the gift of understanding is not distinguished from the other intellectual gifts.

[3] Further, all intellectual apprehension is either speculative or practical. But the gift of intellect has to do with both, as was said.[44] Therefore it is not distinguished from the other intellectual gifts, but comprises all in itself.

BUT TO THE CONTRARY whatever is counted out alongside another must in some way be distinct from it, since distinction is the principle of number. But the gift of intellect is counted out alongside the other gifts, as is clear

[42] Gregory the Great, *Moralia* bk.2 chap.49 sect.77 (PL 75:592D; CCL 143:106.42–44).

[43] In question 1, article 7, above.

[44] In article 3 of this question, above.

in Isaiah 11.[45] Therefore the gift of understanding is distinct from the other gifts.

I ANSWER THAT IT SHOULD BE SAID that the distinction of the gift of understanding from three other gifts, namely, piety, fortitude, and fear, is manifest. The gift of understanding belongs to the cognitive power, while those three belong to the appetitive power. But the difference of the gift of understanding from the other three [gifts], namely, wisdom, knowledge, and counsel, is not so clear. It seems to some[46] that the gift of understanding is distinguished from the gift of knowledge and of counsel in that those two belong to practical apprehension, while the gift of intellect belongs to the speculative. From the gift of wisdom, which also belongs to speculative apprehension, it is distinguished in that judgment belongs to wisdom, while the capacity of intellect for what is proposed—or penetration to their inner [truths]—belongs to understanding. And according to this we assigned the number of gifts above.[47] But examining this more closely, the gift of understanding not only has to do with speculative things, but also with things to be done, as has been said.[48] And similarly also the gift of knowledge has to do with both, as will be said below.[49] And so it is required to take their distinction in another way.

All of the four things mentioned are ordered to supernatural apprehension, which is founded in us by faith. Faith is "from hearing," as is said in Romans 10.[50] So it follows that some things proposed to man for believing are not as if seen, but as if heard, to which one assents by

---

[45] Isaiah 11.2–3.

[46] The reference seems to be to William of Auxerre.

[47] *Summa* 1–2 q.68 a.4. Note that Thomas here explicitly revises—or supplements—his earlier reasoning.

[48] In article 3 of this question, above.

[49] In question 9, article 3, above.

[50] Romans 10.17.

faith. Faith primarily and principally has to do with the first truth; secondarily with certain things to be considered about creatures; and it extends further even to the direction of human works, according as "it works by love," as is clear from what has been said.[51] So two things are required on our part with regard to the things that are proposed for believing by faith. First, that they be penetrated or grasped by intellect; this belongs to the gift of understanding. Second, that a man has right judgment about them, so that he counts them as things to be inhered in and the things opposed to them as things to be avoided. This judgment, as regards divine things, belongs to the gift of wisdom. As regards created things, it belongs to the gift of knowledge. As regards application to single works, it belongs to the gift of counsel.

[1] TO THE FIRST ARGUMENT, THEREFORE, IT SHOULD BE SAID that the difference of the four gifts stated above manifestly agrees with the distinction of those which Gregory puts as opposed to them. Dullness is opposed to acuity. An intellect is called acute by likeness when it can penetrate to the inner [truths] of what are proposed. So by dullness of mind a mind does not suffice to penetrate the inner [truths].—A man is said to be stupid because he judges perversely concerning the common end of life. And so it is properly opposed to wisdom, which makes the right judgment concerning the universal cause.—Ignorance implies a defect about any particular things whatever. And so it is opposed to knowledge, by which man has right judgment concerning particular causes, namely about creatures.—Hastiness is manifestly opposed to counsel, since by it man does not proceed to action before the deliberation of reason.

[2] To the second it should be said that the gift of understanding is about the first principles of graced appre-

---

[51] In article 3 of this question and in question 4, article 2, reply [3], both above.

hension, but differently than faith is. For it belongs to faith to assent to them; it belongs to the gift of understanding to penetrate by mind the things that are said.

[3] To the third it should be said that the gift of understanding belongs to both apprehensions, namely speculative and practical, not as regards judgment, but as regards apprehension, that what is said may be grasped.

Article 7. [Whether the gift of understanding answers to the sixth beatitude, namely, "Blessed are the clean of heart, since they will see God."]

One proceeds in this way to the seventh query. IT SEEMS that the gift of understanding does not answer to the sixth beatitude, namely, "Blessed are the clean of heart, for they shall see God."[52]

[1] Cleanness of heart seems most of all to belong to the affective power. But the gift of understanding does not belong to affective power, but rather to intellect. Therefore the named beatitude does not answer to the gift of understanding.

[2] Furthermore, it is said in Acts 15, "by faith purifying their hearts."[53] But cleanness of heart is acquired by purification of heart. Therefore the named beatitude belongs more to the virtue[54] of faith than to the gift of understanding.

[3] Furthermore, the gifts of the Holy Spirit complete a man in the present life. But the vision of God does not belong to the present life, for it makes [us] blessed, as was had above.[55] Therefore the sixth beatitude, containing the vision of God, does not belong to the gift of understanding.

---

[52] Matthew 5.8.

[53] Acts 15.9.

[54] Some versions read "to the truth of faith."

[55] *Summa* 1 q.12 a.1.

BUT TO THE CONTRARY Augustine says, *The Lord's Sermon on the Mount*, that the sixth working of the Holy Spirit, which is understanding, "comes to the clean of heart, who with a purged eye can see what the eye does not see."[56]

I ANSWER THAT IT SHOULD BE SAID that in the sixth beatitude, as in the others, two things are contained: one in the way of merit, namely cleanness of heart; and another in the way of reward, namely the vision of God, as was said above.[57] And both belong in a certain way to the gift of understanding. There is a twofold cleanness. One is preparatory and dispositing to the vision of God, which is the cleansing of the affective power from disordered affections. This cleanness of heart is brought about by the virtues and gifts that belong to the appetitive power. Another cleanness of heart is as it were completing with respect to the divine vision. This is the cleanness of the mind cleansed of all phantasms and errors, namely so that the things proposed be not accepted in the way of bodily phantasms, nor according to heretical perversities. And this cleanness is brought about by the gift of understanding.

Similarly the vision of God is twofold. One complete, by which the essence of God is seen. The other incomplete, by which, even if we do not see what God is, we see nonetheless what he is not; we apprehend God the more completely in this life the more we understand him to exceed whatever is comprehended by intellect. And both visions of God belong to the gift of understanding. The first to the gift of consummated understanding, as it will be in the homeland; the second, to the gift of inchoate understanding, which is had on the journey.

---

[56] Augustine, *De serm. Dom. in monte*, bk.1 chap.4 sect.11 (PL 34:1235; CCL 35:10.214–217).

[57] *Summa* 1–2 q.69 a.2.

And by this the answer is clear to what was objected. For the first two reasons proceed with regard to the first cleanness. The third, with regard to the complete vision of God. The gifts both complete us here according to a first beginning and also will be fulfilled in the future, as was said above.[58]

Article 8. [Whether among the fruits, faith answers to the gift of understanding.]

One proceeds in this way to the eighth query. IT SEEMS that among the fruits, faith does not answer to the gift of understanding.

[1] Understanding is the fruit of faith, as is said according to another version of Isaiah 7, "If you have not believed, you will not understand,"[59] where we have, "If you have not believed, you will not persevere." Therefore faith is not the fruit of understanding.

[2] Furthermore, the prior is not the fruit of the posterior. But faith seems to be prior to understanding, since faith is the foundation of the whole spiritual building, as was said above.[60] Therefore faith is not the fruit of understanding.

[3] Furthermore, there are more gifts belonging to understanding than to the appetite. But among the fruits there is put only one belonging to understanding, namely faith. All the others belong to appetite. Therefore faith does not seem to answer more to understanding than to wisdom or knowledge or counsel.

BUT TO THE CONTRARY the end of any thing is its fruit. But the gift of understanding seems principally to be ordered to the certainty of faith, which is put as a

---

[58] *Summa* 1-2 q.69 a.2.

[59] Isaiah 7.9, alternate version.

[60] In question 4, article 7, objection [4], above.

fruit. For the Gloss says about Galatians 5 that faith, which is a fruit, is "the certainty of invisible things."[61] Therefore among the fruits faith answers to the gift of understanding.

I ANSWER THAT IT SHOULD BE SAID that the "fruits of the Holy Spirit" are certain final and delectable things that come to us by the power of the Holy Spirit, as was said above when the topic was the fruits.[62] The last delectable thing has the notion of the end, which is the proper object of the will. And so it follows that what is last and delectable in the will is in some way a fruit of all the other things that belong to the other powers. According to this, therefore, the genus of a gift or of a virtue perfecting some power can have a fruit in two ways: one belongs to its power; the other belongs to the will and is last as it were. And according to this it is to be said that faith answers to the gift of understanding as its proper fruit—namely, the certainty of faith; but joy answers to it as its last fruit, since it belongs to the will.

[1] TO THE FIRST ARGUMENT, THEREFORE, IT SHOULD BE SAID that understanding is the fruit of the faith that is a virtue. "Faith" is not taken in this way when it is said of the fruit, but for certainty of faith, to which man comes by the gift of understanding.

[2] To the second argument it should be said that faith cannot universally precede understanding; for man cannot assent to some proposed things through believing unless he understands them somewhat. But the completion of understanding follows upon the faith that is a virtue, to which completion of the understanding there follows a certainty of faith.

[3] To the third argument it should be said that the fruit of practical apprehension cannot be in itself, since such apprehension is not for itself, but for another. But specu-

---

[61] *Glossa interlin.* on Galatians 5.22 (Strasbourg 4).

[62] *Summa* 1-2 q.70 a.1.

lative apprehension has a fruit in itself, namely the certainty of the things about which it is. And so no proper fruit answers to the gift of counsel, which belongs only to practical apprehension. To the gifts of wisdom, understanding, and knowledge, which can also belong to speculative apprehension, there corresponds only one fruit, which is the certainty signified by the name of faith. Many other fruits are posited as belonging to the appetitive part, since, as has been said, the notion of the end, which is implied in the name "fruit," belongs more to the appetitive power than to the intellective.

Question 9
[The Gift of Knowledge]

One should next consider the gift of knowledge. Four queries are raised with regard to this. (1) Whether knowledge is a gift. (2) Whether it is about divine things. (3) Whether it is speculative or practical. (4) What beatitude answers to it.

Article 1. [Whether knowledge is a gift.]

One proceeds in this way to the first query. IT SEEMS that knowledge is not a gift.

[1] The gifts of the Holy Spirit exceed the natural faculty. But knowledge implies a certain effect of natural reason, for the Philosopher says, *Posterior Analytics* 1, that demonstration is a syllogism that makes one know.[1] Therefore knowledge is not a gift of the Holy Spirit.

[2] Furthermore, the gifts of the Holy Spirit are common to all the holy, as was said above.[2] But Augustine says, *On the Trinity* 14, that "many of the faithful are not strong in knowledge, though they are strong in faith itself."[3] Therefore knowledge is not a gift.

---

[1] Aristotle, *Posterior Analytics* bk.1 chap.2 (71b18–19).

[2] *Summa* 1-2 q.68 a.5.

[3] Augustine, *De Trinitate* bk.14 chap.1 sect.3 (PL 42:1037; CCL 50A:424.61–63).

[3] Furthermore, a gift is more perfect than a virtue, as was said above.[4] Therefore one gift suffices for the completion of one virtue. But to the virtue of faith there answers the gift of understanding, as was said above.[5] Therefore the gift of knowledge does not answer to it. Nor does it seem that it answers to any other virtue. Therefore, since the gifts are the completions of virtues, as was said above, it seems that knowledge is not a gift.

BUT TO THE CONTRARY Isaiah 11 counts it among the seven gifts.[6]

I ANSWER THAT IT SHOULD BE SAID that grace is more complete than nature, so that it does not fall short in the things through which a man can be completed by nature. Since man by natural reason assents according to understanding to some truth, he is doubly completed according to that truth: first, since he grasps it; second, since he has certain judgment about it. And so in order that the human intellect completely assent to the truth of faith, two things are required. Of which one is that it healthily grasp the things that are proposed, which belongs to the gift of understanding, as was said above.[7] The other is that it have certain and right judgment about them, namely, discerning what is to be believed from what is not to be believed. And for this the gift of knowledge is necessary.

[1] TO THE FIRST ARGUMENT, THEREFORE, IT SHOULD BE SAID that certainty of apprehension is found in different natures in different ways, according to the condition of each nature. Now man reaches certain judgment of truth by the discourse of reason, and so human knowledge is acquired by demonstrative reason. But in God there is certain judgment of truth by simple intuition

---

[4] *Summa* 1–2 q.68 a.8.

[5] In question 8, article 5, objection [3], above.

[6] Isaiah 11.2–3.

[7] In question 8, article 6, above.

without discourse, as was said in the first [part].[8] And so divine knowledge is not discursive or ratiocinative, but absolute and simple. The knowledge that is posited as a gift of the Holy Spirit is similar to it, since it is a certain participative likeness to it.

[2] To the second it should be said that there can be a twofold knowledge about things to be believed. One by which man knows what he ought to believe, discerning things to be believed from things not to be believed. According to this [kind], knowledge is a gift and belongs to all the holy. Another is the knowledge about things to be believed by which man not only knows what he ought to believe, but also knows how to manifest the faith and how to induce others to believe and to overcome (*revincere*) contradictors. And this knowledge is put among the freely given graces, and it is not given to all, but to some. So Augustine adds, after the quoted words, "It is one thing to know only what man ought to believe, and something else to know this and to teach it well to the pious and to defend it against the impious."[9]

[3] To the third it should be said that the gifts are more complete than the moral and intellectual virtues. They are not more complete than the theological virtues. On the contrary, all the gifts are ordered to the completion of theological virtues as to an end. And so it is not inappropriate if different gifts are ordered to one theological virtue.

Article 2. [Whether the gift of knowledge is about divine things.]

One proceeds in this way to the second query. IT SEEMS that the gift of knowledge is about divine things.

---

[8] *Summa* 1 q.14 a.7.

[9] Augustine, *De Trinitate* bk.14 chap.1 sect.3 (PL 42:1037; CCL 50A:424.63–66).

[1] Augustine says, *On the Trinity* 14, that faith is begotten, nourished, and strengthened by knowledge.[10] But faith is about divine things, since the object of faith is the first truth, as was had above.[11] Therefore the gift of knowledge is also about divine things.

[2] Furthermore, the gift of knowledge is worthier than acquired knowledge. But some acquired knowledge is about divine things, such as the knowledge of metaphysics. Much more, then, is the gift of knowledge about divine things.

[3] Furthermore, as it is said in Romans 1, "The invisible things of God are disclosed, being understood by the things that are made."[12] If there is knowledge about created things, it seems that there is also knowledge about divine things.

BUT TO THE CONTRARY there is what Augustine says, *On the Trinity* 14: "The knowledge of divine things is properly named 'wisdom'; [to the knowledge] of human things, the name 'knowledge' properly applies."[13]

I ANSWER THAT IT SHOULD BE SAID that certain judgment about some thing is given most from its cause. And so the order of judgments must be according to the order of causes. As the first cause is the cause of the second, so the second cause is judged by the first cause. About the first cause one cannot judge by any other cause. And so the judgment that is made by the first cause is first and most complete. In those things in which something is most complete, the common name of the genus is appropriated to the things that fall short of the most complete, while another special name is adapted to the most complete thing. This is clear in logic. For in the genus of con-

---

[10] Augustine, *De Trinitate* bk.14 chap.1 sect.3 (PL 42:1037; CCL 50A:424.59–61).

[11] In question 1, article 1, above.

[12] Romans 1.20.

[13] Augustine, *De Trinitate* bk.14 chap.1 sect.3 (PL 42:1037; CCL 50A:423.54–424.56).

vertible [formulas], what signifies "what it is" is called by the special name "definition." Any existing convertible formulas that fall short of this retain the common name; they are called "properties."[14]

Since, then, the name "knowledge" implies a certainty of judgment, as was said, if the certainty of judgment is due to the highest cause, it will have a special name, which is "wisdom." In any genus, he is called wise who knows the highest cause of that genus, by which he can judge all things. The wise man simply speaking is he who knows the highest cause simply, namely God. And so apprehension of divine things is called wisdom. Apprehension of human or created things is called knowledge, a common name as it were, implying the certainty of judgment appropriate to a judgment made by second causes. And so, taking the name of knowledge in this way, it is put as a gift distinct from wisdom. So the gift of knowledge is only about human things or created things.

[1] TO THE FIRST ARGUMENT, THEREFORE, IT SHOULD BE SAID that, even if the things about which there is faith are divine and eternal things, nonetheless faith itself is a temporal thing in the soul of the believer. And so to know what is to be believed belongs to the gift of knowledge. To know the believed things in themselves, by a kind of union with them, pertains to the gift of wisdom. So that the gift of wisdom answers more to charity, which unites the mind of man to God.

[2] To the second it should be said that this reasoning proceeds so far as the name of "knowledge" is commonly taken. In this way, knowledge is not put as a special gift,

---

[14] One thing is convertible with another when it can be exchanged or substituted for the other. In Aristotelian logic, as Thomas knows it, a distinction is made between convertible formulas that express the essence of a thing and those that, while still being convertible, do not express the essence. The former are definitions, the latter are properties.

but according as it is restricted to the judgment that is made by created things.

[3] To the third it should be said that, as was said above,[15] any apprehending habit concerns formally the middle [term] by which something is known; materially it concerns that by which the middle [term] is known. And since what is formal is more powerful, those bodies of knowledge that conclude from mathematical principles about natural matter are more to be counted together with mathematics, as being similar to them. Even if, as regards matter, they agree more with the natural. And on account of this it is said in *Physics* 2 that they are "more natural."[16] And so, since man apprehends God by created things, it seems more to belong to knowledge, to which it formally belongs, than to wisdom, to which it materially pertains. And conversely, since we judge created things according to divine things, this belongs more to wisdom than to knowledge.

Article 3. [Whether the gift of knowledge is practical knowledge.]

One proceeds in this way to the third query. IT SEEMS that the knowledge that is put as a gift is practical knowledge.

[1] Augustine says, *On the Trinity* 12, that the action by which we use exterior things is attributed to knowledge.[17] But the knowledge to which action is attributed is practical. Therefore the knowledge that is a gift is practical knowledge.

[2] Furthermore, Gregory says, *Moral Remarks* 1: "It is not knowledge if it does not have usefulness for piety. . . .

[15] In question 1, article 1, above.

[16] Aristotle, *Physics* bk.2 chap.2 (194a7–8).

[17] Augustine, *De Trinitate* bk.12 chap.14 sect.22 (PL 42:1009; CCL 50:375.7–9).

And piety is most useless if it lack the discrimination of knowledge."[18] From this it is clear that knowledge directs piety. But this [directing] cannot belong to speculative knowledge. Therefore the knowledge that is a gift is not speculative, but practical.

[3] Furthermore, the gifts of the Holy Spirit are not had except by the just, as was had above.[19] But speculative knowledge can be had even by the unjust, according to the end of James, "Knowing good and not doing it, is a sin to him."[20] Therefore the knowledge that is a gift is not speculative, but practical.

BUT TO THE CONTRARY there is what Gregory says, *Moral Remarks* 1: "Knowledge in its day prepares the banquet, since in the stomach of the mind it overcomes the fasting of unknowing."[21] But unknowing is not removed unless by both forms of knowledge, namely both speculative and practical. Therefore the knowledge that is a gift is both speculative and practical.

I ANSWER THAT IT SHOULD BE SAID that the gift of knowledge is ordered to the certainty of faith, as is also the gift of understanding, as was said above.[22] Faith first and principally consists in speculation, namely so far as it inheres in the first truth. But since the first truth is also the last end, on account of which we work, so it is that faith extends itself to action, according to Galatians 5, "Faith works by love."[23] So it follows that the gift of knowledge first and principally has to do with speculation, so far namely as man knows what ought to be held by faith. Sec-

---

[18] Gregory the Great, *Moralia* bk.1 chap.32 sect.45 (PL 75:547C; CCL 143:49.35–38).

[19] *Summa* 1–2 q.88 a.5.

[20] James 4.17.

[21] Gregory the Great, *Moralia* bk.1 chap.32 sect.44 (PL 75:547B; CCL 143:49.18–19).

[22] In article 1 of this question, above.

[23] Galatians 5.6.

ondarily it extends even to operation, according as by the knowledge of believable things, and of the things that follow upon believable things, we are directed in acting.

[1] TO THE FIRST ARGUMENT, THEREFORE, IT SHOULD BE SAID that Augustine speaks of the gift of knowledge as it extends itself to action. He attributes action to it, but not only or exclusively. And in this way it also directs piety.

[2] The answer to the second is clear from this.

[3] To the third it should be said that, as was said of the gift of understanding,[24] not everyone who understands has the gift of understanding, but only one who understands as it were from the habit of grace. So also the gift of knowledge is to be understood in such a way that those only have the gift of knowledge who by the infusion of grace have certain judgment about things to be believed and things to be done, which judgment deviates in nothing from the rightness of justice. And this is the "knowledge of the holy," about which it is said in Wisdom 10 "the Lord leads the just man by right ways and gives to him the knowledge of the holy."[25]

Article 4. [Whether to the gift of knowledge there answers the third beatitude, namely, "Blessed are they who mourn, for they shall be comforted."]

One proceeds in this way to the fourth query. IT SEEMS that the third beatitude, namely, "Blessed are they who weep, for they shall be consoled,"[26] does not answer to knowledge

[1] Just as evil is the cause of sadness and mourning, so also the good is the cause of gladness. But by knowledge

---

[24] In question 8, article 5, above.

[25] Wisdom 10.10, condensed.

[26] Matthew 5.5.

principally are manifested goods rather than evils, which are apprehended by goods. The straight is the judge of itself and of the oblique, as is said in *On the Soul* 1.[27] Therefore the named beatitude does not appropriately answer to knowledge.

[2] Furthermore, the consideration of truth is the act of knowledge. But in the consideration of truth there is not sadness, but rather joy, as is said in Wisdom 8: "His conversation does not have bitterness, nor living with him tedium, but gladness and joy."[28] Therefore the named beatitude does not appropriately answer to the gift of knowledge.

[3] Furthermore, the gift of knowledge consists first in speculation rather than in working. But so far as it consists in speculation, mourning does not answer to it, since the speculative intellect says nothing about what is to be imitated or fled, as it is said in *On the Soul* 3.[29] Nor does it say anything glad or sad. Therefore the named beatitude is not appropriately put as answering to the gift of knowledge.

BUT TO THE CONTRARY there is what Augustine says, *The Lord's Sermon on the Mount*: "Knowledge becomes those who mourn, who have learned . . . by how many evils they were conquered, which they sought . . . as goods."[30]

I ANSWER THAT IT SHOULD BE SAID that to knowledge there properly belongs the right judgment of creatures. Man is occasionally turned away from God by creatures, according to Wisdom 14, "Creatures have become hateful, to trip the feet of the foolish"[31]—to him namely

---

[27] Aristotle, *On the Soul* bk.1 chap.5 (411a5).

[28] Wisdom 8.16.

[29] Aristotle, *On the Soul* bk.3 chap..9 (432b27–31).

[30] Augustine, *De serm. Dom. in monte* bk.1 chap.4 (PL 34:1234; CCL 35:10.203–205).

[31] Wisdom 14.11, condensed.

who does not have right judgment of them, since he holds the opinion that there is complete good in them. By constituting the end in them, these [men] sin and lose the true good. And this loss is made known to man by right judgment of creatures, which is had by the gift of knowledge. And so the beatitude of mourning is put as answering to the gift of knowledge.

[1] TO THE FIRST ARGUMENT, THEREFORE, IT SHOULD BE SAID that created goods do not excite spiritual joy except so far as they are referred to the divine good, from which spiritual good properly arises. And so spiritual peace and the consequent joy answer directly to the gift of wisdom. To the gift of knowledge answers, first, a mourning over past errors; and consequently consolation, when man by right judgment of knowledge orders creatures to the divine good. And so in this beatitude there are put mourning as merit, and consequent consolation as reward. The reward begins in this life, but is completed in the future life.

[2] To the second it should be said that man rejoices in the very consideration of truth, but he can sometimes be saddened by the thing about which he considers truth. And according to this, mourning is attributed to knowledge.

[3] To the third it should be said that no beatitude answers to knowledge so far as it consists in speculation, since the blessedness of man is not constituted by the consideration of creatures, but by the contemplation of God. But somehow the blessedness of man consists in a due use of creatures and an ordered affection for them. And I say this as regards the blessedness of the journey. So to knowledge there is not attributed some beatitude belonging to contemplation, but rather to understanding and to wisdom, which are about the divine.

Question 10
[On Unfaithfulness in General]

One should next consider the opposed vices. And first, unfaithfulness, which is opposed to faith; second, blasphemy, which is opposed to confession; third, ignorance and dullness, which are opposed to knowledge and understanding. On the first point, one should consider unfaithfulness in general; second, heresy; third, apostasy from faith.

Twelve queries are raised about the first point. (1) Whether unfaithfulness is a sin. (2) What it is in the understanding as in a subject. (3) Whether it is the greatest of sins. (4) Whether every action of those who are unfaithful is a sin. (5) On the species of unfaithfulness. (6) On their comparison with each other. (7) Whether one ought to dispute with the unfaithful about faith. (8) Whether they are to be compelled to faith. (9) Whether one is to share community with them. (10) Whether they can stand above the Christian faithful. (11) Whether the rites of the unfaithful are to be tolerated. (12) Whether the children of the unfaithful are to be baptized even when the parents are opposed.

Article 1. [Whether unfaithfulness is a sin.]

One proceeds in this way to the first query. IT SEEMS that unfaithfulness is not a sin.

[1] Every sin is against nature, as is clear in the Damascene, book 2.[1] But unfaithfulness does not seem to be against nature. For Augustine says, *On the Predestination of the Saints*, that "the ability to have faith, just as the ability to have charity, is of the nature of men; but having faith, just as much as having charity, is of the grace of the faithful."[2] Therefore not having faith, which is being unfaithful, is not against nature and so is not a sin.

[2] Furthermore, no one sins in what he cannot avoid, since all sin is voluntary. But it is not in the power of man to avoid unfaithfulness, which he cannot avoid except by having faith. For the Apostle says, Romans 10: "How will they believe him whom they do not hear? How will they hear without a preacher?"[3] Therefore unfaithfulness does not seem to be sin.

[3] Furthermore, as was said above, there are seven capital sins, to which all sins are traced back.[4] But unfaithfulness seems to be contained under none of these. Therefore unfaithfulness is not a sin.

BUT TO THE CONTRARY a vice is contrary to a virtue. But faith is a virtue, to which unfaithfulness is contrary. Therefore unfaithfulness is a sin.

I ANSWER THAT IT SHOULD BE SAID that unfaithfulness can be taken in two ways. In one way, according to pure negation, as if one were to speak of "unfaithfulness" merely because someone does not have faith. In another way unfaithfulness can be understood as contrary to faith, namely, that someone rejects the hearing of faith, or holds it in contempt, according to Isaiah 53, "Who having heard us has believed?" And this properly com-

---

[1] John Damascene, *On the Orthodox Faith* bk.2 chap.4 (PG 94:876A; Buytaert chap.18 sect.1, 75.8–9) and chap.30 (PG 94:976A; Buytaert chap.44 sect.2, 162.18–21).

[2] Augustine, *De praedest. sanct.* chap.5 sect.10 (PL 44:968).

[3] Romans 10.14.

[4] *Summa* 1-2 q.84 a.4.

pletes the account of unfaithfulness. And according to this [account] unfaithfulness is a sin.

If unfaithfulness be understood as pure negation, however, as it is in those who have heard nothing of faith, it does not have the account of sin, but rather of punishment, since such a lack of knowledge about divine things followed upon the sin of the first parents. Those who are unfaithful in this sense are damned for other sins, which cannot be remitted without faith; they are not damned on account of the sin of unfaithfulness. So the Lord says, John 15, "If I had not come and had not spoken to them, they would not have sin."[5] Expounding this, Augustine says that it speaks "of that sin, that they did not believe in Christ."[6]

[1] TO THE FIRST ARGUMENT, THEREFORE, IT SHOULD BE SAID that to have faith is not in human nature. But it is in human nature that the mind of man not reject the inward impulse and the outward preaching of truth. So that the second kind of unfaithfulness is against nature on this account.

[2] To the second it should be said that this reasoning proceeds from unfaithfulness as it implies simple negation.

[3] To the third it should be said that unfaithfulness, so far as it is a sin, arises from pride, from which it happens that man does not want to subject his understanding to the rules of faith and a healthy understanding of the Fathers. So Gregory says, *Moral Remarks* 31, "from empty glory have arisen the presumptions of novelties."[7]

Nonetheless it can be said that, just as the theological virtues are not traced back to the cardinal virtues, but are

---

[5] John 15.22.

[6] Augustine, *In Ioann.* tr.89 sect.2, on John 15.22 (PL 35:1857; CCL 36:549.9–10).

[7] Gregory the Great, *Moralia* bk.31 chap.45 sect.88 (PL 76:621A; CCL 143B:1610.24–25).

prior to them, so also the vices opposed to the cardinal virtues are not traced back to the capital vices.

Article 2. [Whether unfaithfulness is in the intellect as in its subject.]

One proceeds in this way to the second query. IT SEEMS that unfaithfulness is not in the intellect as in its subject.

[1] Every sin is in the will, as Augustine says, *On the Two Souls*.[8] But unfaithfulness is a kind of sin, as was said.[9] Therefore unfaithfulness is in the will, not in the intellect.

[2] Furthermore, unfaithfulness has the account of sin because it holds the preaching of faith in contempt. But contempt belongs to the will. Therefore unfaithfulness is in the will.

[3] Furthermore, with respect to 2 Corinthians 11, "Satan himself transforms himself into an angel of light,"[10] the Gloss says that "if an evil angel feigns to be good, even if someone believes that he is good, the error is not dangerous or morbid, if he does or says things that are congruent to the good angels."[11] The reason for that seems to be his rightness of will, which inheres in his intending to adhere to the good angel. Therefore the whole sin of unfaithfulness would seem to be in perverse will. Therefore it is not in the intellect as in a subject.

BUT TO THE CONTRARY, contraries are in the same subject. But faith, to which unfaithfulness is contrary, is in the intellect as in a subject. Therefore unfaithfulness too is in the intellect.

---

[8] Augustine, *De duabus anim.* chap.10 sect.12 (PL 42:103), chap.11 sect.15 (PL 42:105).

[9] In article 1 of this question, above.

[10] 2 Corinthians 11.14.

[11] *Glossa Lombardi* on 2 Corinthians 11.14 (PL 192:74C).

I ANSWER THAT IT SHOULD BE SAID that sin is said to be in the power that is the principle of the act of sin, as was said above.[12] The act of sin can have a double principle. One is first and universal, which commands all the acts of sin. And this principle is the will, since all sin is voluntary. The other principle of the act of sin is proper and proximate; it elicits the act of sin. The desiring power is the principle of gluttony and luxury, and so gluttony and luxury are said to be in the desiring power. Dissenting, which is the proper act of unfaithfulness, is an act of understanding, but one moved by the will, just as assenting is. And so unfaithfulness, along with faith, is in the understanding as in a proximate subject; it is in the will, however, as in a first mover.[13] And in this way all sin is said to be in the will.

[1] The answer TO THE FIRST ARGUMENT is clear.

[2] To the second it should be said that contempt in the will causes dissent in the intellect, by which the act of unfaithfulness is completed. So the cause of unfaithfulness is in the will, but unfaithfulness itself is in the intellect.

[3] To the third it should be said that he who believes the bad angel to be good does not dissent from what is of faith. "The sense of the body fails, but the mind is not removed from true and right judgment," as the Gloss says in the same place.[14] But if one adheres to Satan "when he begins to lead to the things that are his," that is to evil and false things, then sin will not be lacking, as is said in the same place.

---

[12] *Summa* 1-2 q.74 aa.1-2.

[13] Some versions read "as in a proximate mover."

[14] *Glossa Lombardi* on 2 Corinthians 11.14 (PL 192:74C).

Article 3. [Whether unfaithfulness is the greatest of sins.]

One proceeds in this way to the third query. IT SEEMS that unfaithfulness is not the greatest of sins.

[1] Augustine says, as is had in 6 question 1: "Whether we should prefer a heretic, in whose life, beyond his being a heretic, men do not find anything reprehensible, over a catholic of terrible morals—I do not dare to render judgment."[15] But a heretic is unfaithful. Therefore it is not simply to be said that unfaithfulness is the greatest of sins.

[2] Furthermore, what diminishes or excuses sin does not seem to be the greatest of sins. But unfaithfulness excuses or diminishes sins. The Apostle says, 1 Timothy 1, "Before, I was a blasphemer and persecutor and someone abusive; but I have obtained mercy, since I did this unknowing, in unfaithfulness."[16] Therefore unfaithfulness is not the greatest of sins.

[3] Furthermore, to a greater sin is due a greater punishment, according to Deuteronomy 25, "According to the measure of the sin will be the manner of chastisements."[17] But greater punishment is due to the faithful who sin than to the unfaithful, according to Hebrews 10: "How much worse punishments do you think he merits who has fouled the Son of God, and polluted the blood of the testament, in which he was sanctified?"[18] Therefore unfaithfulness is not the greatest of sins.

BUT TO THE CONTRARY there is what Augustine says, expounding John 15: "If I had not come, and I had not spoken to them, they would not have sin."[19] He says,

---

[15] Augustine, *De bapt. contra Donatist.* bk.4 chap.20 sect.27 (PL 43:171), as quoted in Gratian, *Decretum* part 2 causa.6 q.1 can.21 Quero ergo (Richter-Friedberg 1:559).

[16] 1 Timothy 1.13.

[17] Deuteronomy 25.2.

[18] Hebrews 10.29.

[19] John 15.22.

"He wants a great sin . . . to be understood under the general name. This is the sin," namely unfaithfulness, "by which sins are held together."[20] Therefore unfaithfulness is the greatest of all the sins.

I ANSWER THAT IT SHOULD BE SAID that every sin consists formally in aversion from God, as was said above.[21] So a sin is more serious the more man is separated from God. By unfaithfulness man is most distanced from God, since he does not have true apprehension of God. By false apprehension of him, one does not draw near to him, but rather is distanced from him. Nor can it be that he who has a false opinion about God can apprehend him in some respect. What he thinks to be God is not God. So it is manifest that the sin of unfaithfulness is greater than all sins that occur in the perversity of morals. But this does not hold for those sins that are opposed to the other theological virtues, as will be said below.[22]

[1] TO THE FIRST ARGUMENT, THEREFORE, IT SHOULD BE SAID that nothing prevents a sin that is more serious according to its genus from being less serious according to certain circumstances. And on account of this Augustine does not want to pass judgment on the bad catholic and the heretic who does not sin by other sins. The sin of the heretic, even if it is more serious in genus, can nonetheless be mitigated by certain circumstances. And conversely the sin of the catholic can be aggravated by certain circumstances.

[2] To the second it should be said that unfaithfulness has both a lack of knowledge connected with it and a resistance to[23] the things that are of faith. And in this way it has the account of a most serious sin. On the part of

[20] Augustine, *In Ioann.* tr.89 sect.1, on John 15.22 (PL 35:1856–1857; CCL 36:549.25–28).

[21] *Summa* 1–2 q.71 a.6.

[22] *Summa* 2–2 q.34 a.2 ao.2, q.39 a.2 ao.3.

[23] Some versions read "a dissent from."

lack of knowledge it has some reason for excuse, and most of all when someone does not sin from malice, as happened in the Apostle.

[3] To the third it should be said that someone who is unfaithful on account of the sin of unfaithfulness is punished more seriously than another sinner for any other sin, considering the genus of sin. But for another sin, such as adultery, if it be committed by someone faithful and by someone unfaithful, other things being equal, the faithful person sins more than the unfaithful—both on account of awareness (*notitia*) of the truth from faith, and also on account of the sacraments of faith by which he is imbued, against which he expresses abusiveness by sinning.

Article 4. [Whether every action of someone unfaithful is sin.]

One proceeds in this way to the fourth query. IT SEEMS that any action of someone unfaithful is a sin.

[1] With regard to Romans 14, "Everything that is not from faith is a sin,"[24] the Gloss says, "Every life among the unfaithful is sin."[25] But to the life of the unfaithful belongs all that they do. Therefore every action of someone unfaithful is a sin.

[2] Furthermore, faith directs intention. But there can be no good that is not from right intention. Therefore in the unfaithful no action can be good.

[3] Furthermore, the prior being corrupted, the posterior are corrupted. But the act of faith precedes the act of all the virtues. Therefore, since in the unfaithful there is no act of faith, they cannot do any good work, but sin in every one of their acts.

---

[24] Romans 14.23.

[25] *Glossa Lombardi* on Romans 14.23 (PL 191:1520A).

BUT TO THE CONTRARY there is what was said about Cornelius, that even while he was someone unfaithful, his offerings were acceptable to God.[26] Therefore not every action of someone unfaithful is a sin, but some action of his is good.

I ANSWER THAT IT SHOULD BE SAID that mortal sin takes away the grace that makes one pleasing, but it does not completely corrupt the good of nature, as was said above.[27] So, since unfaithfulness is a mortal sin, the unfaithful lack grace, but there remains in them some good of nature. So it is manifest that the unfaithful cannot do the good works which are of grace, namely meritorious works. Nonetheless they can somehow do the good works for which the good of nature suffices. They need not sin in every one of their actions; rather whenever they do some work from unfaithfulness, then they sin. Someone who has faith can commit a sin in act that is not referred to the end of faith, sinning either venially or even mortally. So also someone unfaithful can do some good act in what does not refer to the end of unfaithfulness.

[1] TO THE FIRST ARGUMENT, THEREFORE, IT SHOULD BE SAID that the remark is to be understood as saying either that the life of the unfaithful cannot be without sin, since sins are not taken away without faith, or that whatever they do from unfaithfulness is sin. So the text adds: "since everyone living or acting unfaithfully sins vehemently."[28]

[2] To the second it should be said that faith directs intention with respect to the last supernatural end. But the light of natural reason can also direct intention with respect to some connatural good.

---

[26] Acts 10.4.

[27] *Summa* 1–2 q.85 a.2, a.4.

[28] *Glossa Lombardi* on Romans 14.23 (PL 191:1520A).

[3] To the third it should be said that natural reason is not totally corrupted by unfaithfulness in the unfaithful,[29] since there remains in them some true apprehension, by which they can do some work of the genus of goods.

But it should be known about Cornelius that he was not unfaithful, otherwise his act would not have been accepted by God, whom no one can please without faith. He had implicit faith, the truth of the gospel never having been manifested. Peter was sent to him that he might be fully instructed in the faith.

Article 5. [Whether there are several species of unfaithfulness.]

One proceeds in this way to the fifth query. IT SEEMS that there are not several species of unfaithfulness.

[1] Since faith and unfaithfulness are contraries, it follows that they must be about the same thing. But the formal object of faith is the first truth, from which it has unity, granted that it believes many things materially. Therefore the object of unfaithfulness is the first truth; the [particular] things that are disbelieved by someone unfaithful stand in unfaithfulness [only] materially. But a difference according to species is not looked for from material principles, but from formal principles. Therefore there are not different species of unfaithfulness according to the diversity of the things in which the unfaithful err.

[2] Furthermore, someone can deviate from the truth in infinite ways. If then the species of infidelity were to be assigned according to the diversities of errors, it would seem to follow that there would be infinite species of infidelity. And so species of this kind ought not to be considered.

[29] Some versions read "in the faithful."

[3] Furthermore, the same thing is not found in different species. But it happens that someone is unfaithful because he errs according to different things. Therefore the difference of errors does not make different species of unfaithfulness. So then there are not many species of unfaithfulness.

BUT TO THE CONTRARY many species of vice are opposed to each virtue: "the good happens in one way, evil in many," as it clear from Dionysius, *On the Divine Names* chapter 4,[30] and from the Philosopher, *Ethics* 2.[31] But faith is one virtue. Therefore many species of unfaithfulness are opposed to it.

I ANSWER THAT IT SHOULD BE SAID that any virtue consists of attaining to some rule of human apprehension or acting, as was said above.[32] To attain to a rule happens in one way about one matter, but to deviate from a rule happens in many ways. And so to one virtue many vices are opposed. The difference of vices that are opposed to each virtue can be considered in two ways. In one way, according to the different standings to the virtue. And in this way there are determined certain species of vices that are opposed to the virtue. So to moral virtue there is opposed one vice according to excess over the virtue, and another vice according to defect from the virtue.—In another way the difference of vices opposed to one virtue can be considered according to the corruption of the different things that are required for the virtue. And in this way there are opposed to one virtue, such as temperance or fortitude, infinite vices, as the different circumstances of the virtue are corrupted in infinite ways, and recede from the rightness of virtue. And so the Pythagoreans stated that evil was infinite.

---

[30] Ps-Dionysius, *Divine Names* chap.4 sect.1 (PG 3:732; Chevallier 1:302–303).

[31] Aristotle, *Nicomachean Ethics* bk.2 chap.6 (1106b35).

[32] *Summa* 1–2 q.64.

In this way therefore it should be said that, if unfaithfulness is attended to according to the comparison with the end, the species of unfaithfulness are different and of determinate number. Since the sin of unfaithfulness consists in resisting faith, this can happen in two ways. Either the faith being resisted was never accepted, and such is the unfaithfulness of the pagans or gentiles. Or an accepted Christian faith is renounced, either in figure, and such is the unfaithfulness of the Jews, or in the very manifestation of truth, and such is the unfaithfulness of heretics. And so in general there can be assigned the three mentioned species of unfaithfulness.—If the species of unfaithfulness are distinguished according to error about the different things that belong to faith, then there are no determinate species of unfaithfulness. Errors can be multiplied to infinity, as is clear from Augustine, *On Heresies*.[33]

[1] TO THE FIRST ARGUMENT, THEREFORE, IT SHOULD BE SAID that the formal account of any sin can be taken in two ways. In one way, according to the intention of the sinner. And in this way what the sinner turns to is the formal object of the sin, and the species of sin are differentiated according to it. In another way, according to the account of evil. And thus that from which one recedes is the formal object of sin. But in this way sin does not have species; it is rather the privation of species. So it is to be said that the object of unfaithfulness is the first truth as that from which it recedes; but the formal object as that from which it turned is the false judgment that is followed. And in this way its species are differentiated. So just as charity is one, by which it inheres in the highest good, there are nonetheless opposed to charity different vices, which, by turning to different temporal goods, recede from the one highest good, and again according to

[33] Augustine, *De haeresibus* epilogue (PL 42:50; CCL 46:344–345).

different disordered standings to God. So also faith is one virtue, since it adheres to the one first truth. But the species of unfaithfulness are many, since the unfaithful follow different false judgments.

[2] To the second it should be said that the objection proceeds from the distinction of species of unfaithfulness according to the different things about which it errs.

[3] To the third it should be said that just as faith is one because it believes many things as ordered to one, so unfaithfulness can be one, even if it errs in many things, so far as all are ordered to one. – Still nothing prevents a man from erring in different species of unfaithfulness, just as one man can suffer different vices and different bodily sicknesses.

Article 6. [Whether the unfaithfulness of the gentiles or pagans is more serious than the others.]

One proceeds in this way to the sixth article. IT SEEMS that the unfaithfulness of the gentiles or pagans is worse than the others.

[1] Just as a bodily sickness is the more serious the more it is contrary to the health of the principal members, so a sin seems to be graver the more it is contrary to what is principal in virtue. But what is principal in faith is the faith in divine unity, from which the gentiles fall away, believing in a multitude of gods. Therefore their unfaithfulness is most serious.

[2] Furthermore, among heretics heresy is the more detestable so far as it contradicts many and the more principal parts of the truth of faith. So the heresy of Arius, which separated divinity, was more detestable than the heresy of Nestorius, which separated the humanity of Christ from the person of the Son of God. But the gentiles are removed from faith in more and more principal things than are

Jews or heretics, since they receive nothing from faith. Therefore their unfaithfulness is most grave.

[3] Furthermore, every good diminishes evil. But there is something good in the Jews, since they confess the Old Testament to be from God. There is also good in heretics, since they venerate the New Testament. Therefore they sin less than the gentiles, who detest both Testaments.

BUT TO THE CONTRARY there is what is said in 2 Peter 2, "It would be better for them not to apprehend the way of justice than to turn backwards after having apprehended it."[34] But the gentiles did not apprehend the way of justice, while the heretics and the Jews, apprehending it somewhat, [then] deserted it. Therefore their sin is more serious.

I ANSWER THAT IT SHOULD BE SAID that in unfaithfulness two things can be considered, as was said.[35] Of which one is its comparison to the end. And in this way someone sins more seriously against faith if he resists the faith that he had received, than if he resists faith never received. Just so someone sins more seriously who does not fulfill what he had promised, than if he does not fulfill what he never promised. And according to this the unfaithfulness of heretics, who accepted the faith of the gospel and renounced it by corrupting it, is a more serious sin than that of the Jews, who never took up the faith of the gospel. But since they took up its figure in the old law, which they corrupted by badly interpreting it, so even their unfaithfulness is more serious than the unfaithfulness of the gentiles, who in no way took up the faith of the gospel.—Another thing that is considered in unfaithfulness is the corruption of the things that belong to faith. And according to this, since the gentiles erred in more things than the Jews, and the Jews in more than the heretics, the unfaithfulness of the gentiles is more serious than

[34] 2 Peter 2.21.

[35] In article 5 of this question, above.

that of the Jews, and that of the Jews than that of the heretics—except perhaps that of some heretics, such as the Manichees, who err even more than the gentiles about believable things.—Of these two kinds of seriousness the first outweighs the second in the account of fault. Unfaithfulness has the account of fault, as was said above,[36] more from its renouncing faith than from its not having the things that are of faith. The latter seems, as was said, to belong more to the notion of penalty. So, simply speaking, the unfaithfulness of heretics is the worst.

[1]-[3] And from this is clear the answer TO WHAT WAS OBJECTED.

Article 7. [Whether one ought to dispute publicly with the unfaithful.]

One proceeds in this way to the seventh query. IT SEEMS that one ought not to dispute publicly with the unfaithful.

[1] For the Apostle says, 2 Timothy 2: "Do not contend in words; it is useful for nothing except the ruin of those who hear."[37] But public disputation with the unfaithful cannot be done without contention of words. Therefore one ought not to contend publicly with the unfaithful.

[2] Furthermore, the law of Marcianus Augustus, confirmed by the canons, says, "He does damage to the judgment of the most holy synod if he contends in order to reconsider and publicly dispute what has already been judged and rightly disposed."[38] But all the things that belong to the faith have been determined by the holy councils. Therefore someone sins seriously, and does damage to the synod, if he presumes to dispute publicly about the things that are of faith.

---

[36] In article 1 of this question, above.

[37] 2 Timothy 2.14.

[38] Compare the Council of Chalcedon, *Edictum Valentini et Marciani* (Mansi 7:475).

[3] Furthermore, disputation is done with certain arguments. But an argument is a reason producing faith about something doubtful. But the things that are of faith, since they are most certain, are not to be drawn into doubt. Therefore one ought not to dispute publicly about the things that are of faith.

BUT TO THE CONTRARY there is what is said in Acts 9, that "Saul grew strong and confounded the Jews" and that "he spoke to the gentiles and disputed with the Greeks."[39]

I ANSWER THAT IT SHOULD BE SAID that two things are to be considered in disputation about faith: one on the part of the disputer; the other on the part of the hearers. On the part of the disputer one ought to consider intention. If one disputes as doubting faith, and not as supposing the truth of faith to be certain, but intending to test it by arguments, without doubt he sins as one who is doubtful in faith and [so] unfaithful. If someone disputes about faith to confound errors, however, or even as exercise, it is laudable.

On the part of the hearers one ought to consider whether those who hear the disputation are instructed and firm in faith, or simple and hesitant in faith. In front of the wise who are firm in faith there is no danger in disputing about faith. But one must distinguish in regard to the simple. Either they are solicited and buffeted by the unfaithful, such as Jews or heretics or even pagans, who try to corrupt faith in them; or they are not solicited at all about this, as happens in lands in which there are none of the unfaithful. In the first case it is necessary to dispute publicly about faith, so long as there are found some who are sufficient and upright for this, who can [in fact] confute errors. Through this the simple will be made firm in faith, and the capacity of deception in the unfaithful will be

---

[39] Acts 9.22,29.

taken away. The very taciturnity of those who ought to resist perverters of the truth of faith would be a confirmation of error. So Gregory in *Pastoral Rule* 2: "Just as incautious speaking leads to error, so indiscreet silence leaves those who could be taught in error."[40] In the second case it is most dangerous to dispute publicly about faith before the simple. Their faith is firmer because they have heard nothing different from what they believe. And so it is not expedient for them to hear the words of the unfaithful in conversation[41] against the faith.

[1] TO THE FIRST ARGUMENT, THEREFORE, IT SHOULD BE SAID that the Apostle does not completely prohibit disputation, but [only] disordered disputation, which makes more for contention of words than firmness of judgments.

[2] To the second it should be said that this law prohibits public disputation about faith that proceeds from the doubting of faith, not disputation that is for the conservation of faith.

[3] To the third it should be said that one ought not to dispute about the things that are of faith as if doubting them, but in order to make truth manifest and to confute errors. The confirmation of faith requires sometimes disputing with the unfaithful; sometimes defending the faith, according to 1 Peter 3, "Be always prepared to satisfy anyone asking you to give a reason of what is in you by hope and faith";[42] sometimes convincing those who err, according to Titus 1, "that it may be powerful to exhort in healthy doctrine, and to argue with those who contradict."[43]

---

[40] Gregory the Great, *Regula pastoralis* part.2 chap.4 (PL 77:30A–B).
[41] Some versions read "in disputation."
[42] 1 Peter 3.15.
[43] Titus 1.9.

Article 8. [Whether the unfaithful are to be compelled to the faith.]

One proceeds in this way to the eighth query. IT SEEMS that the unfaithful are in no way to be compelled to faith.

[1] It is said in Matthew 13 that the servants of the head of the household in whose field weeds had been seeded asked him, "Should we go gather them up?" He answered: "No. Perhaps at the same time you collected weeds, you would stamp out wheat."[44] Chrysostom says of this passage: "The Lord says this to prevent killings. One should not kill heretics, for if you kill them, many of the saints will necessarily be destroyed at the same time."[45] Therefore it seems that by a similar reasoning neither are some of the unfaithful to be compelled to faith.

[2] Furthermore, in the *Book of Decrees* distinction 45, it says this: "Of the Jews, the holy synod teaches that not one is to be led by force to believing."[46] Therefore by similar reasoning neither should the other unfaithful be compelled to faith.

[3] Furthermore, Augustine says that a man can do other things without willing them, "but not believe without willing it."[47] Therefore it seems that the unfaithful are not to be compelled to faith.

[4] Furthermore, in Ezechiel 18 it says, in the person of God, "I do not will the death of a sinner."[48] But we ought to conform our will to the divine, as was said above.[49] Therefore we too should not will to kill the unfaithful.

---

[44] Matthew 13.28–29.

[45] John Chrysostom, *On Matt.* hom.46 sect.2 (PG 58:477), though the quotation is not exact.

[46] Gratian, *Decretum* part.1 dist.45 can.5 De Iudeis (Richter-Friedberg 1:161).

[47] Augustine, *In Ioann.* tr.26 sect.2, on John 6.44 (PL 35:1607; CCL 36:620.14).

[48] Ezechiel 18.23,32.

[49] *Summa* 1–2 q.19 aa.9–10.

BUT TO THE CONTRARY there is what is said in Luke 14, "Go out into the ways and paths and compel them to enter, that my house may be full."[50] But men enter into the house of God, that is into the Church, by faith. Therefore some are to be compelled to faith.

I ANSWER THAT IT SHOULD BE SAID that, of the unfaithful, some never took up faith, such as the gentiles and the Jews. And these are not in any way to be compelled to faith, that they might believe, since to believe is of the will. They are to be compelled by the faithful, if there is the capacity (*facultas*) to do so, not to impede faith either by blasphemies, or bad persuasions, or even open persecutions. And on account of this the faithful of Christ frequently wage war against the unfaithful, not that they should compel them to believing (since even if they conquer them and take them captive, they should leave them their freedom about whether to believe), but in order to compel them not to impede the faith of Christ.

Others of the unfaithful at one time accepted faith and profited from it, such as heretics or whoever is apostate. And these are to be compelled even bodily to fulfill what they promised and to hold what they once took up.

[1] TO THE FIRST ARGUMENT, THEREFORE, IT SHOULD BE SAID that some have understood this authoritative text to prohibit not the excommunication of heretics, but their killing, as is clear from the adduced authority of Chrysostom. And Augustine, writing to Vicentius, says about himself: "This was my first opinion, that no one should be compelled to the unity of Christ; it was to be done by word, fighting by disputation. . . . But this opinion of mine was overcome not by the contradiction of words, but by the demonstration of examples. . . . The terror of the laws . . . was so profitable that many say, 'Thanks to the Lord, who broke our chains.' "[51] How

---

[50] Luke 14.23.

[51] Augustine, *Epist.* ep.93 chap.5 sect.17–18 (PL 33:329–330; CCL

what the Lord says should be understood, "Let both grow until the harvest," appears from what is added: "That, collecting weeds, you should not perhaps eradicate also with it the wheat."[52] Augustine says, "Where he shows satisfactorily, when this fear is not present . . . , that is, when the crime of each is known and it appears execrable to all, such that either none is defending it, or that he does not have such defenders that a schism could arise from them, the severity of discipline should not sleep."[53]

[2] To the second it should be said that the Jews, if they have not in any way accepted faith, should not be compelled to faith. If they accepted the faith before, "they should be compelled to retain the faith," as it says in the same chapter.[54]

[3] To the third it should be said that, just as "to vow is of the will, to fulfill is nonetheless of necessity,"[55] so also to accept the faith is of the will, but to hold it once accepted is of necessity. And so heretics are to be compelled to hold the faith. Augustine says to Count Bonifacius: "How is it that they are accustomed to cry out, 'It is free to believe or not to believe: whom does Christ lead by force?' In Paul I recognize Christ first compelling and then teaching."[56]

[4] To the fourth it should be said that, as Augustine says in the same letter, "no one of us wants the heretic to perish. But otherwise the house of David will not merit to have the peace of God, unless Absalom his son be extinguished in the war led against the fatherland. So the catholic Church, if it collects the rest by means of the per-

---

34:461.22–463.5), though much is omitted.

[52] Matthew 13.29.

[53] Augustine, *Contra epist. Parmen.* bk.3 chap.2 sect.13 (PL 43:92).

[54] Gratian, *Decretum* part.1 dist.45 can.5 De Iudeis (Richter-Friedberg 1:162).

[55] *Glossa Lombardi* on Psalm 75.11 (PL 191:709A), paraphrased.

[56] Augustine, *Epist.* ep.185 chap.6 sect.22 (PL 33:803; CCL 57: 21.8–11).

dition of some, heals the pain of its maternal heart by the liberation of so many people."[57]

Article 9. [Whether one can share community (*communicari*) with the unfaithful.][58]

One proceeds in this way to the ninth query. IT SEEMS that one can share community with the unfaithful.

[1] The Apostle says, 1 Corinthians 10, "If one of the unfaithful calls you to dinner, and you wish to go, eat whatever is put in front of you."[59] And Chrysostom says, "If you wish to go to the table of pagans, we permit it without any prohibition."[60] But to go to dinner with anyone is to share community with him. Therefore it is licit to share community with the unfaithful.

[2] Furthermore, the Apostle says, 1 Corinthians 5, "Is it my business to judge those who are outside?"[61] The unfaithful are outside. Since the faithful are inhibited from dealings with others by the judgment of the Church, it would seem that the faithful are not inhibited from having dealings with the unfaithful.

[3] Furthermore, a lord cannot use a servant except by having dealings with him at least in words, since the lord

---

[57] Augustine, *Epist.* ep.185 chap.8 sect.32 (PL 33:807; CSEL 57:29. 12–19).

[58] In Thomas's Latin, *communicari* can mean "to take communion" in the sacramental sense, that is, to partake of the Eucharist. But Thomas's sense in this article is much broader. As will be seen from the examples, he has in mind not the sacramental sense of *communio* as "communion," but the civic or social sense of *communio* as "community." The force of the question is to ask whether believers can have any dealings—familial, social, political—with unbelievers.

[59] 1 Corinthians 10.27.

[60] John Chrysostom, *On Hebr.* chap.11 hom.25 (PG 63:176), as in Gratian, *Decretum* part 2 causa.11 q.3 can.24 Ad mensam (Richter-Friedberg 1:650).

[61] 1 Corinthians 5.12.

moves the servant by his will. But Christians can have unfaithful servants, either Jews or even pagans or Saracens. Therefore they can licitly share community with them.

BUT TO THE CONTRARY there is what is said in Deuteronomy 7, "Do not make an alliance with them, do not have mercy on them, nor enter into marriage with them."[62] And with reference to Leviticus 15, "A woman who at the return of the month,"[63] the Gloss says: "Thus one ought to abstain from idolatry, that we do not touch idolaters nor their disciples, nor have community with them."[64]

I ANSWER THAT IT SHOULD BE SAID that community with any person is interdicted to the faithful in two ways: in one way, as punishment to him from whom the community of the faithful is withdrawn; in another way, as a caution to those to whom it is interdicted, that they do not share community with the others. And both causes can be taken from the words of the Apostle, 1 Corinthians 5. After he gives a judgment of excommunication, he adds as reason: "Do you not know that a little ferment corrupts the whole mass?"[65] And later he adds a reason on the part of the penalty inflicted by the judgment of the Church, when he says, "Can't you judge the things that are within?"[66]

In the first way, the Church does not interdict to the faithful community with someone unfaithful who in no way received the faith of Christ, namely, with pagans and Jews. It does not have spiritual judgment over them, but [only] temporal judgment, in the case when, living among Christians, they commit some fault and are temporally

---

[62] Deuteronomy 7.2–3.

[63] Leviticus 15.19.

[64] *Glossa ordinaria* on Leviticus 15.22 (Strasbourg 1, "Qui[cumque] tetigent," col. b).

[65] 1 Corinthians 5.3,6.

[66] 1 Corinthians 5.12.

punished by the faithful. But in this way, namely as penalty, the Church interdicts to the faithful [any] community with those unfaithful who deviate from a faith they had accepted, either by corrupting faith, like the heretics, or even totally withdrawing from faith, like apostates. In either of these cases, the Church gives the judgment (*sententia*) of excommunication.

But as regards the second way, it seems that one ought to distinguish according to the different conditions of persons and businesses and times. If some were firm in faith, such that from their community with the unfaithful the conversion of the unfaithful were to be looked for rather than the turning away from faith of the faithful, these are not to be prohibited from communicating with the unfaithful who did not receive faith, namely pagans and Jews, and most of all if necessity urges it. If they are simple and weak in faith, however, so that the ruin of faith is probably to be feared, they are to be prohibited from community with the unfaithful. They should especially not have great familiarity with them, or share community with them without necessity.

[1] TO THE FIRST ARGUMENT, THEREFORE, IT SHOULD BE SAID that the Lord teaches this with regard to those gentiles whose land the Jews had entered. These gentiles were prone to idolatry and so it was to be feared that by continual conversation with them the Jews would be alienated from the faith. And so in the same place it is added, "Since she seduces your son so that he does not follow me."[67]

[2] To the second it should be said that the Church does not have judgment over the unfaithful so far as inflicting spiritual punishment on them. But the Church does have judgment over some of the unfaithful so far as inflicting temporal punishment. So that the Church sometimes takes

[67] Deuteronomy 7.4.

away from some of the unfaithful, because of certain special crimes, community with the faithful.

[3] To the third it should be said that it is more probable that the servant, who is ruled by the lord's commanding, will be converted to the faith of the faithful lord, than conversely. And so it is not prohibited that the faithful have unfaithful servants. If the lord should draw immanent danger from community with such a servant, however, he ought to cast him away from him, according to the commandment of the Lord, Matthew 5 and 18, "If your foot scandalizes you, cut it off and throw it from you."[68]

Article 10. [Whether the unfaithful can have superiority (*praelatio*) or lordship (*dominium*) over the faithful.]

One proceeds in this way to the tenth query. IT SEEMS that the unfaithful can have superiority or lordship over the faithful.

[1] The Apostle says, 1 Timothy 6, "Whoever is under a servant's yoke should judge their lords to be worthy of honor."[69] And that he is talking about the unfaithful is clear from his adding, "Those who have faithful lords ought not to hold them in contempt."[70] It is said in 1 Peter 2, "Servants, be subservient to your lords in all fear, not only to the good and modest, but also to the difficult."[71] This would not be set down by apostolic teaching unless the unfaithful could be superior to the faithful. Therefore it would seem that the unfaithful can be superior to the faithful.

---

[68] Matthew 5.30 and 18.8.

[69] 1 Timothy 6.1.

[70] 1 Timothy 6.2.

[71] 1 Peter 2.18.

[2] Furthermore, whoever are of the court[72] of some prince are under him. But certain of the faithful were of the court of unfaithful princes. So it is said in Philippians 4, "Greetings to all of you saints, especially to those who are of the household of Caesar,"[73] namely of Nero, who was unfaithful. Therefore the unfaithful can be over the faithful.

[3] Furthermore, as the Philosopher says, *Politics* 1, the servant is the instrument of the lord in things that belong to human life, just as the artisan's helper is the instrument of the artist in the things that belong to the working of art.[74] But in these things someone faithful can be subjected to someone unfaithful: the faithful can even be workmen[75] of the unfaithful. Therefore the unfaithful can be superior to the faithful as regards lordship.

BUT TO THE CONTRARY it belongs to him who is superior to have judgment over those to whom he is superior. But the unfaithful cannot judge the faithful. For the Apostle says, 1 Corinthians 6, "Does one of you, having a case against another, dare to be judged by the wicked," that is, the unfaithful, "and not by the saints?"[76] Therefore it seems that the unfaithful cannot be over the faithful.

I ANSWER THAT IT SHOULD BE SAID that we can speak of this in two ways. In one way, about the newly instituted lordship or superiority of the unfaithful over the faithful. And this should not be permitted in any way. It leads to scandal and to endangering faith. Those who are subjugated to the jurisdiction of others can be easily

---

[72] Literally, "family." As Thomas knows, it was frequent in antiquity for rulers to give their trusted advisers and friends the title of "brother" or "son," "sister" or "daughter."

[73] Philippians 4.22.

[74] Aristotle, *Politics* bk.1 chap.4 (1253b31–32).

[75] Literally, farmers who till their master's land (*coloni*).

[76] 1 Corinthians 6.1.

changed by those under whom they are, so that they follow their will, unless those who are subject are of great virtue. And similarly the unfaithful hold the faith in contempt if they apprehend any defect among the faithful. And so the Apostle prohibits that the faithful contend in judgment before an unfaithful judge. And so in no way does the Church permit that the unfaithful acquire lordship over the faithful, or that they are superior to them in any way in some office.

In another way we can talk of preexisting lordship or superiority. Here one ought to consider that lordship and superiority were introduced by human law, while the distinction of the faithful and the unfaithful is of divine law. Divine law, which is from grace, does not take away human law, which is from natural reason. And so the distinction of the faithful and the unfaithful, considered by itself, does not take away the lordship or superiority of the unfaithful over the faithful. This lordship or superiority can be justly taken away by the judgment or ordination of the Church, which has authority from God. The unfaithful by the merit of their unfaithfulness merit to lose their power over the faithful, who are changed into sons of God. But sometimes the Church does this and sometimes not. In those unfaithful who are also subjugated by temporal subjection to the Church and its members, this law of the Church stands, that the servant of the Jews, once he is made a Christian, is liberated from servitude, no price being given, if he was homeborn, that is, born in servitude, and similarly if, being unfaithful, he was sold into servitude. If he was bought at a market, however, he must be put up for sale within three months. Nor does the Church do injury in this. Since those Jews are the servants of the Church, it can dispose of their goods, just as secular princes have composed many laws in favor of liberty for their subjects.—In those unfaithful who are not subject temporally to the Church or its members, the Church does not establish the mentioned law, even if it can be instituted by law. And this it does in order to avoid scandal. Just so the Lord, Matthew 17, shows that he could excuse himself from tribute, since "the sons are free," and nonetheless he ordered that tribute be sent in order to avoid scandal.[77] So also Paul, when he said that servants should honor their masters, added, "that the name and teaching of the Lord not be blasphemed."[78]

[1] From this the answer TO THE FIRST ARGUMENT is clear.

[2] To the second it should be said that Ceasar's superiority preexisted the distinction of faithful and unfaithful, so that it was not dissolved by the conversion of some to the faith. And it was useful that some of the faithful had a place in the emperor's court, to defend others of the faithful. Just so blessed Sebastian comforted the souls of Christians that he saw weaken in torments, and for this he hid in military uniform within Diocletian's court.

[3] To the third it should be said that servants are subjected to their lords for the whole of life, and underlings to the prefects for all affairs, but artists' ministers are subordinated to them for certain special works. So it would be more dangerous that the unfaithful accept lordship or superiority over the faithful than that they accept from them ministry in some work. And so the Church permits Christians to cultivate the lands of Jews, since by this they do not have the necessity to converse with them. Solomon too took from the king of Tyre masters of work for felling the timber, as is had in 3 Kings 5.[79]—And yet if from this sharing community or conversation the ruin of faith is feared, it should be entirely interdicted.

[77] Matthew 17.24–26.

[78] 1 Timothy 6.1.

[79] 3 Kings 5.6.

Article 11. [Whether the rites of the unfaithful are to be tolerated.]

One proceeds in this way to the eleventh query. IT SEEMS that the rites of the unfaithful are not to be tolerated.

[1] It is manifest that the unfaithful sin by celebrating their rites. But one who does not prohibit sin when he can prohibit it would seem to consent to it, as is had in the Gloss on Romans 1, "Not only they who do, but also they who consent to the ones doing."[80] Therefore those who tolerate their rites sin.

[2] Furthermore, the rites of the Jews are compared to idolatry. With regard to Galatians 5,[81] "Do not will to be contained again by the yoke of servitude," the Gloss says: "The service of this law is not lighter than idolatry."[82] But it would not be borne that some exercise the rites of idolatry, since Christian princes first closed and then ordered the destruction of the temples of idols, as Augustine tells, *On the City of God* 18.[83] Therefore the rites of the Jews should also not be tolerated.

[3] Further, the sin of unfaithfulness is most serious, as was said above.[84] But other sins are not tolerated, but are punished by law, such as adultery, theft, and others of this kind. Therefore the rites of the unfaithful are not to be tolerated.

BUT TO THE CONTRARY in the *Book of Decrees* distinction 45, the canon *Qui sincera,* Gregory says of the Jews: "They have free license to observe and celebrate all of their festivities, just as they are held to the present, they

---

[80] *Glossa Lombardi* on Romans 1.32 (PL 191:1336A), after Ambrose.

[81] Galatians 5.1.

[82] *Glossa Lombardi* on Galatians 5.1 (PL 192:152C).

[83] Augustine, *De civitate Dei* bk.18 chap.54 (PL 41:620; CCL 48:656–657).

[84] In article 3 of this question, above.

and their fathers having cultivated them for a long time."[85]

I ANSWER THAT IT SHOULD BE SAID that the human regime is derived from the divine regime, and should imitate it. God, however much he is omnipotent and the highest good, permits even so some evil things to be done in the universe, which he could prohibit, since if these things were removed, greater goods would be taken away or even worse evils follow. So also in the human regime those who are superior rightly tolerate some evils, that other goods not be impeded or even that other worse evils not be incurred, as Augustine says, in *On Order* 2, "Taking away prostitutes from human affairs, you would stir up all licentiousnesses."[86] So, however much the unfaithful sin in their rites, they can be tolerated either because of some good that comes from them or because of some evil that is avoided.

From the Jews' observing their rites, in which formerly was prefigured the truth of faith that we hold, this good comes, that we have the testimony to our faith from an enemy, and there is represented to us as if in figure what we believe. And so they are to be tolerated in their rites. The rites of others of the unfaithful, which bring neither truth nor usefulness, are not to be tolerated in any and every way, unless perhaps for avoiding some evil, namely, to avoid the scandal or dissent that might come from this, or the impediment to the salvation of those who slowly, if tolerated, are converted to the faith. On account of this, even the Church sometimes tolerated the rites of heretics and pagans, when there was a great multitude of the unfaithful.

---

[85] Gratian, *Decretum* part 1 dist.45 can.3 Qui sincera (Richter-Friedberg 1:161). Compare Gregory the Great, *Registrum epist.* bk.13 ep.12 Ad Paschasium (PL 77:1268; CCL 140A:1014.23–26).

[86] Augustine, *De ordine* bk.2 chap.4 sect.12 (PL 32:1000; CCL 29:114.39–40).

[1]-[3] From this is clear the answer TO THE OBJECTIONS.

Article 12. [Whether the children of Jews or of others of the unfaithful are to be baptized when their parents are opposed.]

One proceeds in this way to the twelfth query. IT SEEMS that the children of the Jews and of others of the unfaithful are to be baptized even if their parents are opposed.

[1] The bond of marriage is greater than the law of fatherly power over a child. The law of fatherly power can be dissolved by man, when the son of the family is emancipated; but the bond of marriage cannot be dissolved by man, according to Matthew 19, "What God has conjoined let not man separate."[87] But on account of unfaithfulness the matrimonial bond is dissolved. For the Apostle says, 1 Corinthians 7, "If the unfaithful one goes, let him or her go away; a brother or sister is not to be subjugated to servitude in this way."[88] And the canon says that if an unfaithful spouse does not wish to be with the other without abusing his creator, then the other spouse should not cohabit with him. Therefore much more on account of unfaithfulness is the law of fatherly power over children taken away. So their children can be baptized even when they are opposed.

[2] Furthermore, a man should intervene much more when there is danger of eternal death than when there is danger of temporal death. But if someone were to see a man in danger of temporal death and did not lend him aid, he would sin. Since therefore the sons of Jews and others of the unfaithful are in danger of eternal death if they are left to their parents, who will form them in their

---

[87] Matthew 19.6.
[88] 1 Corinthians 7.15.

unfaithfulness, it would seem that they are to be taken away and baptized and instructed in faith.

[3] Furthermore, the sons of servants are servants and under the power of the lord. But Jews are servants of kings and princes. So also their sons. Kings and princes have power to make the sons of Jews do what they will. So there will be no injury if they baptize them even if their parents are opposed.

[4] Furthermore, any man is more of God, from whom he has a soul, than of his parents, from whom he has a body. It is therefore not unjust if the children of Jews are taken from their carnal parents and consecrated to God by baptism.

[5] Furthermore, baptism is more effective for salvation than preaching, since by baptism there is at once taken away the stain of sin and the guilt of punishment, and the doorway of heaven is opened. But if some danger follows from an absence of preaching, it is imputed to him who did not preach, as is had in Ezechiel 3 and 33, about him who "saw a sword coming and did not sound the horn."[89] Therefore if the children of Jews are damned from a lack of baptism, much more will it be imputed as a sin to those who could have baptized them and did not.

BUT TO THE CONTRARY injury is to be done to no man. Injury would be done to the Jews if their children were baptized without their permission, since the law of fatherly power over the sons would be removed once they were faithful. Therefore they are not to be baptized when the parents are opposed.

I ANSWER THAT IT SHOULD BE SAID that the custom of the Church has greatest authority, and it should always be imitated in all things. Even the teaching of the catholic doctors has authority from the Church, so that the authority of the Church is more to be retained

[89] Ezechiel 3.18,20 and 33.6,8.

(*standum*) than that of Augustine or Jerome or any such doctor. It was never the practice of the Church that the sons of Jews should be baptized even if their parents were opposed. There were many, most powerful catholic princes in times past, such as Constantine and Theodosius, whose relatives were most holy bishops, as Sylvester to Constantine and Ambrose to Theodosius; they would in no way have omitted to do this, if it were consonant with reason. And so it seems dangerous to concoct this assertion about baptizing the sons of Jews even if their parents are opposed, as it is beyond the custom of the Church observed up to this time.

And the reason for this is twofold. First, on account of danger to faith. If children were to accept baptism without ever having the use of reason, later, when they would come to maturity, they could easily be induced by their parents to set aside what they accepted unknowingly. This would result in detriment to faith.

The other reason is that it conflicts with natural justice. The son is naturally something of the father. At first he is not distinguished from the parents according to the body, when he is contained in the mother's uterus. Later, after he leaves the uterus, before he has the use of free choice, he is contained by the care of parents as it were in a spiritual womb. So long as the child does not have the use of reason, he does not differ from an irrational animal. Just as an ox or a horse belongs to someone so that it may be used by him as he wills, according to civil law, as his own instrument, so it belongs to natural law that the son, before he has the use of reason, is under the care of the father. So it would be against natural justice if the child, before it has the use of natural reason, be taken away from the care of parents, or that something be ordered for him when the parents were unwilling. After he begins to have the use of free choice, he begins to be his own, and can, with regard to the things that are of divine or natural law, provide for himself. And then he is to be induced to faith not by compulsion, but by persuasion; he can consent to the faith and be baptized when his parents are opposed, but not before he has the use of reason. And so the ancient Fathers say about children that "they are saved in the faith of the parents." By which one is given to understand that it belongs to the parents to provide for the salvation of their sons, especially before they have the use of reason.

[1] TO THE FIRST ARGUMENT, THEREFORE, IT SHOULD BE SAID that in the bond of matrimony either spouse has the use of free choice, and either can assent to faith when the other is opposed. But this is out of place in a child before he has the use of reason. But after he has the use, then the likeness [between the cases] holds, if he wants to be converted.

[2] To the second it should be said that no one is to be snatched away from death against the order of civil law—for example, if someone is condemned to temporal death by his judge, no one should violently snatch him away. So neither should someone violate the order of natural law, which is that a son is under the care of the father, in order to liberate him from the danger of eternal death.

[3] To the third it should be said that the Jews are servants of princes by civil servitude, which does not exclude the order of natural or divine law.

[4] To the fourth it should be said that man is ordered to God by reason, by which he can apprehend him. So the child, before he has the use of reason, is ordered to God in the natural order by the reason of his parents, to whose care he is naturally subject. And divine things are to be done with regard to him according to their disposition.

[5] To the fifth it should be said that the danger that follows from unperformed preaching does not affect any but those to whom the office of preaching is committed. So the remark in Ezechiel is prefaced with this: "I gave

you as a watcher over the children of Israel.''[90] To provide the sacraments of salvation for the children of the unfaithful belongs to their parents. So the danger falls to them if, on account of the removal of the sacraments, the little ones suffer some detriment to salvation.

---

[90] Ezechiel 3.17.

Question 11
[On Heresy]

One should next consider heresy. Four queries are raised with regard to this: (1) Whether heresy is a species of unfaithfulness. (2) What matter heresy is about. (3) Whether heretics are to be tolerated. (4) Whether those who revert are to be received.

Article 1. [Whether heresy is a species of unfaithfulness.]

One proceeds in this way to the first query. IT SEEMS that heresy is not a species of unfaithfulness.

[1] Unfaithfulness is in the intellect, as was said above.[1] But heresy does not seem to belong to the intellect, but rather to the appetitive power. For Jerome says, and it is had in *The Book of Decrees* 24, question 3, "Heresy in Greek means choice, that namely each one chooses for himself the doctrine (*disciplina*) that seems to be better."[2] But choice is an act of the appetitive power, as was said above.[3] Therefore heresy is not a species of unfaithfulness.

[2] Furthermore, a vice takes its species principally from the end. So the Philosopher says in *Ethics* 5 that he who

---

[1] In question 10, article 2, above.

[2] Jerome, *In Gal.* bk.3, on Galatians 5.19 (PL 26:417A), as in Gratian, *Decretum* p.2 causa.24 q.3 can.27 Haeresis grece (Richter-Friedberg 1:997).

[3] *Summa* 1–2 q.13 a.1.

fornicates in order that he may steal is more a thief than a fornicator.[4] But the end of heresy is temporal comfort, and most of all political power (*principatus*) and glory, which pertains to the vice of pride or ambition. For Augustine says in *On the Usefulness of Believing* that "the heretic is . . . he who for the sake of some temporal comfort, and most of all of glory and political power, either begets or follows false and new opinions."[5] Therefore heresy is not a species of unfaithfulness, but rather of pride.

[3] Furthermore, unfaithfulness, since it is in the intellect, does not seem to belong to the flesh. But heresy belongs to the works of the flesh. For the Apostle says, Galatians 5, "The works of the flesh are manifest, which are fornication, uncleanness."[6] And he adds among the others after a little, "dissensions, sects," which are the same as heresies. Therefore heresy is not a species of unfaithfulness.

BUT TO THE CONTRARY falsehood is opposed to truth. But "the heretic is he who either begets or follows false and new opinions."[7] Therefore heresy is opposed to truth, from which faith begins. Therefore it is contained under unfaithfulness.

I ANSWER THAT IT SHOULD BE SAID that the name heresy implies choice, as was said.[8] Choice is of the things that have to do with the end, which is presupposed, as was said above.[9] In the things that ought to be believed, the will assents to something so far as it is its own good, as is clear from what has been said.[10] So whatever is the principal truth has the account of the last end. What are

---

[4] Aristotle, *Nicomachean Ethics* bk.5 chap.2 (1130a24-27).

[5] Augustine, *De util. cred.* chap.1 sect.1 (PL 42:65; CSEL 25:3.6–9), from Peter Lombard, *Sent.* bk.4 dist.13 chap.2 sect.2 (Grottaferrata 1:314.203–315.2).

[6] Galatians 5.19–20.

[7] Augustine, *De util. cred.* chap.1 sect.1 (PL 42:65; CSEL 25:3.8–9).

[8] In objection [1] of this article, above.

[9] *Summa* 1–2 q.13 a.3.

[10] In question 4, article 3 and article 5, reply [1], both above.

secondary truths have the account of the things that have to do with the end. Since whoever believes assents to what someone says, the one to whose saying there is assent seems to be principal in any believing whatever, and as having to do with the end. Those things are as if secondary that someone holds in willing to assent to someone. So he rightly has Christian faith who by his will assents to Christ in the things that truly belong to his teaching. Someone can deviate from the truth of the Christian faith in two ways. In one way, since he does not want to assent to Christ himself, and here he has as it were a bad will towards the end itself. And this belongs to the species of unfaithfulness of the pagans and the Jews. In another way, [one deviates] by this that while he intends to assent to Christ, he rather falls short in choosing the things by which he might assent to Christ. He does not choose the things that are truly handed down by Christ, but the things that his own mind suggests to him. And so heresy is a species of unfaithfulness belonging to those who possess Christ's faith, but who corrupt its dogmas.

[1] TO THE FIRST ARGUMENT, THEREFORE, IT SHOULD BE SAID that in this way choice belongs to unfaithfulness, just as will does to faith, as was said above.

[2] To the second it should be said that vices have their species from a proximate end, but from a remote end they have genus and cause. Just so when someone fornicates in order that he might steal, there is a species of fornication from the proper end and object, but from the final end it is shown that fornication arises from theft, and is contained under it as effect under cause or as species under genus, as is clear from what was said above about acts in common.[11] Similarly in the proposed case the proximate end of heresy is to adhere to one's own false opinion; from this it has its species. But from the remote end it

[11] *Summa* 1–2 q.18 a.7.

should have its cause, namely, that it arises out of pride or cupidity.

[3] To the third it should be said that, just as "heresy" is said from choosing, so "sect" from following, as Isidore says in the *Etymologies*.[12] So heresy and sect are the same. And either belongs to the works of flesh, not as regards the very faith or unfaithfulness in regard to its proximate object, but according to the account of a cause, which is either the appetite for an undue end, according as it arises from pride or ambition, as was said; or else some fantastic illusion, which is the principle of erring, as the Philosopher also says, *Metaphysics* 4.[13] Fantasy belongs in a certain way to the flesh, so far as its act is by means of a bodily organ.

Article 2. [Whether heresy is properly about the things that are of faith.]

One proceeds in this way to the second query. IT SEEMS that heresy is not properly about the things that are of faith.

[1] Just as there are heresies and sects among Christians, so also were there among the Jews and Pharisees, as Isidore says in the *Etymologies*.[14] But their dissensions were not about the things that are of faith. Therefore heresy is not about the things that are of faith as about its proper matter.

[2] Furthermore, the things that are believed are the matter of faith. But heresy is not only about things, but also about words and about the exposition of sacred Scripture. For Jerome says that "whoever understands Scrip-

---

[12] Isidore of Seville, *Etymologiae* bk.8 chap.3 (Lindsay sect.1 and 4, lines 7–8 and 19–20).

[13] Aristotle, *Metaphysics* bk.4 chap.3 (1010b1–3).

[14] Isidore of Seville, *Etymologiae* bk.8 chap.4 title (Lindsay line 7).

ture otherwise than the sense of the Holy Spirit demands, by whom it was written, even if he does not withdraw from the Church, nonetheless can be called a heretic."[15] And elsewhere he says that "heresy is made from words spoken in disorder."[16] Therefore heresy is not properly about the matter of faith.

[3] Furthermore, even about the things that belong to faith the holy doctors are found sometimes to disagree, as Jerome and Augustine about the ceasing of the legal precepts [*legalia*].[17] And yet this happens without the vice of heresy. Therefore heresy is not properly about the matter of faith.

BUT TO THE CONTRARY there is what Augustine says, *Against the Manichaeans*: "Those are heretics who in the Church of Christ conceive something morbid and depraved, and once corrected so that they may conceive what is healthy and right, still resist abusively, and do not wish to emend their plague-bearing and deadly dogmas, but continue to defend them."[18] But plague-bearing and deadly dogmas are none other than the things that are opposed to the dogmas of faith, by which the just man lives, as it is said in Romans 1.[19] Therefore heresy is about the things that are of faith as about its proper material.

I ANSWER THAT IT SHOULD BE SAID that we speak of heresy now according as it implies the corruption of Christian faith. It is not a corruption of Christian faith

---

[15] Jerome, *In Gal.* bk.3, with regard to Galatians 5.19 (PL 26:417A), from Gratian, *Decretum* p.2 causa.24 q.3 can.27 Haeresis grece (Richter-Friedberg 1:998).

[16] *Glossa ordinaria* on Hosea 2.16 (Strasbourg 3, "Et erit in die," col. a), but probably taken from Peter Lombard, *Sent.* bk.4 dist.13 chap.2 sect.1 (Grottaferrata 2:314).

[17] Jerome, *Epist.* ep.112 (PL 22.921); Augustine, *Epist.* ep.82 chap.2 (PL 33:281).

[18] Augustine, *De civitate Dei* bk.18 chap.51 sect.1 (PL 41:613; CCL 48:549).

[19] Romans 1.17.

if someone has a false opinion about the things that are not of faith, for example in geometry or in others of this kind, which cannot belong to faith at all. There is corruption only when someone has a false opinion about the things that belong to faith. Something belongs to faith in two ways, as was said above.[20] In one way, directly and principally, such as the articles of faith; in another way, indirectly and secondarily, such as the things from which would follow the corruption of some article. And there can be heresy about either, in the same way as for faith.

[1] TO THE FIRST ARGUMENT, THEREFORE, IT SHOULD BE SAID that just as the heresies of the Jews and Pharisees were about certain opinions belonging to Judaism or Phariseeism, so also the heresies of Christians are about the things that belong to the faith of Christ.

[2] To the second it should be said that he is said to expound sacred Scripture otherwise than the Holy Spirit demands, who twists sacred Scripture so that it contradicts what was revealed by the Holy Spirit. So it is said in Ezechiel [13.6], about the false prophets who "persevered to confirm the word," namely by false expositions of Scripture. Similarly also by the words that someone speaks to proffer his faith, for confession is an act of faith, as was said above.[21] And so if there is disordered speaking about the things that are of faith, corruption of faith can follow from this. So Pope Leo, in a certain letter to Proterius, Bishop of Alexandria, says: "Since the enemies of the cross of Christ lie in ambush for all our words and syllables, let us give little or no occasion to them by which they might lie so as to make us conformed to the Nestorian sense."[22]

[3] To the third argument it should be said, as Augustine says, and as is had in the *Book of Decrees* 24, question 3:

---

[20] *Summa* 1 q.32 a.4.

[21] In question 3, article 1, above.

[22] Leo the Great, *Epist.* ep.129 Ad Proterium chap.2 (PL 54:1076B).

"If there are some who do not defend their judgment with stubborn animosity [however false or perverse it is] . . . but seek the truth with cautious care, and are ready to be corrected when it is found, in no way are they to be placed among the heretics."[23] Namely, since they do not make the choice to contradict the doctrine of the Church. So some teachers seems to dissent either about things for which it does not matter to faith whether they are one way or another; or even about things belonging to faith that were never determined by the Church. After they were determined by the authority of the universal Church, if someone should stubbornly reject such an ordinance, he would be judged a heretic. This authority principally resides in the supreme pontiff. For it is said [in the *Book of Decrees*] 24, question 1: "However much the reason of faith is discussed, I remind all my brothers and cobishops that it should be referred only to Peter, that is, to the authority of his name."[24] Against the authority of which neither Jerome nor Augustine nor any one of the sacred doctors defended his judgment. So Jerome says, "This is the faith, most blessed Father, which we teach in the catholic Church. In which if there is perhaps something put inexpertly or with insufficient caution, we desire that you emend it, you who hold the faith and the seat of Peter. If this our confession should be approved by your judgment as apostle, however, whoever wishes to fault me, whether uninformed or malevolent, I will account as either not a catholic or a heretic."[25]

---

[23] Augustine, *Epist*. ep.43 chap.1 (PL 33:160; CSEL 34:85.8–13), as in Gratian, *Decretum* part 2 causa.24 q.3 can.29 Dixit Apostolus (Richter-Friedberg 1:998).

[24] Gratian, *Decretum* part 2 causa.24 q.1 can.12 Quotiens fidei (Richter-Friedberg 1:970).

[25] Compare Pelagius, *Libellus fidei ad Innocentium papam* (PL 45:1718). During the Middle Ages, this work was transmitted under several different titles and was attributed (falsely) to several of the Fathers, especially Jerome and Augustine.

Article 3. [Whether heretics are to be tolerated.]

One proceeds in this way to the third query. IT SEEMS that heretics are to be tolerated.

[1] For the Apostle says, 2 Timothy 2, "A servant of God should be gentle, correcting those who resist the truth with modesty, so that when God gives them repentance to apprehend the truth, they should recover their senses from the snares of the devil."[26] But if heretics are not tolerated, but are handed over to death, there will be taken away from them the power of repentance. Therefore this seems to be contrary to the precept of the Apostle.

[2] Furthermore, what is necessary to the Church is to be tolerated. But heresies are necessary to the Church. The Apostle says, 1 Corinthians 11, "There must be heresies, so that the things that are proved should be made manifest in you."[27] Therefore heretics are to be tolerated.

[3] Furthermore, the Lord commands, Matthew 13,[28] that his servants allow the weeds to grow until the harvest, which is the end of this age, as is there expounded.[29] But by "weeds" is signified heretics, according to the exposition of the saints.[30] Therefore heretics are to be tolerated.

BUT TO THE CONTRARY there is what the Apostle says, Titus 3: "After the first and second correction, avoid the heretical man, knowing that he is ruinous in this way."[31]

I ANSWER THAT IT SHOULD BE SAID that two things are to be considered about heretics: one on their part; the other on the part of the Church. On their part there is the sin by which they merit not only to be sepa-

---

[26] 2 Timothy 2.24–26, condensed.

[27] 1 Corinthians 11.19.

[28] Matthew 13.30.

[29] Matthew 13.39.

[30] John Chrysostom, *On Matt.* hom.46 sect.1 (PG 58:476–477).

[31] Titus 3.10–11.

rated from the Church by excommunication, but also to be excluded from the world by death. It is much more serious to corrupt faith, by which the soul has life, than to falsify money, by which temporal life is supported. So if falsifiers of money or other malefactors are justly handed over to death at once by secular princes, much more can heretics, as soon as they are convicted of heresy, not only be excommunicated, but also justly killed.

On the part of the Church there is mercy, for the conversion of the erring. And so they are not condemned at once, but "after the first and second correction," as the Apostle teaches. After that, if the heretic is still found to be stubborn, the Church, not hoping for his conversion, provides for the health of others, separating him from the Church by a sentence of excommunication. And it further relinquishes him to secular judgment in order that he be exterminated from the world by death. For Jerome says, and it is had in 24 question 3: "Rotten flesh is to be cut away, and the scabrous sheep chased from the flock, that the whole house, mass, body, and flock not burn, be corrupted, putrefy, and perish. Arius was one spark in Alexandria: but since he was not extinguished at once, the whole world was peopled by his flame."[32]

[1] TO THE FIRST ARGUMENT, THEREFORE, IT SHOULD BE SAID that it belongs to this modesty that the heretic be corrected a first and a second time. But if he does not wish to turn back, he must be held as one already lost, as is clear in the cited authority of the Apostle.

[2] To the second it should be said that the usefulness that comes from heresies is beyond the intention of the heretics—the usefulness, namely, that the constancy of the faithful is proved, as the Apostle says, and that we might shake off laziness, looking into the divine Scriptures more

---

[32] Jerome, *In Gal.* bk.3, with regard to Galatians 5.9 (PL 26:403B), as from Gratian, *Decretum* part 2 causa.24 q.3 can.16 Secandae sunt (Richter-Friedberg 1:995).

attentively, as Augustine says.[33] But it is of their intention to corrupt the faith, which produces great damage. And so one ought to respect what is *per se* of their intention, and so exclude them, rather than what is beyond their intention, and so permit them.

[3] To the third it should be said that, as is had in the *Book of Decrees* 24, question 3, "excommunication is one thing, eradication another. Someone is excommunicated for this, as the Apostle says, 'that his spirit be saved in the day of the Lord.' "[34]—If heretics are totally eradicated by death, however, even this is not against the command of the Lord. The command is to be understood as applying to that case when the weeds cannot be destroyed without destroying the wheat, as was said above, when discussing the unfaithful in general.[35]

Article 4. [Whether those who revert from heresy ought to be received by the Church.]

One proceeds in this way to the fourth query. IT SEEMS that those reverting from heresy ought to be received by the Church in every way.

[1] It says in Jeremiah 3, in the person of Lord, "You have fornicated with many lovers, nonetheless come back to me, says the Lord."[36] But the judgment of the Church is the judgment of God, according to Deuteronomy 1, "Listen to the small as to the great, neither prefer any person, since it is the judgment of God."[37] Therefore if

---

[33] Augustine, *De Genesi contra Manich.* bk.1 chap.1 sect.2 (PL 34:173).

[34] Gratian, *Decretum* part 2 causa.24 q.3 can.37 Notandum est (Richter-Friedberg 1:1000).

[35] In question 10, article 8, reply [1], above.

[36] Jeremiah 3.1.

[37] Deuteronomy 1.17.

some were fornicators because of unfaithfulness, which is spiritual fornication, nonetheless they ought to be received.

[2] Furthermore, the Lord commands Peter, Matthew 18, that he forgive his sinning brothers not only seven times, "but seventy times seven."[38] By which it is to be understood, according to the exposition of Jerome,[39] that however many times someone sins, it ought to be forgiven to him. Therefore, however many times someone has relapsed into heresy, he should be received by the Church.

[3] Furthermore, heresy is an unfaithfulness. But others of the unfaithful wanting to be converted to the Church are received. Therefore heretics too ought to be received.

BUT TO THE CONTRARY there is what the *Book of Decrees* says, that "if some after abjuring error were caught having fallen back into the abjured heresy, they are to be given to the secular judgment."[40] Therefore they ought not to be received by the Church.

I ANSWER THAT IT SHOULD BE SAID that the Church, according to divine institution, extends its charity to all, not only to friends, but also to enemies and persecutors, according to Matthew 5, "Love your enemies, do good to those who hate you."[41] Charity requires that someone both want and work the good of his neighbor. The good is twofold. One spiritual, namely the salvation of the soul, with which charity has principally to do; everyone should will this for others out of charity. So that according to this, reverting heretics, however many times they have relapsed, are to be received by the Church for repentance, by which there is gained for them the way of salvation.

---

[38] Matthew 18.22.

[39] Jerome, *In Matt.* bk.3, with regard to Matthew 18.22 (PL 26:132C; CCL 77:163.669–671).

[40] *Decretal. Gregor.* IX, bk.5 tit.7 chap.9 Ad abolendam (Richter-Friedberg 2:781).

[41] Matthew 5.44.

Another is the good with which charity has to do secondarily, namely temporal good, such as is temporal life, earthly possession, and good fame, and ecclesiastical or secular dignity. We are not held by charity to will this for others except as ordered to their eternal salvation and that of others. So that if some good of this kind existing in one can impede the eternal salvation in many, we need not will this kind of good for him from charity, but rather we ought to will that he lack it. As much because eternal salvation is to be preferred to temporal good, as because the good of the many is to be preferred to the good of one. If reverting heretics were always to be received in such a way that they be conserved in life and in other temporal goods, it could be prejudicial to the salvation of others. As much because if they fall again, they can infect others; or also because, if they escaped without penalty, others would more securely fall again into heresy, as it is said in Ecclesiastes 8, "Because judgment is not passed on evils quickly, the sons of men perpetrate evils without any fear."[42] And so the Church at first not only receives those who revert from heresy for repentance, but also conserves them in life; and meanwhile restores them by dispensation to the ecclesiastical dignities that they previously had, if they seem truly to be converted. And one reads that for the good of peace this was frequently done. But when those who have been received relapse again, it seems to be a sign of their inconstancy about faith. And so coming back again they are received for repentance, but are not freed from the judgment of death.

[1] TO THE FIRST ARGUMENT, THEREFORE, IT SHOULD BE SAID that those who return are always received in the judgment of God, since God inspects hearts and apprehends those who truly return. But the Church cannot imitate this. It presumes that those do not truly

---

[42] Ecclesiastes 8.11.

return who, once they were received, relapse again. And so it does not deny them the way of salvation, but does not preserve them from the danger of death.

[2] To the second it should be said that the Lord speaks to Peter of a sin committed against him, which is always to be forgiven, that a brother who returns be spared. It is not to be understood of a sin committed against neighbor or God, which is "not in our judgment to forgive," as Jerome says.[43] But in this there is a measure established by law, according as it is congruent with the honor of God and the usefulness of neighbors.

[3] To the third it should be said that the others of the unfaithful, who never accepted faith, once converted to faith never show a sign of inconstancy about faith, as do relapsed heretics. And so there is no similar reasoning about the two.

---

[43] Jerome, as in *Glossa ordinaria* on Matthew 18.15 (Strasbourg 4, "Si peccaverit in te," col. a).

Question 12
[On Apostasy]

One should next consider apostasy. Two queries are raised with regard to this: (1) Whether apostasy belongs to unfaithfulness. (2) Whether subjects are absolved from the lordship of apostate leaders (*praesidentes*) because of apostasy.

Article 1. [Whether apostasy belongs to unfaithfulness.]

One proceeds in this way to the first query. IT SEEMS that apostasy does not belong to unfaithfulness.

[1] What is the principle of all sin does not seem to belong to unfaithfulness, since many sins exist without unfaithfulness. But apostasy seems to be the principle of all sin, since it is said in Sirach 10, "The beginning of man's pride is to apostatize from God";[1] and then further on is added, "The beginning of all sin is pride."[2] Therefore apostasy does not belong to unfaithfulness.

[2] Furthermore, unfaithfulness is constituted in the intellect. But apostasy seems rather to be constituted in an outward work of speech or even in an inward will. For it is said in Proverbs 6: "An apostate man is a useless man, going about with a perverse mouth, he winks with his eyes, he taps with his foot, he speaks with his finger, in a depraved heart he machinates evil, and at all times sows

[1] Sirach 10.14.
[2] Sirach 10.15.

quarrels."[3] If someone circumcises himself, or adores the tomb of Mohammed, he is reputed an apostate. Therefore apostasy does not belong directly to unfaithfulness.

[3] Furthermore, heresy, which belongs to unfaithfulness, is a determinate species of unfaithfulness. If then apostasy were to belong to unfaithfulness, it would follow that it would be some determinate species of unfaithfulness. Which it does not seem to be, according to what has been said.[4] Therefore apostasy does not belong to unfaithfulness.

BUT TO THE CONTRARY there is what is said in John 6, "Many of his disciples drew back,"[5] which is to apostatize, about whom the Lord earlier says, "There are some of you who do not believe."[6] Therefore apostasy belongs to unfaithfulness.

I ANSWER THAT IT SHOULD BE SAID that apostasy implies a retreating from God. This happens in different ways, according to the different ways in which man is joined to God. For man is first joined to God by faith; second, by a due will subject to obeying his precepts; third, by special things belonging to supererogation, such as by religion or clerical standing or sacred order.[7] When the latter [ways of being joined to God] are taken away, the former remains, but not conversely. So it happens that someone apostatizes from God by withdrawing from the religion that he had vowed, or from the order that he received; and this is called apostasy from religion or from an order. It also happens that someone apostatizes from

---

[3] Proverbs 6.12–14.

[4] In question 10, article 5, above.

[5] John 6.67.

[6] John 6.65.

[7] That is, by taking vows in the religious life or by being ordained to minor or major orders, such as deacon and priest. The reference is not to membership in a religious order. For the use and meaning of the word "religion," see above, introduction, pp.3-4.

God by a mind that rejects the divine commands. Even after these two apostasies, a man can still remain joined to God by faith. But if he falls away from faith, then he seems to withdraw from God entirely. And apostasy simply and unqualifiedly speaking is that by which someone falls away from faith, which is called the apostasy of treachery. And in this way apostasy is said simply to belong to faith.

[1] TO THE FIRST ARGUMENT, THEREFORE, IT SHOULD BE SAID that the objection proceeds from the second [kind of] apostasy, which implies a will resisting the commands of God. This is found in every mortal sin.

[2] To the second it should be said that faith contains not only trusting belief (*credulitas*) in the heart, but also the profession of inward faith by outward words and deeds, since confession is an act of faith. And in this way some outward words and works also belong to unfaithfulness, so far as they are signs of unfaithfulness, in the way in which a sign of health is said to be healthy. The adduced authority, even if it can be understood of every apostasy, is most truly appropriate to apostasy from faith. Faith is the "first foundation of things to be hoped for," and "without faith it is impossible to please God."[8] When faith is taken away, nothing remains in man that can be useful to eternal salvation. And because of this it is said first, "An apostate man is a useless man." Faith is also the life of the soul, according to Romans 1, "The just man lives by faith."[9] When bodily life is taken away, all the members and parts of man withdraw from their due disposition; so when the life of justice that exists by faith is taken away, disorder appears in all the members. And first in the mouth, by which the heart is most made manifest; second, in the eyes; third, in the instruments of motion; fourth, in the will, which tends to evil. And from this it follows that he

[8] Hebrews 11.1,6.

[9] Romans 1.17.

sows quarrels, intending to separate others from the faith, just as he has withdrawn from it.

[3] To the third it should be said that the species of any quality or form is not differentiated by being an end of motion from which or to which, but, conversely, the ends of motion are to be looked for from the species. Apostasy receives[10] unfaithfulness as the end from which there is the motion of withdrawing from faith. So that apostasy does not imply a determinate species of unfaithfulness, but only a certain aggravating circumstance, according to 2 Peter 2, "It would be better for them not to apprehend the truth than to retreat from it after becoming acquainted with it."[11]

Article 2. [Whether a prince by apostasy from faith gives up lordship over his subjects, so that they are not held to obey him.]

One proceeds in this way to the second query. IT SEEMS that a prince by apostasy from faith does not give up lordship over his subjects, as though they were not held to obey him.

[1] Ambrose says,[12] and it is had in [the *Book of Decrees*] 9 question 4,[13] that "the Emperor Julian, however much he was an apostate, nonetheless had Christian soldiers under him, who obeyed him when he said, 'Produce your steel in defense of the republic.'" Therefore subjects are not absolved from a prince's lordship because of his apostasy.

---

[10] Other versions read "stands in respect to."

[11] 2 Peter 2.21.

[12] Compare Augustine, *Enarr. in Ps.* ps.124 sect.7, with regard to Psalm 124.3 (PL 37:1654; CCL 40:1841.52–58).

[13] Gratian, *Decretum* part 2 causa.11 q.3 can.94 Iulianus inperator (Richter-Friedberg 1:669).

[2] Furthermore, an apostate from the faith is someone unfaithful. But there are found some holy men who faithfully served unfaithful masters, such as Joseph under Pharoah, and Daniel under Nebuchadnezzar, and Mardochaeus to Assuerus [i.e., Cambyses]. Therefore one should not deny because of apostasy from faith that a prince is still to be obeyed by his subjects.

[3] Furthermore, just as one withdraws from God by apostasy of faith, so also by any sin whatever. If then because of apostasy from faith princes were to lose the right of commanding faithful subjects, by the same reasoning this [right] would be cut off because of other sins. But it is clear that this is false. Therefore one ought not to withdraw from obedience to princes because of apostasy from faith.

BUT TO THE CONTRARY there is what Gregory VII says: "Holding to the statutes of our holy predecessors, by apostolic authority we absolve from the oath (*sacramentum*)[14] those who are bound by fealty or oaths to those who are excommunicated, and we prohibit in all ways that they observe faithfulness to them, until they come to satisfaction."[15] But the excommunicate are apostate from the faith, as heretics also are, as the *Book of Decrees* says in [the text] "In order to abolish. . . . "[16] Therefore one ought not to obey those who are apostate from faith.

I ANSWER THAT IT SHOULD BE SAID that unfaithfulness by itself does not contradict lordship, given that

---

[14] The word *sacramentum,* ordinarily translated as "sacrament," can also mean—indeed, originally meant—a solemn oath or agreement. Thomas himself prefers to call an oath *iuramentum,* as he will below.

[15] Compare Gratian, *Decretum* part 2 causa.15 q.6 can.4 Nos sanctorum (Richter-Friedberg 1:756).

[16] *Decretal. Gregor. IX,* lib.5 tit.7 cap.9 Ab abolendam (Richter-Friedberg 2:780).

lordship was introduced by the law of peoples, which is human law, as was said above.[17] But the distinction between faithful and unfaithful is of divine law, by which human law is not taken away. But someone sinning by unfaithfulness can put off the right of lordship by judgment (*sententialiter*), just as sometimes also happens because of other faults. It does not belong to the Church to punish those who never accepted faith, according to the Apostle, 1 Corinthians 5, "What business is it of mine to judge of those who are outside?"[18] But the unfaithfulness of those who accepted faith it can punish by judgment. And they are appropriately punished by being denied lordship over faithful subjects; for this can lead to great corruption of faith. Since, as was said, "the apostate man machinates evil in his heart and sows quarrels,"[19] intending to separate men from the faith. And so as soon as someone is denounced by a decree as excommunicated because of apostasy from faith, by that very fact his subjects are absolved from his lordship and the oath (*iuramentum*) of faithfulness by which they are held to him.

[1] TO THE FIRST ARGUMENT, THEREFORE, IT SHOULD BE SAID that in that time the Church, in its newness, never had the power to compel earthly princes. And so it tolerated the faithful obeying Julian the Apostate in the things that were not against faith, so that a greater danger to faith should be avoided.

[2] To the second it should be said that another reasoning holds for the other unfaithful, who never accepted faith, as was said.[20]

---

[17] In question 10, article 10, above.

[18] 1 Corinthians 5.12.

[19] Proverbs 6.14, paraphrased by condensing, as from article 1 of this question, objection [2], above.

[20] In the body of this article.

[3] To the third it should be said that apostasy from faith separates man from God completely, as was said.[21] This does not happen in any other sins whatever.

[21] In article 1 of this question.

Question 13
[On Blasphemy in General]

One should next consider the sin of blasphemy, which is opposed to the confession of faith. And, first, blasphemy in general; second, the blasphemy that is said to be the sin against the Holy Spirit.

Four queries are raised with regard to the first point. (1) Whether blasphemy is opposed to the confession of faith. (2) Whether blasphemy is always a mortal sin. (3) Whether blasphemy is the greatest sin. (4) Whether there is blasphemy among the damned.

Article 1. [Whether blasphemy is opposed to the confession of faith.]

One proceeds in this way to the first query. IT SEEMS that blasphemy is not opposed to the confession of faith.

[1] Now to blaspheme is to hurl abuse or reproach at the creator as an injury to him. But this belongs more to malevolence against God than to unfaithfulness. Therefore blasphemy is not opposed to the confession of faith.

[2] Furthermore, on Ephesians 4, "Let blasphemy be taken away from you,"[1] the Gloss says, "which is done against God or against the saints."[2] But confession of faith does not seem to be about anything but the things that belong to God, who is the object of faith. There-

---

[1] Ephesians 4.31, condensed.

[2] *Glossa Lombardi* on Ephesians 4.31 (PL 192:208B).

fore blasphemy is not always opposed to the confession of faith.

[3] Furthermore, some say[3] that there are three species of blasphemy: the first, when something is attributed to God that is not appropriate to him; the second, when something is taken away from him that is appropriate to him; the third, when there is attributed to a creature what is appropriate to God. And so it seems that blasphemy is not only about God, but also about creatures. But faith has God for its object. Therefore blasphemy is not opposed to the confession of faith.

BUT TO THE CONTRARY there is what the Apostle says, 1 Timothy 1, "Earlier I was a blasphemer and persecutor," and further on he adds, "not knowing I did this in unfaithfulness."[4] From which it seems that blasphemy belongs to unfaithfulness.

I ANSWER THAT IT SHOULD BE SAID that the name "blasphemy" seems to imply a detracting from any excellence or goodness, and especially from the divine. For God, as Dionysius says, is by his essence goodness.[5] So that whatever is appropriate to God belongs to his goodness; and whatever does not belong to him is far away from the account of complete goodness, which is his essence. Whoever then either negates something of God that is appropriate to him, or asserts of him what is not appropriate to him, derogates the divine goodness. This can happen in two ways: in one way, according to the opinion of the intellect alone; in another way, as conjoined with a certain detestation in the affective power, just as on the contrary faith in God is completed by loving him. This kind of detracting from the divine good is either

---

[3] The reference seems to be to the *Summa Halensis* part 2 sect.474 (Quaracchi 3:464).

[4] 1 Timothy 1.13.

[5] Ps-Dionysius, *Divine Names* chap.1 sect.5 (PG 3:593C; Chevallier 1:39–40).

according to understanding alone, or also by the affective power. If it is constituted in the heart alone, it is blasphemy of the heart. If it proceeds outside into speech, it is blasphemy of the mouth. And according to this blasphemy is opposed to confession.

[1] TO THE FIRST ARGUMENT, THEREFORE, IT SHOULD BE SAID that he who speaks against God, intending to hurl an insult, detracts from the divine goodness not only according to the truth of understanding, but also according to depravity of the will, detesting and impeding the divine honor so far as can be done. This is complete blasphemy.

[2] To the second it should be said that just as God is praised in his saints, so far as those works are praised which God does in his saints; so also the blasphemy that is done against the saints redounds in consequence to God.

[3] To the third it should be said that different species of the sin of blasphemy cannot be distinguished properly speaking according to these three [headings]. To attribute to God what is not appropriate to him and to remove from him what is appropriate to him do not differ except as affirmation and negation. This difference does not distinguish the species of a habit, since a habit recognizes by the same knowledge the falsity of affirmations and negations, and by the same lack of knowledge errs in either way, since negation is proved by affirmation, as is had in *Posterior Analytics* 1.[6] Attributing the things that are proper to God to creatures, moreover, seems to belong with attributing to him something that is not appropriate to him. Whatever is proper to God is God himself; therefore to attribute something that is proper to God to any creature is to predicate God himself of that creature.

---

[6] Aristotle, *Posterior Analytics* bk.1 chap.25 (86b27–28).

Article 2. [Whether blasphemy is always a mortal sin.]

One proceeds in this way to the second query. IT SEEMS that blasphemy is not always a mortal sin.

[1] About Colossians 3, "Now however you put away" and so on,[7] the Gloss says, "After the larger [sin] he prohibits the smaller."[8] And yet he goes on about blasphemy. Therefore blasphemy is to be counted among the smaller sins, which are venial sins.

[2] Furthermore, every mortal sin is opposed to some precept of the decalogue.[9] But blasphemy does not seem to be opposed to any one of them. Therefore blasphemy is not a mortal sin.

[3] Furthermore, sins that are committed without deliberation are not mortal. For this reason the first movements [towards sin] are not mortal sins, since they precede the deliberation of reason, as is clear from what was said.[10] But blasphemy sometimes proceeds without deliberation. Therefore it is not always a mortal sin.

BUT TO THE CONTRARY there is what is said in Leviticus 24, "He who blasphemes the name of the Lord, shall die by death."[11] But the penalty of death is not imposed except for mortal sin. Therefore blasphemy is a mortal sin.

I ANSWER THAT IT SHOULD BE SAID that mortal sin is what separates man from the first principle of spiritual life, which is the charity of God, as was said above.[12] So that whatever things reject charity, are mortal sins by their genus. Blasphemy according to its genus rejects divine charity, since it detracts from the divine goodness, which

---

[7] Colossians 3.8.

[8] *Glossa Lombardi* on Colossians 3.8 (PL 192:281C).

[9] That is, to one of the Ten Commandments.

[10] *Summa* 1–2 q.74 a.3 ao.3.

[11] Leviticus 24.16.

[12] *Summa* 1–2 q.72 a.5.

is the object of charity, as was said.[13] And so blasphemy is a mortal sin by its genus.

[1] TO THE FIRST ARGUMENT, THEREFORE, IT SHOULD BE SAID that the Gloss is not to be understood as saying that all the things that are added are small sins. But since [Paul] had earlier not expressed anything else but large sins, afterwards he also adds certain small sins, among which he also puts some large ones.

[2] To the second it should be said that, since blasphemy is opposed to the confession of faith, as was said,[14] its prohibition is traced back to the prohibition against unfaithfulness, which is understood when it is said, "I am the Lord your God" and so on.[15]

Or blasphemy is prohibited when it is said, "Do not take the name of your God in vain."[16] He who affirms something false of God takes the name of God in vain even more than he who confirms something false by [using] the name of God.

[3] To the third it should be said that blasphemy can proceed without deliberation, by surprise, in two ways. In one way, when someone does not notice that what he says is blasphemy. This can happen when someone erupts quickly from some passion into words he has imagined, but the significance of which he does not consider. And then it is a venial sin, and does not properly have the account of blasphemy. In another way, when he notices that this is blasphemy, considering what is signified by the words. And then it cannot be excused from mortal sin, just as someone who because of a sudden motion of anger kills someone else sitting next to him is not excused from murder.

---

[13] In article 1 of this question.

[14] In article 1 of this question.

[15] Exodus 20.2.

[16] Exodus 20.7.

Article 3. [Whether the sin of blasphemy is the greatest sin.]

One proceeds in this way to the third query. IT SEEMS that the sin of blasphemy is not the greatest sin.

[1] What causes damage is called evil, according to Augustine in the *Enchiridion.*[17] But the sin of murder, which destroys the life of man, causes more damage than the sin of blasphemy, which can inflict no damage on God. Therefore the sin of murder is more serious than the sin of blasphemy.

[2] Furthermore, whoever commits perjury invokes God as a witness to falsity, and so seems to assert that God is false. But no blasphemer whatever goes so far as to assert that God is false. Therefore perjury is a more serious sin than blasphemy.

[3] Furthermore, on the psalm, "Do not raise up your horn to the heights,"[18] the Gloss says, "The greatest vice is excusing sin."[19] Therefore blasphemy is not the greatest sin.

BUT TO THE CONTRARY there is what the Gloss says on Isaiah 18 says, "To the terrifying people" and so on.[20] The Gloss says, "Every sin, compared to blasphemy, is less serious."[21]

I ANSWER THAT IT SHOULD BE SAID that blasphemy is opposed to the confession of faith, as was said above.[22] And so it has in itself the seriousness of unfaithfulness. And the sin is aggravated if there is added the

---

[17] Augustine, *Enchiridion* chap.4 sect.12 (PL 40:237; CCL 46: 54.13–14).

[18] Psalm 74.6.

[19] *Glossa Lombardi* on Psalm 74.6 (PL 191.700).

[20] Isaiah 18.2.

[21] *Glossa ordinaria* on Isaiah 18.2 (Strasbourg 3, "Ite angeli veloces," col. b).

[22] In article 1 of this question, above.

detestation of the will, and even more if it erupts into words. Just so the praise of faith is increased by love and confession. So, since unfaithfulness is the greatest sin according to its genus, as was said above,[23] it follows that blasphemy too is the greatest sin, belonging to the same genus and aggravating it.

[1] TO THE FIRST ARGUMENT, THEREFORE, IT SHOULD BE SAID that if murder and blasphemy are compared according to the object in which one sins, it is clear that blasphemy, which is directly a sin against God, outweighs murder, which is a sin against one's neighbor. If they are compared according to the effect of damage, in this way murder outweighs; murder causes more damage to a neighbor than blasphemy does to God. But because one looks for the seriousness of a fault more in the intention of the perverse will than in the effect of the work, as is clear from what has been said;[24] thus, since blasphemy intends to inflict damage to the divine honor, simply speaking it sins more seriously than murder. But murder holds first place among sins that are committed against one's neighbor.

[2] To the second it should be said that with regard to Ephesians 4, "Take away blasphemy from yourselves,"[25] the Gloss says, "It is worse to blaspheme than to perjure."[26] He who perjures does not say or tell anything false about God, as does the blasphemer. But he invokes God as a witness to falsity not because he thinks that God is a false witness, but because he hopes that God will not [really] testify about this by some other evident sign.

[3] To the third it should be said that the excusing of sin is a circumstance aggravating all sin, even blasphemy. And

---

[23] In question 10, article 3, above.

[24] *Summa* 1–2 q.73 a.8.

[25] Ephesians 4.31.

[26] *Glossa ordinaria* on Ephesians 4.31 (Strasbourg 4, "Blasphemia," col. a).

so it is said to be the greatest sin, since it makes anything greater.

Article 4. [Whether the damned blaspheme.]

One proceeds in this way to the fourth query. IT SEEMS that the damned do not blaspheme.

[1] Some of the evil [among the living] are held back from blaspheming by fear of future punishments. But the damned experience these punishments, so that they abhor them even more. Therefore much more are they restrained from blaspheming.

[2] Furthermore, blasphemy, since it is a most serious sin, takes away most from merit. But in the future life there is no state of meriting or taking away merit. Therefore there is no place for blasphemy.

[3] Furthermore, Ecclesiastes 11 says, "in whatever place wood fell, there shall it be."[27] From which it is clear that after this life neither a merit nor a sin grows in man that he did not have in this life. But many are damned who in this life were not blasphemers. Therefore neither in the future life will they blaspheme.

BUT TO THE CONTRARY it is said in Revelations 16, "Men were burned with a great heat, and they blasphemed the name of the Lord who had power over these plagues."[28] The Gloss says that "those placed in hell, however much they know that they are punished with merit, grieve that God has so much power that he can cast plagues upon them."[29] This would be blasphemy in the present. Therefore also in the future.

---

[27] Ecclesiastes 11.3, condensed.

[28] Revelation 16.21.

[29] *Glossa ordinaria* on Revelation 16.21 (Strasbourg 4, "Et blasphemaverunt").

I ANSWER THAT IT SHOULD BE SAID that, as was said above,[30] detestation of the divine will belongs to blasphemy. Those who are in hell will retain a perverse will, opposed to the justice of God, so far as they love the things for which they are punished, will to use them if they could, and hate the pains that are inflicted for sins of this kind. They grieve for the sins that they bewail, not because they hate them, but because they are punished for them. Such a detestation of the divine will is in them an inward blasphemy of the heart. And it is believable that after the resurrection there will be in them even vocal blasphemy, as there will be vocal praise of God in the saints.

[1] TO THE FIRST ARGUMENT, THEREFORE, IT SHOULD BE SAID that men are deterred from blasphemy in the present on account of the fear of punishment that they believe they can evade. But the damned in hell do not hope that they can evade these punishments. And so, being so desperate, they are carried to everything that their perverse wills suggest to them.

[2] To the second it should be said that to merit and to take away from merit belong to the state of the journey. So good things are meritorious in journeyers, bad things against merit. In the blessed, however, good things are not meritorious, but belong to their reward of blessedness. And similarly evil things are not against merit in the damned, but belong to the punishment of damnation.

[3] To the third it should be said that whoever dies in mortal sin carries with him a will that detests divine justice with regard to something. And according to this there can be blasphemy in him.

---

[30] In article 1 and 3 of this question, both above.

Question 14

[On Blasphemy against the Holy Spirit]

One should next consider in particular blasphemy against the Holy Spirit. And four queries are raised about this: (1) Whether blasphemy or sin against the Holy Spirit is the same as sin from confirmed malice (*certa malitia*). (2) On the species of this sin. (3) Whether it is unforgivable. (4) Whether someone can sin against the Holy Spirit from the very beginning, before he commits other sins.

Article 1. [Whether the sin against the Holy Spirit is the same as sin from confirmed malice.]

One proceeds in this way to the first query. IT SEEMS that the sin against the Holy Spirit is not the same as sin from confirmed malice.

[1] The sin against the Holy Spirit is the sin of blasphemy, as is clear from Matthew 12.[1] But not every sin from confirmed malice is a sin of blasphemy. It happens that many other genera of sins are committed from confirmed malice. Therefore the sin against the Holy Spirit is not the same as sin from confirmed malice.

[2] Furthermore, sin from confirmed malice is divided from sin from ignorance and sin from weakness. But the sin against the Holy Spirit is divided from the sin against

[1] Matthew 12.31.

the Son of man, as is clear from Matthew 12.[2] Therefore the sin against the Holy Spirit is not the same as sin from confirmed malice. Things whose opposites are different are themselves also different.

[3] Furthermore, the sin against the Holy Spirit is a certain genus of sin to which determinate species are assigned. But the sin from confirmed malice is not a special genus of sin, but a condition or general circumstance that can have to do with all genera of sins. Therefore the sin against the Holy Spirit is not the same as the sin from confirmed malice.

BUT TO THE CONTRARY there is what the Master says, *Sentences* book 2 distinction 43, that one sins against the Holy Spirit "whom malice pleases on account of itself."[3] This is to sin from confirmed malice. Therefore the sin from confirmed malice seems to be the same as the sin against the Holy Spirit.

I ANSWER THAT IT SHOULD BE SAID that some speak in three ways about sin or blasphemy against the Holy Spirit. The ancient teachers, namely Athanasius, Hilary, Ambrose, Jerome, and Chrysostom,[4] say that there is sin against the Holy Spirit when, literally, some blasphemy is said against the Holy Spirit—whether "Holy Spirit" is taken as it is an essential name appropriate to the whole Trinity, of which every person is a spirit and is also holy; or so far as it is the personal name of one person of the Trinity. And according to this [view], blasphemy against the Holy Spirit is distinguished, Matthew

---

[2] Matthew 12.32.

[3] Peter Lombard, *Sent.* bk.2 dist.43 chap.1 (Grottaferrata 1:533).

[4] Athanasius, *Fragm. on Matt.,* with respect to Matthew 12.32 (PG 27:1386B-1387A); Hilary, *In Matt.,* on Matthew 12.32 (PL 9:989A-C); Ambrose, *In Luc.* bk.7, on Luke 12.9 (PL 15:1729D); Jerome, *In Matt.* bk.2, on Matthew 12.32 (PL 26:81A-B; CCL 77:94–95); John Chrysostom, *On Matt.* hom. 41 (PG 57:449).

12,[5] from blasphemy against the Son of man. Christ worked some things humanly, eating, drinking, and doing other things of this kind; and some divinely, namely, casting out demons, raising the dead, and others of this kind. The latter he did both by the power of his own divinity, and by the operation of the Holy Spirit, with which he was filled according to his humanity. The Jews first spoke blasphemy against the Son of man, when they called him "voracious, a drinker of wine and lover of publicans," as is had in Matthew 11.[6] Afterwards they blasphemed against the Holy Spirit, when they attributed the works he did by the power of his own divinity and by the operation of the Holy Spirit to the prince of demons. And according to this they are said to blaspheme against the Holy Spirit.

But Augustine, in *On the Word of the Lord*, says that blasphemy or sin against the Holy Spirit is final impenitence, namely when someone perseveres in mortal sin until death.[7] This someone does not only by word of mouth, but also by word of heart and of work, not in one [thing only], but in many. This remark, taken thus, is said to be against the Holy Spirit, since it is against the remission of sins, which is done by the Holy Spirit, who is the charity of the Father and the Son. Nor does the Lord say this to the Jews as if they sinned against the Holy Spirit, for they were never finally impenitent. But he admonished them, speaking in this way, that they would come to sin against the Holy Spirit. And so one ought to understand what is said in Mark 3, where, after he said, "He who blasphemes against the Holy Spirit" and so on,[8] the evangelist adds, "For they had said, 'He has an unclean spirit.' "[9]

---

[5] Matthew 12.32.

[6] Matthew 11.19.

[7] Augustine, *Serm. ad popul.* serm.71 chap.12 sect.20 (PL 38: 455–456).

[8] Mark 3.29.

[9] Mark 3.30.

Others take it yet otherwise,[10] saying that the sin against the Holy Spirit comes when someone sins against the good appropriated to the Holy Spirit, to whom is appropriated goodness, just as power is appropriated to the Father and wisdom to the Son. So they call it sin against the Father when there is sin from weakness; sin against the Son, when there is sin from ignorance; and sin against the Holy Spirit, when there is sin from confirmed malice, that is, by the very choice of evil, as was expounded above.[11] This happens in two ways. In one way, from the inclination of a vicious habit, which is said to be malice; in this sense to sin from malice is not the same as to sin against the Holy Spirit. It happens in another when what would impede the choice of sin is cast aside and removed by contempt—as hope [is cast aside] through despair, and fear through presumption, and certain others of this kind, as will be said below.[12] All these things that impede the choice of sin are effects of the Holy Spirit in us. And to sin from malice in this sense is to sin against the Holy Spirit.

[1] TO THE FIRST ARGUMENT, THEREFORE, IT SHOULD BE SAID that just as the confession of faith consists not only in the protestation of the mouth, but also in the protestation of works; so also blasphemy against the Holy Spirit can be considered in the mouth, in the heart, and in the work.

[2] To the second it should be said that blasphemy against the Holy Spirit in the third sense is distinguished from blasphemy against the Son of man so far as the Son of man is also the Son of God, namely, "the power and wisdom of God."[13] According to this, sin against the Son of man will be sin from ignorance and from weakness.

---

[10] The reference seems to be to Richard of St.-Victor, *De Spir. blasphemiae* (PL 196:1187).

[11] *Summa* 1–2 q.78 a.1, a.3.

[12] In the following article of this question.

[13] 1 Corinthians 1.24.

[3] To the third it should be said that sin from confirmed malice so far as it comes from the inclination of a habit, is not a special sin, but a certain general condition of sin. So far as it is from special contempt of the effect of the Holy Spirit in us, it has the account of a special sin. And according to this also the sin against the Holy Spirit is a special genus of sin. And similarly according to the first exposition. According to the second exposition, it is not a special genus of sin; for final impenitence can be a circumstance of any genus of sin.

Article 2. [Whether six species of sin against the Holy Spirit are appropriately assigned.]

One proceeds in this way to the second query. IT SEEMS that six species of the sin against the Holy Spirit are inappropriately assigned, namely, despair, presumption, impenitence, obstinacy, fighting against known truth, and envy of fraternal grace, which species the Master puts in *Sentences* book 2 distinction 43.[14]

[1] To negate divine justice or mercy pertains to unfaithfulness. But by despair someone rejects divine mercy; by presumption, divine justice. Therefore each one of them is rather a species of unfaithfulness than of the sin against the Holy Spirit.

[2] Furthermore, impenitence seems to regard past sin; obstinacy, future sin. Past and future do not differentiate species of virtues and vice. According to the same faith by which we believed Christ was born, the ancients believed that he was to be born. Therefore obstinacy and impenitence should not be put as two species of sin against the Holy Spirit.

---

[14] Peter Lombard, *Sent.* bk.2 dist.43 chap.1 (Grottaferrata 1:536).

[3] Furthermore, "truth and grace came by Jesus Christ," as is had in John 1.[15] Therefore it seems that fighting against known truth and envy of fraternal grace belong more to blasphemy against the Son of man than to blasphemy against the Holy Spirit.

[4] Furthermore, Bernard says, in *On Dispensation and Precept,* that not to obey is "to resist the Holy Spirit."[16] The Gloss also says, on Leviticus 10, that "simulated penitence is blasphemy of the Holy Spirit."[17] Schism seems to be directly opposed to the Holy Spirit, by whom the Church is united. And so it seems that the species of sin against the Holy Spirit are not sufficiently handed down.

BUT TO THE CONTRARY Augustine says, in *On Faith to Peter*, that those who despair of the indulgence of sins, or who presume without merits on the mercy of God, sin against the Holy Spirit.[18] In the *Enchiridion* he says that "he who in obstinacy of mind closes the limit to God, is guilty of sin against the Holy Spirit."[19] And in *On the Word of the Lord* he says that impenitence is a sin against the Holy Spirit.[20] And in *On the Sermon on the Mount* he says that "to fight brotherhood with the flames of envy" is to sin against the Holy Spirit.[21] And in *On the One Baptism* he says that he who holds the truth in contempt either bears malice against his brothers, by whom the truth is revealed, or is ungrateful to God, by whose

---

[15] John 1.17.

[16] Bernard, *De praecept. et dispensat.* chap.11 (PL 182:876B).

[17] *Glossa ordinaria* on Leviticus 10.16 (Strasbourg, 1, "Inter hec hyrcum," col. 2).

[18] Rather, Fulgentius, *De fide ad Petrum* chap.3 sect.40 (PL 65:690–691; CCL 91A:738).

[19] Augustine, *Enchiridion* chap.83 (PL 40:272, CCL 46:95.31–33).

[20] Augustine, *Serm. ad Popul.* serm.71 chap.12 sect.20 (PL 38: 455–456), chap.13 sect.23 (PL 38:457), chap.21 sect.34 (PL38:464).

[21] Augustine, *De serm. Dom. in monte* bk.1 chap.21 sect.73 (PL 34:1266; CCL35:82.1792–1794).

inspiration the Church is instructed,[22] and so it seems that he sins against the Holy Spirit.

I ANSWER THAT IT SHOULD BE SAID that, when the sin against the Holy Spirit is taken in the third way, the mentioned species are appropriately assigned to it. These are distinguished by the removal of or the contempt for the things by which man can be impeded from the choice of sin. These things are either on the part of divine judgment; or on the part of the divine gifts; or even on the part of the very sin. Man is averted from the choice of sin by consideration of the divine judgment, which has justice with mercy, and by hope, which arises from consideration of the mercy of the one remitting sins and rewarding goods; and this is taken away by despair. And again [he is held back] by fear, which shoots up from consideration of the divine justice of the one punishing sins; and this is taken away by presumption, namely when someone presumes that he will receive glory without merits, or pardon without penance.

The gifts of God by which we are called back from sin are two. One is acquaintance with truth: against which is put fighting against known truth, namely, when someone fights against a known truth of faith, so he might sin more boldly (*licentius*). The other is the help of inward grace: against which is put envy of fraternal grace, namely when someone not only envies the person of a brother, but even envies the grace of God growing in the world.

On the part of the sin there are two things than can recall a man from sin. Of which one is the disorder and ugliness of the act, the consideration of which often induces penance over the committed sin in a man. And against this is put impenitence, not in the sense of permanence in sin until death, as impenitence was taken above[23] (in this

---

[22] Augustine, *De bapt. contra Donatis.* bk.6 chap.35 sect.67 (PL 43:219).

[23] In article 1 of this question, above.

sense it is not a special sin, but a certain circumstance of sin); but impenitence is taken here according as it implies a resolution not to be penitent. The other is both the smallness and briefness of the good that someone seeks in sin, according to Romans 6, "What fruit did you have in the things of which you are now ashamed?"[24] The consideration of this often induces man to have a will that is not firm in sin. And this is taken away by obstinacy, namely when a man makes his resolution firm in inhering in sin. And of these [species], two are spoken of in Jeremiah 8: "There is no one who repents of his sin, saying, What did I do?"[25] as regards the first; and, "All are turned to the course like a horse going in motion to the prize," as regards the second.

[1] TO THE FIRST ARGUMENT, THEREFORE, IT SHOULD BE SAID that the sin of despair or presumption is not constituted by not believing the justice or mercy of God, but by having contempt for them.

[2] To the second it should be said that obstinacy and impenitence differ not only according to past and future, but according to certain formal accounts [deriving] from the different consideration of the things that can be considered in sin, as was said.[26]

[3] To the third it should be said that Jesus Christ made grace and truth by the gifts of the Holy Spirit, who gave gifts to men.

[4] To the fourth it should be said that not to will to obey belongs to obstinacy; simulation of penance to impenitence; schism to the envy of fraternal grace, by which the members of the Church are united.

---

[24] Romans 6.21.

[25] Jeremiah 8.6.

[26] In the body of this article.

Article 3. [Whether the sin against the Holy Spirit is unforgivable.]

One proceeds in this way to the third query. IT SEEMS that the sin against the Holy Spirit is not unforgivable.

[1] Augustine says, in *On the Word of the Lord*, "One ought not to despair of anything so long as the patience of the Lord leads to repentance."[27] But if some sin is unforgivable, the sinner ought to despair of something. Therefore the sin against the Holy Spirit is not unforgivable.

[2] Furthermore, no sin is forgiven except because the soul is healed by God. But "there is no languor that is incurable for the omnipotent physician," as the Gloss says[28] on the psalm, "He who heals all your sicknesses."[29] Therefore the sin against the Holy Spirit is not unforgivable.

[3] Furthermore, free choice has to do with good and evil. But so long as the state of this life lasts, one can fall from any virtue whatever, since even the angel fell from heaven. So it says in Job, "In his angels he discovered depravity; how much more those who inhabit houses of clay?"[30] Therefore by the same reasoning someone can go back from any sin whatever to the state of justice. Therefore the sin against the Holy Spirit is not unforgivable.

BUT TO THE CONTRARY there is what is said in Matthew 12, "He who speaks a word against the Holy Spirit, it cannot be forgiven him, neither in this age nor in the future."[31] About which Augustine says, in *On the Lord's Sermon on the Mount*, that "the devastation of this sin is

---

[27] Augustine, *Serm. ad popul.* serm.71 chap.13 (PL 38:457).
[28] *Glossa Lombardi* on Psalm 102.3 (PL 191:920A).
[29] Psalm 102.3.
[30] Job 4.18–19.
[31] Matthew 12.32.

so great that it cannot tolerate the humility of one who beseeches."[32]

I ANSWER THAT IT SHOULD BE SAID that according to the different senses of the sin against the Holy Spirit, it is said to be unforgivable in different ways. If final impenitence is called the sin of the Holy Spirit, it is then called unforgivable because it will not be forgiven in any way. A mortal sin in which man perseveres until death, since it is not forgiven in this life by repentance, will also not be forgiven in the future.

According to the other two senses, it is said to be unforgivable, not because it will not be forgiven in any way, but because, as regards it itself, it merits not being forgiven. And this in two ways. In one way, as regards punishment. He who sins out of ignorance or weakness, merits lesser punishment; but he who sins out of confirmed malice has no excuse by which his punishment might be diminished. Similarly one who blasphemed against the Son of man, when his divinity had not yet been revealed, can have a certain excuse from the weakness of flesh which he saw in him, and so a lesser punishment might be merited. But he who blasphemed divinity itself, attributing the works of the Holy Spirit to the devil, has no excuse by which his punishment might be diminished. And so it is said, according to Chrysostom's exposition,[33] that this sin of the Jews would not be forgiven in this age or in the future, since for it they suffered punishment both in the present life by the Romans, and in the future life in the pains of hell. So also Athanasius adduces the example of their parents,[34] who first quarreled with Moses for the lack of water and bread. This the Lord patiently sustained,

---

[32] Augustine, *De serm. Dom. in monte* bk.1 chap.22 sect.74 (PL 34:1266; CCL 35:84.1817–1818).

[33] John Chrysostom, *On Matt.* hom.41 sect.3 (PG 57:449).

[34] Athanasius, *Epist.* ep.4 sect.16 (PG 26:662A-B).

for they had the excuse of weakness of flesh. Then they sinned more seriously, blaspheming as it were against the Holy Spirit, attributing the benefits of God, who led them out of Egypt, to an idol, when they said, "These are your gods, Israel, that led you out of the land of Egypt."[35] And so the Lord made them to be punished temporally, since "they killed in that day almost three thousand men,"[36] and planned punishment for them in the future, saying, "But I will visit this sin of theirs in the day of vengeance."[37]

It can be understood in another way as regards fault. A disease is said to be incurable from the nature of the disease, when it takes away that by which the disease can be cured, for example, when the disease takes away the power of nature or induces fastidiousness about food and medicine. Even so, God can cure this disease. So a sin against the Holy Spirit can be said to be unforgivable according to its nature, so far as it excludes the things by which the forgiveness of sins is brought about. This does not preclude, however, the path of forgiveness and healing from the omnipotent and merciful God, by which sometimes those are spiritually healed as it were miraculously.

[1] TO THE FIRST ARGUMENT, THEREFORE, IT SHOULD BE SAID that one ought to despair of nothing in this life, considering the omnipotence and mercy of God. But considering the condition of sin, some are said to be "sons of diffidence," as is had in Ephesians 2.[38]

[2] To the second it should be said that the reasoning proceeds on the part of the omnipotent God, not according to the condition of the sin.

[3] To the third it should be said that free choice remains always changeable in this life, but sometimes it throws

[35] Exodus 32.4.

[36] Exodus 32.28.

[37] Exodus 32.34.

[38] Ephesians 2.2.

away that by which it can be changed to the good, so far as lies in its power. So that on its part the sin is unforgivable, though God can forgive it.

Article 4. [Whether man can sin first against the Holy Spirit, other sins not being presupposed.]

One proceeds in this way to the fourth query. IT SEEMS that man cannot first sin against the Holy Spirit, other sins not being presupposed.

[1] The natural order is that someone be moved from the incomplete to the complete. And this order appears in the good, according to Proverbs 4, "The path of the just like a splendid light grows and flourishes until complete day."[39] But in evil things the complete is said to be what is most evil, as is clear by the Philosopher, *Metaphysics* 5.[40] Since then the sin against the Holy Spirit is most serious, it seems that man comes to it through other, smaller sins.

[2] Furthermore, to sin against the Holy Spirit is to sin from confirmed malice or from choice. But man cannot do this all at once, before he has sinned many times. For the Philosopher says, *Ethics* 5,[41] that if a man can do unjust things, he nonetheless cannot work at once as the unjust man does, namely, from choice. So it seems that the sin against the Holy Spirit cannot be committed except after other sins.

[3] Furthermore, repentance and impenitence are about the same thing. But repentance is only about past sins. Therefore also impenitence, which is a species of the sin against the Holy Spirit. Therefore the sin against the Holy Spirit presupposes other sins.

BUT TO THE CONTRARY "it is easy in the sight of God to make the poor man honorable," as it is said in

---

[39] Proverbs 4.18.

[40] Aristotle, *Metaphysics* bk.5 chap.16 (1021b25–28).

[41] Aristotle, *Nicomachean Ethics* bk.5 chap.6 (1134a17–23).

Sirach 11.[42] Therefore on the contrary it is possible, by the malice of suggesting demons, that someone at once be led into the most serious sin, which is against the Holy Spirit.

I ANSWER THAT IT SHOULD BE SAID that to sin against the Holy Spirit in one way is to sin from confirmed malice, as was said above.[43] It can happen that one sins from confirmed malice in two ways, as was said.[44] In one way, from the inclination of a habit, which is not properly to sin against the Holy Spirit. And in this way to sin from confirmed malice does not happen at the beginning. It is necessary that [other] acts of sin precede, by which a habit is caused that inclines one to sin.

In another way someone sins from confirmed malice by casting down in contempt the things by which a man is brought back from sin. This is properly to sin against the Holy Spirit, as was said.[45] And this also presupposes many other sins, since, as is said in Proverbs 18, "the impious man, when he comes to the depth of sins, has contempt."[46] It can happen, however, that someone in the first act of sin sins against the Holy Spirit by contempt, either from free choice, or also because of many preceding dispositions, or even because of some vehement motive to evil and man's weak affect for the good. In complete men it can hardly ever or never happen that they sin at once and from the beginning against the Holy Spirit. So Origen says, in *On First Principles* 1: "I do not think that one of those who are in the highest degree of completion should suddenly be withdrawn or fall away; but it is necessary for him to fall slowly and by stages."[47] And the

---

[42] Sirach 11.23.
[43] In article 1 of this question, above.
[44] In article 1 of this question, above.
[45] In article 1 of this question, above.
[46] Proverbs 18.3, modern versions differ.
[47] Origen, *On First Principles* bk.1 chap.3 (PG 11:155B-C).

same reasoning holds if sin against the Holy Spirit is taken literally as blasphemy against the Holy Spirit. For such blasphemy of which the Lord speaks always proceeds from the contempt of malice.

If by sin against the Holy Spirit is understood final impenitence, as it is understood by Augustine, there is no question, since the sin against the Holy Spirit requires the continuation of sins until the end of life.

[1] TO THE FIRST ARGUMENT, THEREFORE, IT SHOULD BE SAID that in the good as in the bad—just as in most matters—things proceed from the incomplete to the complete, so far as man avows either the good or the bad. And nonetheless in either [case] one [man] can begin from a greater point than another. And so that from which someone begins can be complete in good or in evil according to its genus; even if it is incomplete according to the series of the progression of man avowing the better or the worse.

[2] To the second it should be said that, if [this sin] is taken as impenitence, according to the intention of Augustine, that is, as it implies permanence in sin until the end, then it is plain that impenitence presupposes sins, just as does repentance. But if we speak of habitual impenitence, as it is put as a species of sin against the Holy Spirit, then it is manifest that impenitence can also be before [other] sins. He who never sins can have the purpose of repenting or not repenting, if it happens that he should sin.

Question 15
[On Blindness of Mind and Dullness of Sense]

One should next consider the vices opposed to knowledge and understanding. And since not knowing, which is opposed to knowledge, was spoken about above when dealing with the causes of sins, the question now to be asked is about blindness of mind and dullness of sense, which are opposed to the gift of understanding.

Three queries are raised with regard to this. (1) Whether blindness of mind is a sin. (2) Whether dullness of sense is a sin different from blindness of mind. (3) Whether these vices arise from sins of the flesh.

Article 1. [Whether blindness of mind is a sin.]

One proceeds in this way to the first query. IT SEEMS that blindness of mind is not a sin.

[1] What excuses from sin does not seem to be a sin. But blindness of mind excuses from sin. For it is said in John 9, "If you were blind, you would not have sin."[1] Therefore blindness of mind is not a sin.

[2] Furthermore, punishment differs from fault. But blindness of mind is a certain punishment, as is clear from

[1] John 9.41.

what is had in Isaiah 6, "Make the heart of this people blind."[2] Therefore blindness of mind is not a sin.

[3] Furthermore, every sin is voluntary, as Augustine says.[3] But blindness of mind is not voluntary. As Augustine says, *Confessions* 10, "all love" to apprehend "the shining truth,"[4] and it is said in Ecclesiastes 11, "Light is sweet, and it is delightful for eyes to see the sun."[5] Therefore blindness of mind is not a sin.

BUT TO THE CONTRARY Gregory, *Moral Remarks* 31, puts blindness of mind among the vices that are caused by luxury.[6]

I ANSWER THAT IT SHOULD BE SAID that just as bodily blindness is a privation of what is the principle of bodily vision or light, so also mental or intellectual blindness is the privation of what is the principle of mental or intellectual vision. The principle is threefold. One is the natural light of reason. And this light, since it belongs to the species of the rational soul, is never taken away from the soul. It is sometimes impeded from its proper act, however, by impediments of the lower powers, which the human understanding needs to understand, as is clear in the mindless and the insane, as was said in the first [part].[7]

Another principle of intellectual vision is a certain habitual light added to the natural light of reason. And this light is from time to time taken from the soul. And such privation is the blindness that is a punishment, in the sense that the privation of the light of grace is put as a punish-

---

[2] Isaiah 6.10.

[3] Augustine, *De vera religione* chap.14 sect.27 (PL 34:133; CCL 32:204:11–12).

[4] Augustine, *Confessiones* bk.10 chap.23 sect.34 (PL 32:794; CCL 27:204.4,11–12).

[5] Ecclesiastes 11.7.

[6] Gregory the Great, *Moralia* bk.31 chap.45 sect.88 (PL 76:621; CCL 27:173.29–30).

[7] *Summa* 1 q.84 aa.7–8.

ment. So it is said of some, Wisdom 2, "Their malice blinds them."[8]

The third principle of intellectual vision is a certain intelligible principle by which man understands other things. The mind of man can intend or not intend this intellectual principle. And it truly happens that it does not intend it in two ways. Sometimes because [a man] has a will that spontaneously turns him away from the consideration of such a principle, according to the psalm, "He did not wish to understand that he might do well."[9] In another way by occupying the mind with the things that it loves more, by which the mind is turned from the inspection of that principle, according to that psalm, "The fire dazzled them," the fire namely of desire, "and they did not see the sun."[10] And in both ways blindness of mind is a sin.

[1] TO THE FIRST ARGUMENT, THEREFORE, IT SHOULD BE SAID that the blindness that excuses from sin is that which happens from the natural defect of one not able to see.

[2] To the second it should be said that the reasoning proceeds from the second blindness, which is punishment.

[3] To the third it should be said that to understand the truth is in itself lovable for anyone. But it can be accidentally hateful to someone, so far, namely, as a man is impeded by it from the things that he loves more.

Article 2. [Whether dullness of sense is different from blindness of mind.]

One proceeds in this way to the second query. IT SEEMS that dullness of sense is not different from blindness of mind.

---

[8] Wisdom 2.21.

[9] Psalm 35.4, after the Septuagint.

[10] Psalm 57.9, after the Septuagint.

[1] One thing is contrary to one thing. But dullness is opposed to the gift of understanding, as is clear from Gregory, *Moral Remarks* 2.[11] To this is also opposed blindness of mind, in that the principle of intellect is designated as something like sight (*visivum*). Therefore dullness of sense is the same as blindness of mind.

[2] Furthermore, Gregory, speaking of dullness in *Moral Remarks* 31, names it "dullness of sense about intelligence."[12] But for sense to be dull about intelligence seems to be nothing other than to lack understanding, which belongs to blindness of mind. Therefore dullness of sense is the same as blindness of mind.

[3] Furthermore, if they differ in something, they seem to differ most of all in this, that blindness of mind is voluntary, as was said above,[13] while dullness of sense is natural. But a natural defect is not a sin. Therefore according to this dullness of sense is not a sin. This is against Gregory, who counts it among the vices that arise from gluttony.[14]

BUT TO THE CONTRARY different causes have different effects. But Gregory, *Moral Remarks* 31, says that dullness of mind arises from gluttony, while blindness of mind arises from luxury.[15] Therefore they are different vices.

I ANSWER THAT IT SHOULD BE SAID that the dull is opposed to the sharp (*acutum*). Something is said to be sharp because it is penetrating. So something is said to be dull because it is obtuse, not serving well for pene-

---

[11] Gregory the Great, *Moralia* bk.2 chap.49 sect.77 (PL 75:592D; CCL 143:106.42).

[12] Gregory the Great, *Moralia* bk.31 chap.45 sect.88 (PL 76:621B; CCL 143B:1610.33–34).

[13] In the preceding article of this question.

[14] Gregory the Great, *Moralia* bk.31 chap.45 sect.88 (PL 76:621B; CCL 143B:1610.32–34).

[15] Gregory the Great, *Moralia* bk.31 chap.45 sect.88 (PL 76:621B; CCL 143B:1610.32–34).

trating. By a kind of likeness, bodily sense is said to penetrate the medium so far as it perceives its objects across some distance, or so far as it can perceive what is hidden in a thing as if by penetrating it. So in bodily things someone is said to be acute of sense who can perceive something sensible from distant things, whether by seeing or hearing or smelling. On the contrary, he is said to be dull in sense who does not perceive anything but sensible things that are near and large.

By likeness to bodily sense, there is also said to be a sense about intelligence, which is of certain "first extremes," as is said in *Ethics* 6,[16] just as sense apprehends sensibles as certain principles of apprehension. This sense that is about intelligence does not perceive its object through a medium of bodily distance, but by some other medium, just as it perceives the essence of a thing through its property, and perceives a cause through its effect. He is said to be sharp in sense about intelligence who comprehends at once the nature of the thing when he has apprehended its property or even its effect, and so far as he attains to the smallest conditions of the thing to be considered. He is said to be dull about intelligence who cannot attain to apprehending the truth of the thing except by much exposure to it, and even then cannot attain to considering completely all that belongs to the account of the thing.

Thus dullness of sense about intelligence implies a certain weakness of mind about the consideration of spiritual goods, while blindness of mind implies a privation of their apprehension in every way. And both are opposed to the gift of understanding, by which man apprehends in grasping spiritual goods and subtly penetrates to what is hidden in them. Dullness has the account of sin just as does blindness of mind, so far namely as it is voluntary, as is clear in

[16] Aristotle, *Nicomachean Ethics* bk.6 chap.11 (1143a26–28).

him who, moved by fleshly things, dislikes or neglects to speak subtly about spiritual things.

[1]-[3] From this the answer TO THE OBJECTIONS is clear.

Article 3. [Whether blindness of mind and dullness of sense arise from sins of the flesh.]

One proceeds in this way to the third query. IT SEEMS that blindness of mind and dullness of sense do not arise from fleshly vices.

[1] Augustine says, in the *Reconsiderations*, reconsidering what he said in the *Soliloquies*, "God who did not will that any but the clean should know truth,"[17] says, "It could be answered that many who are not clean know many true things."[18] But men are made most unclean by fleshly vices. Therefore blindness of mind and dullness of sense are not caused by fleshly vices.

[2] Furthermore, blindness of mind and dullness of sense are certain defects about the understanding part of the soul; but the fleshly vices belong to the corruption of the flesh. The flesh does not act on the soul, but rather conversely. Therefore fleshly vices do not cause blindness of mind and dullness of sense.

[3] Furthermore, each one suffers more from what is near than from what is far. But spiritual vices are nearer the mind than fleshly vices. Therefore blindness of mind and dullness of sense are rather caused from spiritual vices than from fleshly vices.

BUT TO THE CONTRARY there is what Gregory says, *Moral Remarks* 31,[19] that dullness of sense about

---

[17] Augustine, *Soliloquia* bk.1 chap.1 sect.2 (PL 32:870).

[18] Augustine, *Retractationes* bk.1 chap.4 sect.2 (PL 32:589; CCL 57:14.13–14).

[19] Gregory the Great, *Moralia* bk.31 chap.45 sect.88 (PL 76:621B; CCL 143B:1610.32–34).

intelligence arises from gluttony, blindness of mind from luxury.

I ANSWER THAT IT SHOULD BE SAID that completeness of the operation of understanding in man is constituted by a certain abstraction from sensible phantasms. And so the more the intellect of man was free from such phantasms, the more powerfully he could consider intelligibles and order all sensibles things. Just so Anaxogoras said that it was necessary that the mind be unmixed so that it would rule, since in acting it was necessary that it dominate over matter so that it could move it, as the Philosopher says, *Physics* 8.[20] It is manifest that delighting applies intention to the things in which someone delights. So the Philosopher says, *Ethics* 10, that everyone works best in the things in which he delights; in contrary things, not at all or weakly.[21] Fleshly vices, namely gluttony and luxury, are constituted by the delights of touch, namely of food and sexual things, where there are the most vehement among all bodily pleasures. And so by this vice man's intention is most of all applied to bodily things, and in consequence man's working with intelligibles is weakened. More by luxury than by gluttony, just so far as the delights of sexual matters are more vehement than those of food. And so blindness of mind arises from luxury, which almost totally excludes the apprehension of spiritual things; from gluttony there arises dullness of sense, which renders man weak concerning intelligibles of this kind. And conversely the opposed vices, namely abstinence and chastity, most of all dispose man to the completion of intellectual operation. So it is said, Daniel 1, that "God gave knowledge and instruction in every book and wisdom to these children,"[22] namely to the abstinent and continent.

[20] Aristotle, *Physics* bk.8 chap.5 (256b25–28).

[21] Aristotle, *Nicomachean Ethics* bk.10 chap.5 (1175a30–b2).

[22] Daniel 1.17.

[1] TO THE FIRST ARGUMENT, THEREFORE, IT SHOULD BE SAID that, however much some can subdue fleshly vices at times by speculating subtly on some [points] about the intelligibles, because of the goodness of natural ingenuity or some superadded habit, nonetheless it is necessary that the intention be withdrawn from the subtlety of the contemplation of those things most often because of bodily pleasures. And so the unclean can know some true things, but by their uncleanness they are impeded in this.

[2] To the second it should be said that flesh does not act on an intellectual part by altering it, but by impeding its operating in the way already said.

[3] To the third it should be said that just as fleshly vices are more distant from the mind, so much more do they distract its intention from distant things. So also they impede the mind more from contemplation.

Question 16

[On the Precepts of Faith, Knowledge, and Understanding]

One should next consider the precepts belonging to the things already mentioned. Two queries are raised with regard to this: (1) On the precepts[1] belonging to faith. (2) On the precepts belonging to the gifts of knowledge and of understanding.

Article 1. [Whether in the old law precepts about believing should have been given.]

One proceeds in this way to the first query. IT SEEMS that in the old law precepts of believing should have been given.

[1] A precept is about what is due and necessary. But it is most necessary to man that he believe, according to Hebrews 11, "Without faith it is impossible to please God."[2] Therefore it was most necessary to give precepts about faith.

[2] Furthermore, the New Testament is contained in the Old, as the figured in a figure, as was said above.[3] But in

---

[1] I have put *praeceptum* halfway into English as "precept" in order to retain the important ambiguity of the Latin, which can mean both command and teaching.

[2] Hebrews 11.6.

[3] *Summa* 1-2 q.107 a.1, a.3.

the New Testament there are put express commands (*mandata*) about faith, as is clear in John 14, "Believe in God, and believe in me."[4]

[3] Furthermore, it belongs to the same reasoning to teach the act of virtue and to prohibit the opposed vices. But in the old law there are put many precepts prohibiting unfaithfulness, such as Exodus 20, "Do not have any foreign Gods before me."[5] And again Deuteronomy 13 commands that they hear not "the words of the prophet or the dreamer" who wishes to turn them away from faith in God.[6] Therefore in the old law too precepts about faith should have been given.

[4] Furthermore, confession is an act of faith, as is said above.[7] But precepts are given in the old law about confession and the promulgation of faith. It is commanded in Exodus 12 that when their sons ask, they should give the reason for the Passover observance;[8] and in Deuteronomy 13 it is commanded that someone who spreads teaching against the faith should be killed.[9] Therefore the old law should have had precepts about faith.

[5] Furthermore all the books of the Old Testament are contained under the old law. So the Lord says in John 15[10] that it is written in the law, "They hated me without cause," which is however written in Psalms.[11] But in Sirach 2 it is said, "You who fear the Lord, believe him."[12] Therefore in the old law there were to be given precepts of faith.

---

[4] John 14.1.
[5] Exodus 20.3.
[6] Deuteronomy 13.3.
[7] In question 3, article 1, above.
[8] Exodus 12.27.
[9] Deuteronomy 13.5.
[10] John 15.25.
[11] Psalm 34.19.
[12] Sirach 2.8.

BUT TO THE CONTRARY the Apostle in Romans 3 names the [old] law "the law of works" and divides it against the "law of faith."[13] Therefore precepts of faith were not to be given in the old law.

I ANSWER THAT IT SHOULD BE SAID that a law is only imposed by a lord on his subjects. And so the precepts of the law presuppose that any recipient of the law is subjected to him who gives the law. The first subjection of man to God is by faith, according to Hebrews 11, "Coming to God one must believe that he exists," and so faith is presupposed to the precepts of the law.[14] And on account of this in Exodus 20, what is of faith is put before the precepts of the law when it is said, "I am the Lord your God, who led you from the land of Egypt."[15] And similarly Deuteronomy 6 puts first, "Hear O Israel: The Lord your God is one," and then at once it begins to deal with the precepts.[16] In faith many things are contained [that are] ordered to the faith by which we believe that God exists, which is the first and principal thing among all believable things, as was said.[17] Faith in God being presupposed, by which the human mind is subjected to God, precepts can be given about other things to be believed. So, expounding that text in John, "This is my precept,"[18] Augustine says that "many things are commanded us about faith."[19] But in the old law the secrets of the faith were not to be expounded to the people. And so, faith in the one God being presupposed, no other precepts were given in the old law about faith.

---

[13] Romans 3.20–22.

[14] Hebrews 11.6.

[15] Exodus 20.2.

[16] Deuteronomy 6.4.

[17] In question 1, articles 1 and 7, above.

[18] John 15.12.

[19] Augustine, *In Ioann.* tr.83 sect.3, on John 15.12 (PL 35:1846; CCL 36:535.9–10).

[1] TO THE FIRST ARGUMENT, THEREFORE, IT SHOULD BE SAID that faith is necessary as the principle of spiritual life and so is presupposed for receiving the law.

[2] To the second it should be said that, even in that text the Lord presupposes something of faith, namely faith in the one God, when he says, "Believe in God." And he teaches something else, namely faith in the incarnation, by which God and man are one. This way of making faith explicit belongs to the faith of the New Testament. And so he adds, "And believe in me."

[3] To the third it should be said that prohibitive precepts have to do with sins, which corrupt virtue. Virtue is corrupted by particular defects, as was said above.[20] And so faith in the one God being presupposed in the old law, they were prohibited from those particular defects by which [that] faith could be corrupted.

[4] To the fourth it should be said that even the confession or teaching of faith presupposes the subjection of man to God by faith. So more precepts could be given in the old law about confession or the teaching of faith, than about that faith itself.

[5] To the fifth it should be said that in that very authoritative text the faith is presupposed, by which we believe that God exists. So that it puts first, "You who fear God," which cannot happen without faith. When it adds, however, "Believe him," this is to be referred to certain special believable things, and principally to what God promises to those who obey him. So the text adds, "And your mercy will not be taken away."

---

[20] *Summa* 1–2 q.18 a.4 ao.3 and so on.

Article 2. [Whether in the old law there are appropriately handed down precepts about knowledge and understanding.]

One proceeds in this way to the second query. IT SEEMS that in the old law there are inappropriately handed down precepts about knowledge and understanding.

[1] Knowledge and understanding belong to apprehension. Apprehension precedes action and directs it. Therefore the precepts belonging to knowledge and understanding should precede the precepts belonging to action. Since the first precepts of the law are the precepts of the decalogue,[21] it seems that among the precepts of the decalogue there should be given some precepts about science and understanding.

[2] Furthermore, learning precedes teaching. First a man learns from another what he [then] teaches to yet another. But certain precepts about teaching are given in the old law. Both affirmative [precepts], as it is taught in Deuteronomy 4, "Teach your sons, and your nephews,"[22] and also prohibitive [precepts], as it is said in Deuteronomy 4, "Do not add to the word which is spoken to you, nor take away from it."[23] Therefore it seems that some precepts should be also given inducing man to learn.

[3] Furthermore, knowledge and understanding seem more necessary to a priest than to a king. So it is said in Malachi 2, "The lips of the priest keep knowledge, and they seek the law from his mouth,"[24] and it is said in Hosea 4, "Because you rejected knowledge, so I reject you, so that you will not perform your priesthood for

---

[21] That is, of the Ten Commandments.

[22] Deuteronomy 4.9.

[23] Deuteronomy 4.2.

[24] Malachi 2.7.

me."[25] But the king is commanded to learn knowledge of law, as is clear in Deuteronomy 17.[26] Therefore much more should it be precepted in law, that the priest learn the law.

[4] Furthermore, meditation on the things that belong to knowledge and understanding cannot take place in one who sleeps. It is also impeded by external occupations. Therefore Deuteronomy 6 inappropriately teaches, "You will meditate on these things while sitting in your house, and walking along the path, while sleeping, also rising."[27] Therefore precepts about knowledge and understanding are inappropriately handed on in the old law.

BUT TO THE CONTRARY there is what is said in Deuteronomy 4: "That when the world hears this precept, it should say, 'Here is a wise and understanding people.' "[28]

I ANSWER THAT IT SHOULD BE SAID that three things can be considered about knowledge and understanding [considered as one]: first, its acceptance; second, its use; third, its conservation. Now acceptance of knowledge and understanding is done by learning and is taught in either law [that is, old and new]. It is said in Deuteronomy 6, "These words will be in your heart, which I teach to you."[29] What belongs to learning belongs also to the learner, that he apply the things that are said to his heart. So what is added, "And you will tell them to your sons,"[30] belongs to teaching. The use of knowledge or understanding is the meditation on the things that someone knows or understands. And as regards this there is added: "And you will

---

[25] Hosea 4.6.
[26] Deuteronomy 17.18.
[27] Deuteronomy 6.7.
[28] Deuteronomy 4.6.
[29] Deuteronomy 6.6.
[30] Deuteronomy 6.7.

meditate while sitting in your house,"[31] and so on. Conservation is done by the memory. As regards this there is added, "And you will tie these things as a sign on your hand, and they will be there and will move between your eyes; and write them on the doorpost and the entrances to your house."[32] By which [things] it signifies all the things commanded by the Lord in the yoke of memory, those namely, which continually occur to our senses, either to touch, such as those that we have in the hand, or to sight, such as those that we have continually before our eyes, or to the things to which it is necessary for us to return often, such as the entry to the house. These cannot be removed from our memory. And Deuteronomy 4 says more manifestly, "Do not forget the words, which your eyes saw, and let them not be removed from your heart all the days of your life."[33] And this is read even more abundantly in the New Testament, as much in the evangelical doctrine as in the apostolic commandments.

[1] TO THE FIRST ARGUMENT, THEREFORE, IT SHOULD BE SAID, as is said in Deuteronomy 4, "This is your wisdom and your understanding before the peoples."[34] From which it is given to understanding that the knowledge and understanding of God's faithful is constituted by the precepts of the law. So first the precepts of the law are to be proposed; and then later men are to be induced to knowing or understanding them. And so the precepts given first should not be put among the precepts of the decalogue, which are first.

[2] To the second it should be said that precepts belonging to learning are also put in the law, as was said.[35] Teaching is more expressly precepted than learning, since

---

[31] Deuteronomy 6.7.

[32] Deuteronomy 6.8.

[33] Deuteronomy 4.9.

[34] Deuteronomy 4.6.

[35] In the body of this article.

teaching belongs to the greater ones, who are their own right (*ius*), living immediately under the law, by whom the precepts of the law should be given. Learning belongs to the lower ones, to whom the precepts of the law should come from the greater.

[3] To the third it should be said that the knowledge of the law is so far annexed to the office of the priest, that there should be understood immediately together with the injunction to that office the injunction to knowledge of the law. And so it was not necessary to give special precepts on the instruction of the priest. But the teaching of the law of God is not so much annexed to the royal office, since the king is constituted above the people in temporal things. And so it is specially precepted that the king be instructed by priests about the things that belong to the law of God.

[4] To the fourth is should be said that this precept of the law is not to be understood [as saying] that a man should meditate on the law of God while sleeping, but that when sleeping, that is when going to sleep, he should meditate on the law of God. Men while sleeping receive better phantasms so far as they go through the motions of watchfulness before sleeping, as is clear from the Philosopher in *Ethics* 1.[36] Similarly it is commanded that someone mediate on the law in his acting, not that he always think of the law while acting, but that all things that he does be moderated according to the law.

---

[36] Aristotle, *Nicomachean Ethics* bk.1 chap.13 (1102b10–11).

Index of Authoritative Sources

This index gathers, in two lists, all of the authoritative texts cited by Thomas in the *Summa*'s questions on faith. The first list is for citations to Scripture, the second for nonscriptural citations. For each textual citation, in Scripture or outside it, the index gives the places where it appears in Thomas. The places are identified by question (q., qq.), article (a., aa.), and part of article. The following abbreviations are used for the parts of articles: ob. = *obiecta*, the preliminary numbered arguments; sc. = *sed contra*, the counterargument, usually single, beginning "But to the contrary . . . "; co. = *corpus*, the body of the argument, beginning "I answer that . . . "; ao. = *ad obiecta*, the numbered replies to the preliminary arguments, beginning "To the first. . . . " So, for example, "q.1 a.2 ao.3" refers to question 1, article 2, reply [3]; and "q.10 a.9 sc." refers to question 10, article 9, counterargument.

The abbreviations used for parts of works other than the *Summa* should be interpreted as follows: bk. = book; causa = *causa*, that is, a topical division in legal codifications; can. = canon; chap. = chapter; col. = column; dist. = distinction; ep. = epistle; hom. = homily; pros. = prose; sect. = section; serm. = *sermo*, that is, a sermon or speech; tit. = title; tr. = treatise.

No attempt has been made to give in this index the intermediate sources from which Thomas may have gathered these citations. The most important of the intermediaries are mentioned, however, in the footnotes to the text. Texts written in Latin are cited by their Latin titles; texts originally in other languages are cited by their customary

English titles. Information about Latin translations known to Thomas is provided in the notes.

Readers should use the detailed list of articles given in the table of contents as an index of topics. Indeed, one of the aims of the arrangement of the table of contents is to encourage something like a medieval approach to the text. The reader should see this section of the *Summa* as the dialectical engagement of a structure of topics and a selection of authoritative sources.

Scriptural Citations*

(according to the traditional order of books in the Septuagint)

*Scriptural citations marked with an asterisk are those for which Thomas seems primarily to be interested in an attached gloss or comment rather than the text itself. These should be compared with the entries for the glosses in the list of nonscriptural citations, below.

Nonscriptural Citations

(alphabetically by author and work)